The Long Shorter Way

The Long Shorter Way
Discourses on Chasidic Thought

A D I N S T E I N S A L T Z

Edited and translated
by
Yehuda Hanegbi

JASON ARONSON INC.
Northvale, New Jersey
London

First softcover printing—1993

Library of Congress Cataloging-in-Publication Data

Steinsaltz, Adin.
  The long shorter way.

  Transcriptions of talks on the Tanya originally delivered 1977–1980 in Hebrew.
  1. Shneur Zalman, of Lyady, 1745–1813. Likute
amarim. 2. Hasidism. I. Hanegbi, Yehuda. II. Title.
BM198.S483S74 1987   296.8'33   87-26909
ISBN 0-87668-992-6 (hb)
ISBN 1-56821-144-9 (pb)

Manufactured in the United States of America. Jason Aronson Inc. offers books and cassettes. For information and catalog write to Jason Aronson Inc., 230 Livingston Street, Northvale, New Jersey 07647.

Contents

Acknowledgments

To Milton I. Taubman of San Francisco, California, whose consistent support, faith, and friendship over a period of several years made it possible for us to undertake and complete the work on this book.

Adin Steinsaltz
Yehuda Hanegbi

Translator's Preface

In spite of growing interest in Chasidism as a religious revival movement in Judaism and the concurrent translation into modern languages of the words of the Tzadikim, there remains a certain lack of understanding of the more profound contents of this movement. This may well be due to the Chasidic masters themselves, who had a strong objection to any kind of written codification or explanation. One of the few exceptions is the *Tanya* by Rabbi Schneur Zalman of Liadi, which is a classic text of the Chabad school of Chasidism.

Rendered in the spirit of an age-old tradition of commentary on Torah, the following chapters are derived from weekly lectures on the *Tanya*, delivered in Hebrew, by Rabbi Adin Steinsaltz between 1977 and 1980 to a small group of Jerusalemites interested in Chabad philosophy.

Part of the difficulty in these talks is related to their authenticity. Rabbi Steinsaltz expresses the ideas and the spirit of Jewish thought in a way that one can describe as traditional. His thoughts are profoundly original and are organic extensions of Torah as well. He passes freely from one topic to another, keeps coming back to the original idea without belaboring it, and uses a wide variety of modes of explanation from philosophic logic, textual exegesis, and scientific illustration to symbolism, story, parable, thought association, and so forth. But, of course, there is more to Rabbi "Adin" than repetition of old wisdom. To hear him is a challenge that increasing numbers of people are eager to assume. To read him is exhilarating, if one is prepared to risk the turbulent flow of his ideas. True, one may have to forgo a preference for a certain academic neatness. But what one gains is a taste of the genuine. It is important also to bear in mind that the translation, for all its striving to be faithful, necessarily has to relinquish some of the clarity and pungency of the original discourses. Thus, even though Rabbi Steinsaltz reviewed the English, we beg the reader's indulgence.

The names of the chapters are my own, but the numbers of the chapters correspond to those of the Hebrew text of the *Tanya*.

Yehuda Hanegbi

Introduction

The *Tanya* is the first part of the *Book of Selected Writings* (*Likutei Amarim*) by Schneur Zalman of Liadi. The author also called it *Book of the Intermediates* (*Sefer shel Benonim*). The concept of "Intermediate" man is altogether original and certainly does not point to any sort of class or type of personality. Historically, one may view it as a turning away from the ideal image of the Jew in the moralistic *musar* literature which preceded Chasidism and as an endeavor to come to grips with something more tangible, if not closer to the limited abilities of common humanity. The term "Intermediate" (Benoni) is thus quite an accurate description of the subject of the book.

The author, following the traditional Jewish precedent of avoiding the public eye, does not claim to have composed a book. He says he has merely put it together. Although, to be sure, there is an unusual originality about the book, and it is relatively sparing about the use of quotations. Nevertheless, the author maintains that the *Tanya* was collated from the works of saintly authors. Among other sources, it is surmised, the *Tanya* does borrow from the Maharal, a scholar of great learning and power, especially in the esoteric wisdom. Also felt is the influence of the *musar* writings, especially *Shnei Luchot HaBrit* and *Reishit Chochmah*. The author's direct teachers were the Maggid of Mezritch and his son, Avraham HaMalach ("The Angel"), and Rabbi Menachem Mendel of Vitebsk, who later moved to Eretz Yisrael, where he became the leader of the Chasidic movement there. It may be mentioned that Chasidism, which until then had been more or less under a single head, divided at that time into two main parts: the Galician branch, under the guidance of Reb Elimelech of Lisansk, and the Ukrainian branch, under the leadership of the grandson of the Baal Shem Tov and others. Afterwards, the Polish sections of the movement developed under the leadership of other Tzadikim, including the Seer of Lublin and his pupils. The region of White Russia and the north, which was adjacent to the Lithuanian stronghold of the Mitnagdim, was more vulnerable to anti-Chasidic pressures and developed under the influence of Rabbi Schneur Zalman of Liadi. It was here, in this particular generation and center of great learning, that Rabbi Schneur Zalman had to prove himself—so that not even his enemies could deny his greatness—and establish a school of Chasidism on the basis of a systematic work: the *Tanya*.

Understandably, the purpose of this profound work was not to impress the scholars but to show Jews that "the thing is very nigh unto thee, in your mouth and in your heart to do it." This theme is a consistent, underlying refrain of the *Tanya*: that a person can create his life, change himself and direct his experience, his feelings, and his thoughts toward ever higher levels. The message that knowledge of God is close to one and given to fulfillment is not a mere quotation from Scripture (Deuteronomy 30:14), flung out to the spiritually hungry masses, but a rationally expounded conviction.

Of course, the way is not easy, and it may even be wise to choose the more difficult route of hard work and discipline rather than the quicker and more perilous path of inspiration. This long way is the shorter one because it is based on one's own efforts, which, even though we rely on God for everything, remains a necessary factor for success. Somehow, too, there is more room for hope on a way that is based on work.

The aim of the introduction to the *Tanya* is to explain why such books (of spiritual guidance) should not be written and to apologize for having written one nevertheless. Because the Chasidic movement put such store on the intimate relations with the Rebbe or teacher, it was felt that writing only created a barrier. There was something dead about a book in contrast to the direct communication between master and disciple, teacher and pupil. Not only were the true problems of the soul left unresolved, but the very essence of the message was somehow lost, as the following story about the Baal Shem indicates. When a volume of the sayings of the founder of the Chasidic movement came out, and this still in his lifetime, the Baal Shem Tov dreamed that he saw a devil walking about with a book under his arm, and when the Baal Shem Tov asked him what it was, the devil replied, not without a smile of satisfaction, "It is a book by you, yourself." The next day, the venerable teacher called his disciples together and demanded to know who dared to write books in his name. When he was shown the volume of his sayings, he read it and said, "There isn't a single word here that I actually spoke." All of the first Chasidic masters were very sensitive about the need to keep the essential message pure by transmitting it directly from soul to soul. Writing may have value for others, but not for them, the Chasidim.

As an interesting aside, let us compare this approach with that of the Rambam, whose book on Halachah, like the *Tanya*, was also an original work and, in fact, similar to it in many ways. One of the chief differences was in the introduction by the Rambam, in which he apologized for writing another book on the subject and justified it by explaining that his book could supplant all the previous ones.

The Baal HaTanya, on the other hand, apologizes for writing altogether. Because one is not really passive when reading a book, one is constantly interpreting according to one's previous knowledge and understanding. Two persons can study the same text, and when asked to relate what they have read, they will present two very different versions. The reason for this is the different viewpoint of every reader, each with his or her intellectual and emotional prejudices, and each with a different capacity to grasp what is being taught. With all the best intentions in the world and the finest rapport, one can still fail to comprehend what one is reading; or else one grasps only a part of the text. It is very much a function of basic attitude as well as of intelligence. How often have we not met the very keen and rational mind who simply cannot read a page of a religious book. Just as those who contemplate the stars of heaven may react differently, some with awe or wonder or humility, others with intellectual interest and excitement, and still others with fear and terror. The more one knows, the greater the sense of genuine awe and fear. In any case, the books of spiritual inspiration, which aim at some awakening of the heart, may often fail to inspire because the writer is human and tends to talk to people like himself.

It is written in the Talmud that when one sees 600,000 Jews together, one should say a special blessing: "Blessed is the Wise One of Secrets." This is because there were 600,000 opinions and nuances of disagreement at Sinai, and no book could speak equally to all. Concerning this, it was said (Numbers 27:15–23) that Moses demanded of God that He choose someone with the Divine Spirit in him to go about and explain the Torah to each and everyone. Someone with a Divine Spirit being the one who can understand each and every person and thereby direct his explanations accordingly.

Two living persons can commune together; one can teach the other by orienting himself to the other's spirit. If there is any barrier to their communion, such as a lack of understanding on the part of the listener, the speaker can adjust himself to the situation and overcome it. Otherwise, he would not be fulfilling his role of teacher. After all, what is the task of the spiritual guide? Is it not to feel the state of mind of the listener, even while he speaks, and constantly take it into consideration? The important thing is the act of comprehension, of genuine absorption. True, only too often this is lacking between two persons who are close.

But where there is more than one listener, the problem becomes increasingly complex. An audience of many requires an adjustment which only the true leader can make. He has to make himself understood by each one, as illustrated in the following story told by Solomon Maimon, who was not even a believer in the Chasidic Way. He was a guest at the table of the

Maggid of Mezritch, where, as he relates, the Maggid called each of the company by name and place of origin (without having been told beforehand, it seems) and then asked each one to quote a passage, whatever first came into his head. Afterwards, the Maggid thought for a moment and delivered a sermon combining all of the disconnected passages quoted by the guests. He did so with the greatest of ease and coherence. What was most astonishing was that each of his listeners was convinced that the Maggid was talking to him, and only to him, in connection with what he himself had spontaneously quoted, and that it was in some intimate way profoundly related to his life.

This is a sample of what a Maggid was: someone who could speak (maggid) to all people, each one feeling that he was being addressed personally. And this, our author maintains, no book can do, and it is a reason not to write books.

THE SEFIROT: THEIR STRUCTURE AND HUMAN CORRESPONDENCES

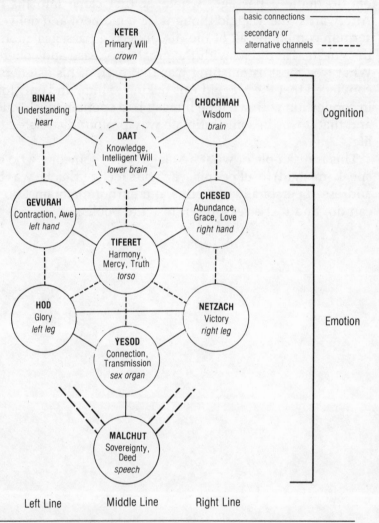

Malchut can be considered above as well as below the others, first as well as last. The broken lines from Malchut indicate that it connects itself to each of the Sefirot.

Daat and Keter are "interchangeable"; it is one or the other. Beyond cognition, there is no Daat; within cognition, Keter is not apprehendable.

This is only one version of the many possible diagrammatic representations of the Sefirot.

English translations of the names of the Sefirot: Keter, Crown; Chochmah, Wisdom; Binah, Understanding; Daat, Knowledge; Chesed, Grace; Gevurah, Strength; Tiferet, Splendor; Netzach, Victory; Hod, Glory; Yesod, Foundation; Malchut, Kingdom.

WORLDS

ATZILUT (EMANATION) —Divine Sefirot

BRIAH (CREATION) —Chariot (Holy Intelligence)

YETZIRAH (FORMATION) —Angels (Holy Speech)

ASIYAH (ACTION) —Man (Holy Deed)

(Unholy Worlds) | Klipat Nogah (Shell of Light) | Asiyah Ruchanit (Spiritual Action)
| Klipot Temayot (Impure Shells) | Asiyah Gashmit (Physical Action)

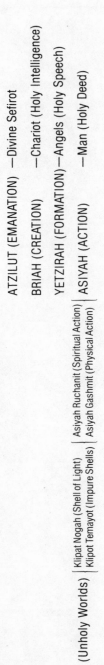

THE LEVELS OF SOUL

Level of Soul		World to Which It Corresponds
YECHIDAH	——	The Divine Spark
CHAYAH	——	Emanation
NESHAMAH	——	Creation
RUACH	——	Formation
NEFESH		
• HANEFESH HASICHLIT (Intelligent Spirit)	——	Action
• HANEFESH HACHIYUNIT (Animal Spirit)		

unrevealed

revealed

DIVINE SOUL

ANIMAL SOUL

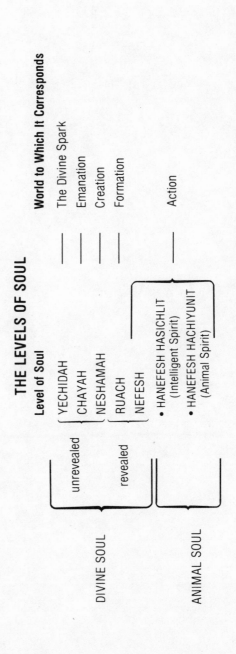

The Long Shorter Way

1

The Vital Soul

It is written in the Kabbalah (Etz Chaim 50,2) that in every Jew there are two souls, irrespective of the nature of the person. And the differences between people—in breadth of outlook or goodness of character—can perhaps be traced to the quality of one or another of these two souls. In any event, they are bound to one another and integral to every human being.

In order to better understand what is meant here by the word soul—and in Jewish tradition there are at least five different souls, all of them difficult to translate into other languages—let us define the present usage loosely as the spiritual entity that gives life to a person and of which the body is its material aspect. The two souls are the one that comes from the holy and the one that is derived from uncleanness; that is, the Divine Soul and the one belonging to the other side—the Sitra Achra. However, the one deriving from the unclean is merely the shell, the part of life which can be discarded after the fruit, which is the goodness, is extracted. This suggests that the shell also has a positive function, to protect the fruit while it is ripening, and only thereafter is it a hindrance and an obstacle.

In other words, the "other side" is not necessarily evil. This

1

does not mean that it is neutral, somewhere between the holy and the unholy. Because things must be either one or the other; either holy or unholy—there is no in-between. There is a difference, however, between the unclean or the unholy that can be corrected by Tikun and the unholy that is beyond repair.

True, in the Halachic code of law there are things that are indifferent or neutral, belonging neither to the commanded nor the forbidden; but, fundamentally, these permitted areas outside the fold of the mitzvah may be seen to belong to the Sitra Achra (the other side) and not to the Sitra diKedusha (the side of holiness).

There seems to be a more profoundly incisive question behind all this, as Moses put it (Exodus 32:26): Who is for the Lord? And whosoever is not for Him is neither neutral nor hesitant nor for anything else; he is against Him. But how much? Can anyone be totally against God?

This leads us to the difference between the "shell" and the "Sitra Achra"—for they are not merely two terms for the same thing. The Sitra Achra is that which defines the world as having two sides: one belonging to God and all that recognize His sovereignty, and the other side, Sitra Achra—all the rest. Whereas the term "shell" does not merely point to the two aspects of existence, it denotes something of the relations between them as well, outer and inner, darkness and light. Although, as previously said, there cannot be any in-between state. Things are either darkness or light; and though there may be more or less light, there cannot be anything that is neither one nor the other.

A shell is a concentric structure in space, the holiness being contained within the outer covering. The meaning of the distinction between shell and Sitra Achra is that one can pass through the shell to the holiness. And there are even certain sanctities that can be obtained only by piercing the shell. The point here is that, as we shall see later in practical ethics, one can scarcely achieve any light by breaking or piercing the darkness; the darkness can yield nothing but darkness; the negative cannot produce the positive. However, when one puts the matter in terms of the shell, it makes it possible to break through to reach the fruit. Of course there may be ways, as described elsewhere, of pounding the darkness with such force and persistency that it is ground into something else. However, within the context of ordinary life, light and darkness are different, each with its own functions and tasks.

It is written that the soul clothes itself in the blood of the man. The concept of a garment or clothing in Jewish wisdom is intended to indicate that which serves both to cover or hide and to manifest or reveal. It is the way in which a person is concealed and protected from the outer world and the way in which he is seen and apprehended by the world. It may also be—to get beyond physical terms—the relation between speech and thought, for example. Thought clothes itself in speech, with speech revealing thought, serving as its vehicle of expression, and yet at the same time, hiding the thought, unable to transmit it completely, and thus becoming its substitute. Hence, the soul that clothes itself in the blood of the man is to be understood as the animal-soul, the blood being the symbol of the natural, the vital aspect, of creaturely existence.

The statement (to which we are referring) goes on to say that this animal-soul which envelops us as a garment is the source of the negative qualities in us which may be divided into four main categories. The division corresponds to the ancient world's straightforward grasp of things as solid, liquid, gas, and fire (energy) and provides a corresponding framework for moral categories. Thus, there are bad qualities that, having the attributes of fire, always tend to rise. Anger and pride, for example, which are connected in some way, veer upwards. Moreover, unlike other qualities, they increase the more they are stirred up and the more they are interfered with. Other qualities will tend to diminish as one gets more involved with them, not so pride and anger. In Hebrew, this redundance is indicated by using the reflexive tense, *mitragez* and *mitgaeh*, to define such a state. The appetite for pleasure corresponds to the element of Water, frivolity and boasting to the element of Air, and sloth and melancholy to the element of Earth.

What is important to realize in this division is the view that bad qualities are not necessarily of one sort; they are not absolute qualities of the soul itself. They are more in the nature of modes of expression. For instance, there is a general

consensus of opinion among moralists that whereas depression
is evil, a little melancholy is a good thing; that while joy is
certainly positive, an excess of good spirits is rather dangerous,
and so forth. The emphasis is not on specific qualities, but on
right measure, on the correctness of application. Even love and
compassion can be bad when exercised without discrimination.
God made both the light and the darkness, the good and the
evil.

Therefore, the holiness and the shell cannot be distinguished
as clearly as we would wish. It all depends on the use made of
them, on the relationships with everything else, not on anything intrinsic. Like poisons, which when used in certain doses
become medicines, and vice versa. As someone once remarked
of a certain Chasid: "He was untainted by sin only because of
his pride; he wouldn't let himself be shamed into committing a
misdemeanor."

The question is asked, therefore, whether it is permissible to
make judgments. And the answer is that one does have to
judge things all the time. It is forbidden to accept things en bloc
without investigating deeply into each matter specifically.
Every person and situation has to be examined in the context of
a surrounding reality and adjudged good or bad.

As for the nature of man, it should be remembered that there
are also good qualities in the shell which seem to belong to the
body itself, without second thoughts or self-awareness. Lust,
anger and the like are part of the animal–soul structure of man;
they belong to the life force itself. And they make a man what
he is without any consideration of good or evil. But so too does
philosophy belong to this same category of the animal-soul. For
the mental is no indication of holiness in man; it too belongs to
what is closer to his biological aspect.

We have said that everything has its life force expressed as
the animal-soul which animates it. Each such soul in man is
extremely complex and made up of thoughts and fine emotions
as well as instinctual drives. The vital, animal-soul of Israel, in
this respect, is rather special, just as the souls of Tzadikim
within Israel are special. This means that there is a genealogical
factor; just as a person is born a Jew, so is a Tzadik born with
the potential to be a saint. To be sure, education is a decisive

factor. Nevertheless, there is little doubt that certain qualities are given at birth, and there is no need for education to do more than restrain them or develop them somewhat.

A person of Israel is said to be born with three such basic qualities: pity, shyness, and kindness. And it cannot be explained by comparing greater or lesser individuals or even by pointing to generations of teaching; it is something that every Jew has, a character structure which belongs to the paradigm of Israel. Thus, a person who does not exhibit these qualities is said to be not of the seed of Abraham, Isaac, and Jacob—even though he may be a proper Jew in the sense that he performs the mitzvot.

There is a story in the Talmud of someone who went to Babylon and asked for help; and the Jews there did not come to his assistance, either with money or anything else, and he wrote saying that these were evidently not Jews, but a mongrel community, because they failed to show kindness. He did not inquire whether they prayed or put on *tefillin* or wore *tzitzit*; the fact that they did not act naturally and spontaneously with kindness was decisive.

It is not that the Jew is a better person or that he may be necessarily characterized as a good person; it is rather that the qualities of pity and shyness and kindheartedness are an intrinsic part of him: they may even be considered his weaknesses. Just as some people have a sensitive, musical ear, others have a "weakness" for other modes of experience.

This may be explained by the nature of the vital soul of Israel which is of the Nogah Shell, containing a mixture of good and evil. Actually, everything has some good in it—otherwise, it could not be said to exist. The question is: how much good, or rather, what proportion of good to evil, and what is the capacity to release the good? Because certain things can release positive qualities while others cannot. As, for instance, in chemistry, the element aluminum, which is one of the commonest components in earth and clay, can be extracted only with the greatest difficulty and then only from bauxite which is relatively rare. Bauxite will release the aluminum while other substances will not.

The difference between the Nogah Shell and other shells is

that the others do not readily release the good in them. The Nogah Shell is more ready and open to the influence that engenders such a release. In this sense, the vital soul of Israel is a Nogah Shell which is not holy but contains certain elements of good natural to it that can be released by exerting the right kind of pressure. The point is that a Jew does certain things, not necessarily because he chooses the good and recoils from evil, but because they are natural or almost instinctive to him. In the soul of the other nations, this is not as pronounced—which does not mean that a non-Jew cannot be compassionate, shy, and kindly. In the same way, there are qualities which are a function of one's relation to God, like a certain kind of joy (on the Sabbath), or humility (on the Day of Atonement) which do not come naturally. They are not a part of the vital soul of the Jew, and he can choose to be one thing or another in this respect. However, no matter how much a Jew will surrender to his passion and lower instincts and neglect his duties to holiness, he will still tend to manifest a clear inclination towards pity, shyness, and kindness.

Of course, every people may be said to have its weaknesses as well as its strengths. There are also characteristics which are of a double quality and may be a failing as well as an advantage, depending on the way they are expressed; for example, pride and generosity. And since, as it has been said that the Jews are like unto the heart of the world, they will tend to absorb and express the negative qualities of mankind as well as their own. Thus, a Jew dwelling among a nation of gentiles will be inclined to imbibe the failings as well as the good qualities of that nation.

In any case, just as every person has a vital soul, a life force, which is connected with his being human, a Jew has certain qualities connected with his being Jewish.

2

The Divine Soul

I n addition to the vital soul, every person of Israel has a Divine Soul that can be considered a part of God. Furthermore, there are many thousands of levels of Divine Souls, from the generation of the Patriarchs to the fallen generations preceding the Messiah.

Within each generation, there are also many gradations of soul; and within every person, there are different categories of this spiritual core of existence. The true heads of a generation are not necessarily recognized leaders, but they are the highest and most spiritual souls who may or may not be known, but they are connected to the rest of the souls of Israel like the head to the body.

Besides the simple division of this Divine element in man into Nefesh (Vital Soul), Ruach (Spirit), and Neshamah (Divine Soul), there is the division into many personal souls within a vast range of levels. Yet, all of them are derived from God, just as children of unlike nature can come from the same father. Each person can thus be said to be made up of three aspects: that which comes from the physical mother, that which is derived from the physical father, and that which comes from God.

In the language of the *Tanya*, which is very austere, every word has significance, and when it says that something is actually true, the intention is that it is not symbolic or allegorical or approximate, but is precisely what it says. So when the author writes that the soul of man is bound up in actual truth with the Divine through the Higher Wisdom, it is not a farfetched image, but is like the link between the mind of a human father (source of the "drop" of semen) and the nails of the feet of the son. There is only an apparent gap—the connection is very real and direct. When a person, in his ignorance and boorishness, denies his Father who is in Heaven, it does not alter the fact itself, it merely indicates something about the person; the fatherhood is not a matter of opinion.

The whole of Israel is an entity, with feet and toenails, chest and head, and soul—all drawing upon a source of life and power. To a degree, the rest of the body receives this life and power from the consciousness in the head. And the heads of Israel, as stated, are the souls of men like Tzadikim, who are able to be in some kind of contact with both God and with the people. As it was said of a famous Chasid, if a woman was in labor within 500 miles of him, he was unable to sleep because of the pain. Can a head be real if it does not sense every ache of the body? The connection is also mutual. Even Moses is not the great prophet without the people whom he has to feed like a baby.

Every individual, thus, has a definite function within the people, just as every limb or organ has its function in the body, and one of the chief problems a person has to solve for himself is to know what his function is. There is the story of the Tzadik who said to a rich, if somewhat stingy, disciple of his entourage: "You're in great danger." "Why?" asked the disciple. "Because," said the Tzadik, "every army is composed of many units—regiments, platoons, and so forth—and if a person takes upon himself to move from one unit to another, he is liable to be punished as a deserter. And you, who were supposed to belong to the brigade of philanthropists and givers of charity, have deserted to the brigade of Torah scholars."

In many respects a person may be convinced of doing the

right thing, but it may not be the right thing for him. Although each soul is a part of the Divine, it is also a wholeness in itself; and there is nothing that a person can reasonably avoid by saying, "I am no more than a limb or a part of mankind." And there is a whole order of things that he must do in their entirety, at a specific point and place in the social system, as well as within the world which is his own personal self.

From this, one may also comprehend the purpose of the injunction to love and respect devoted students of the Torah. It is important, especially for those simple persons whose own souls are relatively hidden from sight, to establish an inner relation to the true heads of the people, the highest and most spiritual souls, and in this way receive life force from the source. As for those who are even less able to establish such a connection—and no one is totally unable to do so—life force is received from "behind," unconsciously. The meaning of this odd expression, "from behind," lies in the idea of God's omnipresence. He is everywhere. And the only reason for a person's inability to establish a connection with the Divine, even in terms of relating to saintly persons around him, is that he has turned his back on God. Therefore, the life force that God in His mercy wishes to bestow on him has to be given from "behind," without that person's conscious knowledge. Repentance (Teshuvah) is thus not really a "Return" in that one goes a long way back; it is rather a simple change of direction, a turning about to receive the Divine plenty face to face.

Moreover, concerning this intrinsic nearness of God, there can be no difference between classes of people, like the learned and unlearned. Every human being is born into the world as a free and independent soul clothed in a body. The parents determine the physical vehicle; they give the child their own physical characteristics, but they do not give him his soul. That is given by God. To be sure, the physical garment of the soul is extremely important. The special way a child makes his appearance in life is usually decisive. And even many of the spiritual aspects of personality are largely inherited from parents—a mitzvah is not performed in a vacuum. Modes of behavior and habits of spiritual expression are taught. The soul, of itself, cannot perform any action at all; it has to use whatever means are available to contact holiness. Thus, the garment of the soul is of decisive importance, even though it does not activate the soul or diminish its independence.

In most cases, a great soul does have to be born of parents who are holy. And even then there is usually a constant struggle to overcome the disturbances and the obstacles caused by the inherited garment. To be sure, there may also be an instance of a small soul born to parents of great spirituality, in which case, it is easier to achieve certain things. This is perhaps a justification for the whole tradition of aristocracy or congenital superiority. Even though the soul itself is not inherited, its garment is passed on, and when this includes higher qualities of mind and body, it becomes an important factor for the expression of the soul.

The "garment" may also be called the personality of the individual, that is to say, it is not only a matter of physical characteristics. For the essential quality of a person as parent can be meaningful in many ways when considering what is transmitted to his offspring. There are the stories told of the Rabbi of Ziditzov describing how both he and his mother before him used to wake the children, even the little ones, for the Tikun Chatzot (midnight prayers for spiritual rectification), and how all five of the children turned out to be especially gifted visionaries. Which is to intimate that the more whole and holy the garment of the parents, the easier for the children to be spiritually conscious. It is also true that the same holy garment of the parents can serve as a very serious obstacle to anyone who seeks to live an unclean life; sin becomes not only an anguish of betrayal, but even the very simplicity of an unthinking act becomes impossible. Indeed, there are many people in our generation who, because of their heritage, cannot be entirely at ease with their unbelief or freedom of thought, much less with dubious political action.

On the other hand, there is the frequent birth of a great soul from unworthy parents or degrading situations. And according to the Kabbalistic writings of the School of the Ari, certain exceptional souls cannot come into the world any other way. The development of such a major personality as Rabbi Meir, whose genealogical connections with the royal family of Rome were hardly a sufficient basis for sanctity in the Jewish sense, could be explained by the fact that this particular soul belonged to the root of Esau and had to be born this way. Another example is Rabbi Akiva, who, although he came from a family of proselytes, of very plain and simple stock, had to come into the world the way he did in order to rise, to be "like unto Moses." Even Moses himself, it is said, was born of a questionable marriage. Most conspicuous in this respect is the line of the Messiah, which is certainly problematic—when we consider the instances of Judah and Tamar, Boaz and Ruth, David and Bathsheba, Solomon and Naama, and so on. One may begin to wonder, then, about the way truly great souls emerge, as it is written, from "captivity," and how, in order to do so, they have to slip across the border between the holy and the unclean.

The garment of the great soul is what disturbs it, of course, and therefore, the need for a father and mother is of itself a source of trouble. As Psalm 51 puts it: "Behold, I was shapen in iniquity; and in sin did my mother conceive me." Any soul born of gross or unworthy parents has much pain and many difficulties to overcome; how much more so an unusually great soul. All this clearly confirms that the parents do not determine the soul, no matter whether it is large or small, holy or base. They provide the garment, that is, the body, the personality, even the character traits, and no more. As it is well known, parents are usually not consulted about what they get: A saintly son can be as much a cause of dissatisfaction to certain parents as a vicious son to others. All folklore has a version of the story of the hen sitting patiently on what she believes to be her own eggs, only to hatch a gosling.

From this, it may be gathered that all Jews, no matter who they are—sinners with great souls capable of the noblest of deeds as well as of the basest, or people with small souls incapable of rising above themselves even in piety—are each and all a part of the Divine reality. And at some ultimate point in life, there is no difference between the large and small souls, the good and the bad Jews, they are all equal before God. It is not, of course, a matter of democratic equality; the differences remain, but they are differences between brothers and sisters in the same family. There are more successful and less successful brothers, but the fact that they are sons of the same father is not subject to any influence or change.

3

The Primal Flash of Wisdom

$\overline{\qquad\qquad}$

All the three levels of soul, Vital Soul (Nefesh), Spirit (Ruach), and Divine Soul (Neshamah) have within them at least three levels of the same order. That is to say, Nefesh (Vital Soul), for example, is divided into the Nefesh of the Nefesh, Ruach of the Nefesh, and Neshamah of the Nefesh, and this is only a partial indication of the complexities of the intermediate levels. In life, what characterizes the soul is the way it reflects the Ten Sefirot, which are the fundamental Divine attributes of Creation.

There are two categories of Sefirot: the three higher Sefirot, Wisdom (Chochmah), Understanding (Binah), and Knowledge (Daat), and the seven lower Sefirot, corresponding to the seven days of Creation and reflected in the basic structure of exterior reality. The three higher Sefirot of the intellect are the powers of apprehension and consciousness. They are also the foundation of all thought and emotion, while the lower categories are more like primary forces or impulses—human drives that effect a person as instinctive feelings rather than thoughts. Indeed, they can be readily converted to emotion by way of thought, although this distinction between heart and mind is of course very approximate.

Essentially however, all lower attributes are the results of Chochmah, Binah, and Daat, the Sefirot of the mind, for nothing is possible without consciousness. Love, fear, and all the other human attributes are functions of the intellect, not because of any thought process involved, but because they are products of conscious awareness. There has to be something of which one is conscious before it can become an object of love, fear, and the like.

To be more accurate about the way in which the higher Sefirot of the mind generate the lower attitudes of the soul, it should be stated that the emotion of love, for instance, is not actually born from intellect. Wisdom, understanding, and knowledge may make a person realize that something is good and beautiful and worthy of love; it cannot induce the love itself. That is a mystery of its own; love may or may not arise where one expects it.

To be sure, much has been said of the love that can be evoked by proper contemplation of the Divine. It is important to bear in mind, however, that not always do things work in the same way for different people. For instance, the *Shulchan Aruch* instructs the reader to wake in the morning with the thought that the King of Kings, the Lord Himself, in all His greatness and glory, is standing over him and watching his every move, so that he should bestir himself, jump out of bed, and begin to serve the Lord as best he can. However, as we know, even the wisest of men find this difficult.

For Wisdom itself is no more than a potential, as it is written in Hebrew, "Koach Mah." If we translate *mah* according to the expression of Moses (Exodus 16:7) as "nothing," then Chochmah is the force (*koach*) of nothing, the power of mind which is intellectual but which does not necessarily understand.

To shed some more light on this—since things do tend to get clogged with superfluous mystery—we may refer to one of the many images used by the sages. The wisdom of the soul is called the lightning flash of the mind, that which creates the primal consciousness and which is itself indivisible. After this flash there is the descent into other Sefirot, firstly into Binah (understanding) and then into all the others. In fact, what occurs in the soul transpires so quickly and so instinctively that a person cannot discern the nature of his most intimate inner movements. These inner processes are irrational and extremely rapid, which only adds to the basic difficulty of analyzing them within oneself. It is easier to see them in others. Within oneself, it may be easier to see them when the movement is slowed down, perhaps when emerging from general anesthesia.

Another insight into the dynamics of the inner processes lies in the suddenness and wholeness of the flash of understanding that comes to someone struggling with a problem—and the inability to explain, at that moment, what it is that one has grasped. There is an intuitive leap from the darkness of ignorance into light, but it is not yet understanding; that needs time. This in turn explains why the light of wisdom is said to be like a sudden flash and the quality of understanding is conceived as something almost spatial with dimensions of breadth, height or depth, as well as a large degree of transferability, something which can be communicated. At the level of pure consciousness, only forms can be grasped—or, as we have said, only the potential, the force of the "as-yet" nothing—while at the level of understanding, there is content and substance. Hence, it has been said that Wisdom is connected with vision, and Understanding, with hearing. Wisdom is a complete gestalt, an inclusive view that has to be broken down into its specific components in order for one to be able to relate to them intelligibly, with understanding. True, all the intellectual processes are thus constructed; although the units of comprehension are usually much smaller—a person does not see an entire city—he is able to encompass only small coherent units.

We tend to distinguish between the wise person and the person with understanding as though the latter, the understanding one, was the humanly preferable, being able to distinguish one thing from another, being more discriminating and more subtle than the wise who are able only to grasp the totality of things or to shed light on the obscure and the complex. From this one might deduce that the wise man is essentially passive and that it is the understanding man who possesses the double capacity of the active mind to grasp and to create. Indeed, we may observe that many a sage merely sees the truth, absorbs it, and gives it a certain abstract reality, whereas the understanding person is able to deal with the reality, to give it a variety of forms and to create new, practical realities as a result. In order to absorb truth, a person has to be passive and to realize wisdom as a potential power (Koach Mah); he has to be like Moses. The one who thinks that he knows beforehand what is coming can learn less than the wise. That is to say, the one who has already absorbed a great deal can absorb that much less of the new. No one is so dense that he cannot absorb anything at all, but there is a relationship between the readiness to receive and the capacity to absorb new things. The one who at the time of receiving feels a strong urge to say something, even in response, is absorbing that much less.

One of the recurring paradoxes in Jewish thought is related to the nature of the fool—recognizing that a valid reason for unwisdom (folly) is knowing too much. This is one of the reasons why children are often wise. They have so much of that natural humility which is the capacity to absorb things without having to relate to them critically. Altogether, this may be considered a requirement for creativity of all kinds, artistic and scientific. Even among modern physicists, the period of youth is known to be the time of innovation and creativity, the later years being devoted to elaboration and teaching of the original inspirations.

It seems to be enough then to have this openness in order for wisdom to enter, whereas to gain understanding—which is also the capacity to give expression to wisdom—one usually needs a considerable amount of experience. True, there are individuals who remain in the stage of the "flash" of wisdom, who could have become great artists or scientists had they been able to express themselves with coherence, understanding, and skill. Thus, the wise person is one who grasps knowledge that seems to come to him from outside; the understanding person is the one who comprehends and distinguishes one thing from another by some inner process of absorption and is further able to manipulate or amplify the ingredients of consciousness. To be sure, people are not entirely one thing or another, either wise or understanding; they are always a combination of both, the quality of the individual intellect being determined by the proportions of one attribute to the other.

Incidentally, many philosophic schools have called the primal flash by various names including Consciousness of Light, Truth Awareness, and Cosmic Illumination, all signifying the particular mode of awareness by which one is able to say that one grasps and distinguishes. There seems to be a general agreement that this fundamental experience of Wisdom as a flash of consciousness or as light is the basis for all apprehension of truth.

The consequent amplification of this in understanding and in terms of the power to discriminate is the basis of all human achievement. It is usually broken down into a great many details and becomes a complex matter requiring study. Thus, two things which in the realm of Wisdom are close together (one intuits a connection) may, in the realm of understanding, become far apart; and even elaborate reasoning cannot bridge the gap.

This process of contemplation may be described as a matter of taking the flash of Wisdom and breaking it down, dismantling it, and trying to find its length, breadth and depth, its integral parts, and connections and meanings. In this context, the attributes of Wisdom (Chochmah) and Understanding (Binah) are often considered as father and mother, giving birth to all the elements of life and mind, that is, consciousness, love, and all the other attributes. The relation between Wisdom and Understanding is likened to the birth process with the father providing the sperm cell "flash" and the mother sheltering the embryo until it matures into fullness of form. In the contemplation process, the time involved may be a matter of moments instead of nine months. The important thing is for a certain realization of original form to take place.

One of the ways of interpreting Amalek as a devastating influence is to see the influence as that flaw in man which does not permit freedom of passage from Wisdom to Understanding. A person may be as clever and wise as one could wish, and yet nothing may come of it if it is of the nature of Amalek. Even the most assiduous study of Torah and Scripture and Kabbalah will not alter the situation; the blocking of the passage from mind to heart causes a state of barrenness or unproductivity. That which should be given life never comes forth; the whole process is interrupted in the passage from the mental (or father) stage of thoughts or intentions to the creative (or mother) stage, and never comes to life.

As may be suspected, there are very many variations of the creative process. A person can remain within a circumstantial field of spiritual creativity with all its accompanying bliss, without having it affect the rest of his life. That is to say, the relations between Father (Wisdom) and Mother (Understanding) are seldom perfect. But when they do approach a degree of perfection, the result is Love of God and the awe, or fear, of God.

From Wisdom and Understanding, therefore, come love as well as awe and fear. Awe is intellectual, a knowledge that something is to be approached with great caution and even dread. Fear is the emotional reaction to this holiness, reaching to an almost physical terror and proving that one need not understand its nature in order to feel the dread.

This in turn occurs as a result of the recognition, created by Wisdom and Understanding, of the greatness of God. The quality of this recognition, the height of the Divine qualities which are revealed to one, is a product of the level of consciousness that is brought to bear. For it is evident that there are many planes of love and fear, and the level one reaches will correspond to the nature of contemplation. This is an insight into that which is known in Chabad philosophy as Daat (Knowledge), the mysterious third Sefirah of the acronym Chochmah, Binah, Daat (CHaBaD).

What is being said here is that the fruitful interaction between Chochmah and Binah in contemplation can bring forth thousands of ideas. The very fecundity of the process can render it meaningless and does not ensure the appearance of the desired love and fear of God. The third factor of Daat is necessary, a quality of discrimination and clarity, the ability to know what is needed in a particular situation. The mind creates according to its level of Knowledge, or Daat.

This may be better understood by the answer to the question

at the heart of ethics: How shall a person not sin? If there are so many temptations, a normal person will inevitably fall prey to some of them. If a person's mind is sufficiently occupied with something, there will be an almost automatic response to it in his life. To contemplate the greatness of God will lead to the love and fear of God, but it is much easier to linger on the things of this world—with the results we see around us.

There is a story told about a rabbi, the Zeida of Shpola, who said: "God, Lord of the Universe, you did not make the world correctly. The lusts of this life you put into the very present world, and Hell you put into the book *Reishit Chochmah*. By my beard, I am ready to warrant that had you done the contrary, and put Hell here and our lusts in *Reishit Chochmah*, no man would sin."

4

The Garments of the Soul

The soul can be said to have three garments: thought, speech, and action. The word "garment" here indicates that which conceals and covers, as well as that which is expressed or revealed to the outer world. Thus the garment "thought" is the inner clothing revealing the soul to the person himself. The garment "speech" is the outer expression of the soul in terms of ideas, and the garment "action" is the manifestation of the soul through the instruments of the physical world. Such are the ways in which the soul as a whole is clothed. What are the garments of the Divine Soul, however, that part of the human soul which is of God? And the answer given by the sages is that these are the 613 commandments of the Torah.

In contrast to the relatively straightforward expression of the various aspects of the vital soul, the expressions of the Divine Soul have to be connected somehow to the holy. But what is holy? This is given in the form of Revelation as the 613 commandments of the Torah. This does not mean that just by fulfilling these commandments a person achieves a state of sanctity or even enlightenment. It means that one cannot reach such a contact or cognition of holiness except by way of the commandments. The essential point being made here is that there is no absolute good that is not connected somehow with the Torah. People tend to attribute holiness to certain objects or places or people. Thus, there is the "holiness of the state" and the "holiness of labor" and the "holiness of the right to strike." There are so many "sanctified" things in our world, one suffers the consequences of the inevitable contradictions between them. From this, it may be concluded that, of course, they are not really holy; they are merely very important in one way or another.

The question is whether men can create new sanctities, even within the framework of religion. And it appears to be quite impossible; all such man-made holiness is artificial. Like the efforts of a certain rabbi to lift up the spiritual awareness of his pupils by jests and laughter. Even if he succeeded, the jests could hardly be considered holy.

To be sure, there is a sensitivity to holiness, which may be seen as a human capacity or talent, greater in some than in others. Holiness is not merely that which inspires; it is that which relates to God, and it is only that. And one cannot create this of oneself, even for the sake of God or in His name. All men are caught within a framework of values, of preferences and loves. And the very highest of them is still not holy unless it relates back directly to the Divine. Thus one's finest creations—even if one considers them a total sacrifice to the Lord and the best humanity is capable of producing—is still far from being holy. The gap between the human and the Divine is absolute and is not so easily bridged, neither by the noblest intentions nor the most magnificent efforts. There is no way of overcoming it; and it is with this that the snake tempted Eve when he suggested that the apple could make one "like God, knowing good and evil." It is the chief temptation of all original artists, thinkers, and men of science—the thought that by getting beyond some stage or limitation, one could be like God. Whereas, the only thing that the fruit of the tree of knowledge seems to bring is the heartache of being more aware of God, and of not being closer to God. The Divine Himself, or the actual contact with the absolute, remains out of reach. For it is only when God Himself reaches out to men as Revelation that there is contact; any significant approach to Him is possible only with the means made available by God. It is He Who determines the substance, and the manner of revealing the substance, of what is Holy. Only the Infinite can cross the abyss between man and Divinity.

Thus, Divine holiness has chosen to clothe itself as Torah in all its aspects. From this it is clear that Torah relates to something far beyond the rules of cooking food and far beyond wisdom or folly. Its essence lies in Revelation—the giving of Torah and the providing of a means of contact with the One Who gave it. And its effectiveness lies not in the intensity or devotedness in carrying out the instructions, but in the recognition of the fact that this is what God wants.

To be sure, a single individual cannot be expected to carry out all the 613 mitzvot; there are those that concern only a man or a woman, a priest or a king. Nevertheless, a person can perform them as part of the whole of Israel, as an integral component of a particular generation in time and place. For every generation is a cross section of the timeless entity which is Israel. And even if a person cannot carry out a mitzvah in terms of action, he can perform it in speech and in thought. By reading aloud and studying Torah, all the 613 mitzvot find their expression in the individual whose soul, in turn, finds therein its Tikun or correction.

As this suggests, there are many levels of uniting with Torah, depending on one's capacities. There are those who are limited by their intellects, others by their willpower or their soul roots. That is to say, a person can comprehend something in Scripture and yet be unable to make contact with it somehow, because the root of his soul shrinks from it. All men are conscious of an attraction to certain aspects of Torah and an incapacity to react to others.

There is the well-known anecdote about Rabbi Joseph Karo, one of the greatest thinkers and Kabbalists in Jewish history, who used to fall asleep at the lessons with the Ari, until the latter finally told him that this was not his way. In other words, the root of his soul was not attuned to the Kabbalah of the Ari. To be sure, this is not a common discrepancy, just as there have been instances of persons of poorly endowed intellect who were able to grasp the intricacies of the Ari with ease. Every person seems to have his own preference or talent. It is hardly even a matter of intelligence; it is more a function of the root of the soul which facilitates a direct communication with a certain subject or mode of expression in the Torah. In terms of Halachah, where the doing is important, such a gap between intellectual grasp and emotional identification becomes more obviously a problem. Chasidism is full of stories of the need of the soul for wholeness.

Concerning the mitzvot (commandments) that are specifically related to speech, the most important, perhaps, is the study of the Torah. And like all the positive mitzvot, its spiritual meaning and power is derived from love, the love of God. And one cannot express this love by any sort of spontaneous action; to go out into the street shouting that one's soul thirsts for God, would express no more than one's thirst; it would not bring one any closer to the object of one's love. Thus, the injunction to study: "Come to me all ye who thirst." To be sure, one can always say that the yearning is for God and not the Torah. The answer is that there is no water that can quench the thirst except Torah.

To be more precise, just as the performance of the mitzvah derives its power and meaning from "Devekut," the love of God (otherwise, why do it), so too is the "Devekut" or union with God without much real meaning or force unless it is accompanied by the actual carrying out of the mitzvot (otherwise, one remains with little more than good intentions). True, it may be maintained that the doing or not doing of some small act does not affect the grandeur of this love; nevertheless, love itself does not suffice with only sentiments or wishes; it demands more.

In contrast, the factor of fear or awe of God is vital in other ways. Fear of the consequences of rebelling against the Almighty compels the performance of mitzvot in no uncertain terms. At the same time, this very *yirah* can affect a person, not as fear but as shame. It is perhaps a matter of temperament. There are those who are more inclined to feel awe as a basic mode of response to the Divine and those who tend to be ashamed, remorseful, and even embarrassed by their human weakness. The latter are probably those rare individuals who feel a close relationship, even an intimacy, with God. Like Rabbi Nachman of Bratslav, who, it is said, as a boy, used to blush with shame before the Divine Omniscience every time he did or thought something he considered wrong.

In general, the system of right and wrong is not simply the "rules of the game." It reverts to a more fundamental concept of evil, as that which in its essence nourishes the "Klipah" or shell. In spite of the fact that evil is an intrinsic part of the world, it derives its life and sustenance from man, or more specifically, from the lower levels of the human. Because all the rest of creation lies outside the realm of good and evil. The tiger is no worse than the lamb; both are creatures of nature. On the same premise, the angels are also creatures outside the realm of good and evil, even though they are so much higher than man. For an angel cannot do wrong. It is unthinkable to allow angels the freedom of choice. From this it may be understood that man, for all his smallness and sinfulness, is beyond the comprehension and scope of the angel. Man stands uniquely alone in the universe.

Among the many Chasidic stories on the subject, there is the one told by the saintly Rabbi Ephraim (son of the Chacham Tzvi), about a Jew who, when being judged in Heaven, excused himself and his transgressions on the grounds that he had been given a bad wife. The angel in charge dismissed this as irrelevant, whereupon this same angel was himself sent to live on earth with an uncongenial spouse. His life was so bitter that he became sick unto death, and eventually had to admit that he had learned the true meaning of a bad wife.

All of this confirms that of all the things and creatures in the universe, the only thing that allows evil to flourish is man. With all his many opportunities for choosing the good and the uplifting, man seems to persist in sustaining the sinful. Whether he knows it or not, whenever a man does anything prohibited by the commandments, he nourishes and gives life to one of the forces of evil. In this context, the evil may thus be seen as a parasitic entity, living off of man. Indeed, everything that is not directed to holiness slips off into the other realm of the unholy, into one form or another of what is inimical to good in mind or heart or deed.

The Torah itself is higher than the soul, and a person can thus use the Torah as a bridge to God—although, to be sure, the Torah is not only an instrument. It is the Divine Wisdom and at certain levels is itself Divine, so that it is the perfect vessel of communication between man and God. The problem is that at the level of Divine Wisdom the Torah is just as inaccessible as God Himself. Consequently, Torah has to descend, level by level, so that it can be grasped by ordinary mortals—that is to say, the Torah contains practical actions and specific instructions about life. Comparatively little is left to speculation of a higher level. The Torah bows down to earth in order to enable all men to make contact with it.

As an illustration, let us consider the computer, composed as it is of a large number of levels. At the highest levels, the theory and the details are so intricate only the most expert minds can deal with it. At lower levels, the people with normal education and intelligence can be taught to ask questions of the computer and receive answers. The way in which all this works is again out of the range of those who operate it. Similarly, were the Torah to remain in the world of Briah (Creation), at the level of the Higher Angels, it would be utterly incomprehensible. Whereas if it says that on Purim one should give presents to the poor, the Torah becomes available to all men. Even the whole realm of the abstract Halachah (Code of Law) relating Torah and action—why to give presents to the poor, and what this should consist of, and what if one is poor himself—all this is something an ordinary person need not concern himself with. The one thing required is something that every man can do. Such a genuine contact is the start and basis. Thereafter, the opportunity is given to all who care to enter the Torah to rise level by level to the infinite without ever losing this real contact.

5

The Way of Understanding

Having touched upon the subject of the way a person apprehends the Divine through Torah, it may be necessary to clarify this matter somewhat—especially since the *Patach Eliahu* section of the Zohar says thought cannot grasp Him at all. What do we mean by the term the apprehending or grasping of God? Is this more than an intellectual act?

When the intelligence understands something, that which is so apprehended becomes encompassed by, or contained within, the mind. At the same time, as intelligence encompasses the object, there is an opposite movement in which the intelligence is itself clothed and revealed within the object of thought. Thus, when a person studies some precept of Halachah in the Talmud, the comprehension, when fully realized, means that the precept is now contained within the mind as an intellectual truth. Simultaneously, the intelligence of the student is revealed in the object of thought; that is, when expressed, the precept will now contain the mind of the student. There is a certain mutuality, therefore, in the process of full apprehension—intelligence and object of intelligence encompass each other; or, as the Hebrew image puts it, each becomes clothed in the other. And if the object of inquiry is a precept from the Torah, one's mind grasps something of Divine Will and Wisdom by understanding the precept. Also, when a person is engaged in another sort of problem, such as in mathematics or physics, whether practical or not, the real issue is actually beyond the specific situation because it is concerned with the same kind of truth that exists in Halachah, which also emerged from and went beyond the specific situation.

To be sure, a person only grasps a minute portion of Divine Will and Wisdom in either case; the larger causes and reasons exceed his capacity of understanding. The point is that there is no other way of grasping even this minute portion except by entering into a study of specific problems—by inquiring into the way Divine Will and Wisdom are exercised. One would hardly be able to learn much by abstract meditation, even if one were vouchsafed visions of heavenly angels. The point is that much of what goes on in the mind is so much a product of the mind itself that the apprehension of truth requires at least a certain fulcrum of actuality, no matter how little. This is obtained by studying the words of Torah, by inquiring into a certain incident or example in the Talmud, and by letting the intelligence run into the channels of Divine thought. Divine Wisdom thus clothes itself with the student's thought, even though it is also that which encompasses his thought. Also, the Word of God, Divine Wisdom, becomes a part of the thinker's mind and, in a sense, encompasses it. The union of the two, this mutually encompassing process, is something beyond all material fulfillment. At that moment of union, when a fragment of Torah is understood, the mind of man becomes a divine "mansion" and the identity of thinking between man and the Divine is a source of extreme joy.

To be sure, in performing a mitzvah, there is also an identification with the Divine Will, but in Torah study the wonderful advantage lies in more than saying or even learning the words; it lies in this union of the mind by a mutual encompassing. The mitzvah requires a personal expression. How one performs it is unique; the practical aspect of one's body is intrinsic to it. God clothes the soul of man in the mitzvah, and man reveals himself in the expression of the mitzvah. However, in study, the intelligence itself becomes clothed in Divine Wisdom and this is irrespective of the intellectual level of the student. The words and mind of God become a part of the student's whole being.

In this way, the subject of thought and the thinker become one in the soul; the idea is absorbed entirely into oneself. The learning is not an exterior act of intellectual acquisition; it is a grasping on all levels and forms of being; it encompasses one's life as well as one's mind. Torah has been likened to bread, bread of the soul or sustenance of the soul, whereas the mitzvah is called a garment of the soul, that by which the person is clothed, in the sense that it is the way a person acts and is seen to act. In Torah study, it is not only that one thinks in terms of Torah, but also that the Torah thinks within oneself. It is an object that becomes a subject, capable of expressing itself in one's own thoughts and actions.

That which is known is thus encompassed by the mind, and the mind is clothed by it, so to speak. The knower can also communicate it and transfer it to another. It is largely agreed that whenever there is a difficulty or lack of clarity in making this transfer, in explaining, this reflects a certain lack of understanding, as well as an incapacity to transmit adequately. In either case, this may be due to other factors besides incompetence. For instance, it may be a product of the nature of the gap between communicator and receiver, as between one who knows "too much" and a child or beginner.

On the whole, however, the one who really comprehends can also transmit what he knows to others. It can also be said that the mind is within the object of cognition, as when thinking about something in total fashion so that it seems all-encompassing. The knower is thus wrapped in the object of his thought; he is submerged in it, and it may be communicated or transmitted with or without conscious participation on his part.

6

Klipat Nogah, The Shell of Light

The secular, or that which is not specifically within the limits of the mitzvah, has always been pushed aside in Jewish life. As one Chasidic saying puts it: "That which is forbidden is forbidden, and that which is permitted should not be hurried." Another, even more sharply expressed version of this approach is: "What is forbidden is forbidden, and what is permitted is not needed." There is more here than a hint of the feeling that what is forbidden is unclean, comes from the "Sitra Achra" (the other side), and is beyond repair, while that which we consider permitted is also of the nature of the shell and "Sitra Achra," the difference between them being, not in their belonging to one side or another of the shell, but in their inner essence, in the possibility of correcting or remedying the harm that they may do.

Why should all that is not forbidden—and that which is forbidden can be of many kinds, whether connected with dietary laws of *kashrut* or the ethical rules of behavior—why should this be considered as belonging to the shell? The answer lurks in the relationship to the desires of the body altogether. Even if they are conceded to be permissible and even necessary, they are still of the nature of the shell because they are not

29

for the sake of Heaven. There is no neutral territory; nothing is neither holy nor profane, and there is no in-between state. From this, it follows that an object, a thought, or an action has to belong to one or the other—either to the holy or to the "unclean."

Thus, even the essential needs of man, like minimal food and water, are still of the shell; a person can be greedy if he consumes even a dry crust of bread voraciously. One may not be able to afford the luxuries of meat and drink, and yet, in the simplest and most innocent way, be guilty of gluttony by the mere fact that he is not eating for the "sake of Heaven." Similarly, a person may be clothed in gold and silk and partake of the greatest delicacies, doing so as a mode of Divine worship, in purity and in holiness. It is not the permission granted to perform an action that takes it out of the category of the shell. So long as it remains tied to the needs and desires of the body and not to the explicit desires of God, it is of the category of that which is not holy, that is, of the shell.

There is a story, which may help illustrate this point, about a man who was a famous recluse and ascetic. He was also a great scholar and something of a saint, wearing sackcloth next to his skin and practicing self-abnegation. One day he went to visit one of the great Chasidic rabbis; on arrival, he thought it would be appropriate to open his jacket a little and expose the sackcloth underneath. The rabbi peered at him and kept saying, "How clever he is. How wise he is." After hearing this repeated several times, the ascetic could not refrain from asking, "Who? Who is wise?" And the rabbi answered: "The Evil Impulse—who took such a one as you and put him into a sack." The truth is that a person can remain all his life modest and frugal and decent and can still be doing it entirely for himself. His life then belongs to his animal-soul, that is to the Nogah Shell, the Shell of Light.

As we have said, there are three shells which are impure and one shell, called Klipat Nogah, the Shell of Light, which, although it too is of "Sitra Achra," can be considered to represent its more congenial aspect. The name Klipat Nogah is taken from the Book of Ezekiel in the Bible in which there is a description of darkness and wind and storm and a great fire with a Nogah light about it. There is also the metaphor of the two layers of the shell of a nut; the outer shell is hard and thus inedible, while the inner soft shell is edible, but only to be eaten under duress. This inner soft shell is called a Nogah Shell.

There are many exhortations by the sages about the need to perceive this shell, it being so much more difficult to distinguish than the other shells. A person may do what is permitted and feel quite uplifted as well as justified in all his actions and still be caught in the world of the shell.

It is said that in this World of Action, most of it is bad, and only a little good is mixed into it. This little good can be extracted and used. It is also the basis for the good in the animal-soul of Israel. For the fact is that Israel has an innate tendency to compassion, shyness, and kindness, not only on account of its Divine Soul but also on account of its nature, its animal-soul. Indeed, the Talmud has a whole list of attributes of the beasts of the earth—from the cleanliness of the cat to the hoarding instincts of the ant—all of them are qualities men can learn from, and yet they clearly belong to the realm of nature, the *klipah* or shell.

There is a certain wisdom in placing the Shell of Light, the Klipat Nogah, in the same category as the three unclean shells and not somewhere higher, closer to the realm of holiness. Since there is no in-between layer between holiness and the shell of life, Klipat Nogah has to remain a part of the Shell as a point of departure to holiness; it is not itself a part of the holy. Only after considerable preparation and work, can the transition be made, and one can succeed in elevating things from Klipat Nogah to Holiness.

To do this one has to have acquired a certain level of being. First, one must distinguish clearly between the good and the evil in the things one wishes to raise. Otherwise, it is possible to make a serious mistake and raise something essentially unclean that has good in it. Secondly, the good itself has to be of such a nature that it can merge with holiness. The example is given of eating meat and drinking wine (Klipat Nogah objects) in order to have strength to study Torah. Here, the enjoyment of the things of the Klipah can be of decisive nature. One has to be subtle in discriminating between good and evil—

how one eats, what one takes pleasure in, even with the noblest of intentions. It is also important that in the act some genuine change takes place in the doer. Saying a blessing is obviously not enough to sanctify the act of eating; indeed, there is no formula for the elevation of anything to the realm of holiness. What is needed is a conscious integration of intention and action as a continuous whole "for the sake of Heaven." There has to be an actual elevation of the good in the thing being sanctified. Thus, merely enjoying the three meals of the Sabbath is no more than an outer performance of the mitzvah, if one does not, at the same time, enjoy the holiness of the day with every bite one takes. Only then is one offering a sacrifice to God. The food, which is organic matter of a certain "permitted" order of existence, is raised to the realm of the holy.

The difference between the two kinds of mitzvot lies in something more than intention itself. The intention expresses only one's own subjective view of the act; the higher one's level of being and sincerity, the higher the dimension of the performance. At the highest level, it becomes a sacrifice, an offering; and it has always been a tradition in Israel to remember that before the destruction of the Temple, offering the sacrifice upon the altar in the Holy Temple was able to atone for the transgressions of the people. Now the altar is the table at which the daily meal is eaten. The salt on the table is the symbol of the covenant of the sacrifice; and, similarly, it is a custom to remove all the knives from the table before the blessing which concludes the meal—this in recognition of the prohibition of using any iron implements on the holy altar. Thus, the table where one eats can serve as an atonement, although it is, of course, not enough to place the salt or to remove the knife.

It would obviously be a simplification to say that a person should eat for the sake of Heaven. In this respect, incidentally, the Chasidim do not follow the common custom of wishing "Good appetite" to someone partaking of food. They will say "LaBriut" (for good health). The sharp appetite is often an obstacle in overcoming the physical desire when one is anxious to make eating an integral part of a mitzvah and to raise the food to holiness. Eating is thus not only the instrument of a mitzvah, it can itself become the mitzvah.

Another example of the transforming of the Nogah Shell to holiness is the use of humor to lighten the heart and mind while studying Torah. As it is reported to have been said by Rabbi Aharon of Karlin, as well as by other Chasidic masters, that joy is something that is not a mitzvah in the Torah, and yet it is greater than all the other mitzvot. Sadness is not a transgression; yet it is worse than all the transgressions because it dulls the heart and closes the mind. In jesting too, just as in eating and drinking, a person has to be aware of himself and know what he is doing. There is a whole code and a vast amount of technique involved. A certain Tzadik once said that it was easier for him to study a tractate of Talmud than to eat his dinner properly. He could handle the complexities of the Talmud well enough; the difficulties of his evening meal were more complicated for him, and he really preferred to fast.

In order to attain such a level of consciousness one has to be consistently struggling with the shell in the realm of the permitted, constantly discriminating, constantly aware of the process of raising the action up as a sacrifice. And it is not beyond the powers of an ordinary mortal. One does not have to be an exceptional spiritual being; it is a matter of making the proper effort of consciousness. A person has to be in such a state of mind that everything he does is performed for a higher purpose; and the higher the level of consciousness, the higher the aim, the more the person himself is elevated.

If someone does not do this, if he eats in order to satisfy his hunger, he remains temporarily in the realm of the Shell. But only for the duration of his unawareness, for as soon as he begins to act for the sake of Heaven, then all the previous eating takes on the meaningfulness of the holy. He could not have arrived at this higher level without having eaten, even if mindlessly. There is the story in the Midrash about Chanoch who sewed shoes, and with every stitch he said, "Blessed is the name of the Glory of His Kingdom Forever." Thus, a person can combine a certain intention with every stitch of his life, directing it toward Heaven. This in turn raises him toward

God and makes him something of an angel; but what about the person who does not do this? While sewing shoes, he remains within the shell. The money he earns is, albeit, honestly come by, and some goes to charity, and the rest is spent on the proper demands of the good life—and thus he, too, also approaches the realm of holiness. The real difference seems to lie in the degree of awareness at the moment of action. Perhaps the secular life, at this level, is another shell, connected with impurity in such a loose manner it is easily given to separation.

Similarly, in trying to judge whether a thing is permitted or forbidden, one has to take into consideration whether it has the potential of being raised to holiness. That is, if it can be genuinely corrected or repaired by the influence of human intention. If so, it is permitted; if no such potential exists, it can be considered forbidden.

Someone once asked why are there now apparently so many more prohibitions than in ancient times. Could it be that the Jews of Talmudic times were transgressing unaware? The answer is that it was a matter of the capacity to make use of that which is given. The lower the level of the generation, the more forbidden to it; that is to say, there are many more things it cannot raise up, remedy, or repair. Tentatively, one can say that the greater a person, the more he can accomplish in the way of correcting the world; the smaller a person, the less he can do and, therefore, the greater the number of prohibitions imposed on him. This relationship is, of course, not one-sided. When a person eats, he not only has an effect on the food; the food also has its effect on him. The teller of jokes not only amuses the listener; he is himself affected in one way or another. In the same way, the nearer a thing is to impurity and unholiness, the greater the danger to the one who deals with it. A person gets carried along.

There is the story of Rabbi Elazar ben Arach, a great Talmudic scholar who lived comfortably and well. Rabbi Elazar began to slide downhill because of the good life, and he lost his reputation and his good name. For it is difficult to come in contact with such things and not be influenced by them. In a mood of bitter humor someone once remarked that only God can offer help to sinners without getting dirty. Men always tend to become involved with the forces of good and evil. Even a pupil–teacher relationship is never one-sided so that there are many precautions one must take and many prohibitions to be observed to help one deal with the questionable things that lie "in-between." Of course, there are people who are able to withstand negative influences while dealing with questionable things and people—but these are few.

For example, a person may eat like an animal grazing in the field. Bear in mind that the eating habits of animals are highly commendable: They will not consume more than the body requires nor will they, as a rule, eat what is harmful. Thus, any unholiness or uncleanness accruing to such a person may be considered a part of the universal impurity of nature. Even then, even if the same natural person eats differently, consciously, raising the food to a higher dimension, the act of biting and chewing leaves a scar. This scar can never be entirely eliminated; it is beyond "Tikun" or repair, or at least beyond the repair that leaves no mark. True, most things can be corrected, but few, if any, cracks or ruptures can be put together so well that there will be no impression or scar. This scar on the flesh of man influences the whole structure of human life. In one afternoon meal, a person can lose much of the spiritual refinement of years. On the whole, however, the influence is cumulative in both directions—holy and profane.

The opposite is also true. The body of a saint or Tzadik is not impure, and even in death does not contaminate. For just as eating may add to the impurity of nature, it can also add to holiness. Every bite that transforms food, like every jest that raises the essence of a situation, accumulates and forms something that remains and lasts even in the realm of the physical. As the biblical expression puts it: "And it shall be engraved on your bones." Every act leaves its mark and becomes part of the body.

7

Levels of Repentance

The permitted can be seen as mobile: free to move from one level to another. In such a case, the action of repentance or restoration to holiness, following on the unthinking performance of a permitted act, completely changes its character and transposes that unthinking act from one realm to another. Conversely, when someone performs a forbidden act, that act is beyond repair. Neither the prayers nor the good deeds of that person can correct his transgressions, for the mitzvot are mitzvot and the transgressions remain transgressions. There is no question of blending or mixing, of taking from the one to mitigate the other. Mitzvot and transgressions are neither complementary nor opposite poles, like plus and minus, which cancel each other out. True, there is an ultimate judgment of good and of evil in which an individual life is weighed in the balance. But that judgment examines each separate action by itself. The good deeds do not influence the badness of the bad deeds, and the bad deeds, no matter how many or how terrible, cannot alter the existence or the value of the humblest good. There is simply no common denominator between them.

It has often been said that even the wickedest of the wicked, the most vicious of blasphemers, has also to perform the mitzvot. And if he can keep even one mitzvah, no matter which, it is a genuine mitzvah; and the fact that he is a criminal, bound to end up in perdition, is another matter and has nothing to do with it. There are two separate reckonings, each in a different dimension. The transgression belongs to the domain of evil; it is beyond correction and remains forbidden or taboo. Its only chance for release is the end of days, when death shall be vanquished forever. Thus, it is not even a matter of the coming of the Messiah, but rather of the transformation of the very structure of the world as world. Only when the essence of the world will change, will the spirit of uncleanness pass from the earth; and even then, a selection and purification process will have to take place to release the sparks of holiness that have been imprisoned in the evil. This, clearly, is not given to man to do.

What is it then which nevertheless makes correction possible? How can repentance have any real effect? There are actually two levels of repentance. One is that related to those sins committed in error, which includes sins for which the individual is held responsible, just as though they had been committed deliberately. As the Baal Shem Tov said, when a person repents he places himself on another level of consciousness: "What I know now I was previously unconscious of." One rises to a higher level, in which sins are seen as mistakes. That which was previously considered an action performed in full awareness is now viewed as having been performed in ignorance. As it has been said, "A person does not sin unless the spirit of folly enters into him." With the passing of folly comes the recognition of error. That is one level of repentance, the one in which a person extricates himself from a certain way of life and severs himself from his past in order to reach another level of being.

The second level of repentance is the one in which deliberate sins are transmuted into virtues, when every transgression one has committed is reckoned as though it were a mitzvah. To reach this very high level of repentance, the individual must reach a point in his life equivalent to "the end of days," the edge of time and world. He must change the very essence of himself so drastically that all the facts of his existence, all thoughts or actions, assume an entirely different meaning. He shifts into another field of being. The incalculable difficulty of such a shift may be illustrated with a simple example from the physical world. Let us take the laws of symmetry; while it is mathematically possible to find the correspondence for almost anything in terms of geometrical perspective, it is practically impossible to transform something with a right-hand sym- metry to a left-hand symmetry, like a glove for instance. The whole system of coordinates has to be revolutionized or transcended. To transform the Sitra Achra into holiness, or one's sins into virtues, requires the same sort of total upheaval as changing a left glove to a right glove. Incidentally, one of the expressions used to depict this sort of repentance is "to turn inside out like a seal," the seal consisting today, as in ancient times, of an embossed emblem whose negative face is inscribed when pressed. The negative-positive relationship of the faces of a seal is the same as the left-right relationship of the hands. This extreme transformation requires the most drastic action that the individual can undertake: repentance which is done out of love and not out of fear.

This repentance must come, therefore, from the depths of the heart, not out of its shallowness. In practical terms, one must relate back to that which he truly desires. For the individual has many desires and the question must therefore be: Which one is the true desire? A man may insist that he really wants to grow in spirit and to carry out the command- ments. Does he really want this with all his being, from the depths of his heart? Were he given complete freedom, what would he do?

There has to be a "great love" for a person to lust for the things of the other world. This great love then becomes a passion, like other passions, but even more difficult to bear. As it is written: "My soul thirsts for thee like one in a barren land," that is, without water. Whereas the Tzadik can satisfy his thirst, indulge his passion for the Divine for the duration of his life, the penitent is driven by his accumulated agony of long unsatisfied thirst and his sense of shame. Thus, when the penitent indulges his passion for the Divine, after years in the wilderness, his iniquities are transformed into virtues. Every moment empty of sin can now be filled with something positive and life-giving. Subsequently, when a person has reached such a level of penitence, it may be said that he is transmuting the evil he did previously and making it part of holiness.

There is a Psalm of David concerning the Prophet Nathan, who came to the king with regard to David's infamous conduct with Bathsheba. It is said that the penitent must come to God with the same irrepressible longing as that which brought David to Bathsheba; otherwise he cannot truly be said to have experienced contrition. He who repents must pass through all stages of regret and painful knowledge of his sin, and these stages must often be repeated in order to deepen his comprehension before he can start life anew.

There are many levels of repentance. One person may need to make ever greater and more intense efforts towards Divine unity while another may desire no more than to be able to make an honest living. True, there is also a matter of proportion—the more one has been sunk in sin the greater the pressure to emerge. Just as a dam holds back a body of water, the higher the dam the greater the power which can afterwards be extracted from release. But all this means that the sinner has to go through all the intervening stages of growth and comprehension, and that the more he learns of the magnitude of his past transgressions, the more painful the knowledge and the more effective the transformation.

A person who has sinned for ten, twenty, or fifty years, feels the immense vacuum in that part of his life. Although he strives desperately to fill it, there seems to be an emptiness that nothing can satisfy, and his past evildoing, even if thoroughly repented, becomes part of the structure of his soul in the opposite direction. This is why it is said that, in a way, a true penitent, with that extra power of recollected sin, stands on a higher level than a Tzadik who has never sinned at all. The nature of the transformation is more like a chemical change, a change of essence rather than a change of form or place. Everything that was true of a person is transmuted into a different substance.

To be sure, not everyone is granted such a level of repentance, for it is indeed rare and difficult to attain. A Talmudic story tells of Elazar ben Durdia, a man who was, indeed, such a sinner that there was hardly a single sin that he had not committed, decided one day to repent. He thereupon went about seeking help from the world. He went to the hills and mountains and begged them to ask for mercy on his behalf. The hills replied: "Before we ask for mercy for you, we must plead for mercy for ourselves." He went to the heavens and made a similar request. The heavens also answered: "Before we ask for mercy for you, we have to plead for mercy for ourselves." Ben Durdia therefore realized that the matter depended on his own repentance alone, and it is written that he placed his head between his knees and burst into such weeping and crying that his soul departed. Then a voice from Heaven was heard saying: "Rabbi Elazar ben Durdia is permitted to enter the life hereafter."

In any case, this extraordinary repentance, arising out of great love, heals and makes whole the totality of a personality. There is no need for mortification and self-flagellation; one has primarily to live through the feeling of remorse; the combination of longing and the knowledge of what is lacking to fulfill that longing is as much anguish as one can bear. Everything is overturned.

In relation to Elazar ben Durdia a student asked: "It may be possible for the man to make an upheaval so completely sincere that he experienced complete repentance—but how could he have become a rabbi in that hour? After all, a rabbi must be learned." The reply to this, given by a Chasid, was that a rabbi is one who teaches others. Thus, when Elazar ben Durdia made his heartbreaking repentance, he became a teacher of many generations of penitents by showing them the way. Teaching is transmitted not only by means of rules and doctrines; the Halachah itself can be taught by demonstration. It is true that such extreme repentance cannot be demanded of others, for not everyone is capable of such intensity of feeling; nevertheless one can learn from it to repent out of love. Then, even if one fails to reach higher levels of Divine love, such sincere repentance can be effective and the return to God full of a sense of forgiveness. It is as though God assures us that we have become new people.

Nevertheless, once committed, the bad deeds are unalterable facts. Even their value as actions cannot be made to appear to be anything else; the evil deed remains an evil deed forever. And it does not always matter whether the evil was committed as a thought, as a casually spoken word, or as a shameful act. A transgression is that which creates uncleanness and evil in the world. This uncleanness remains, and the transgressor is responsible for it. When he repents, God releases him from the responsibility for the evil act, but the act itself remains. Remorse may loosen the cord that binds one to the evil deed, but it does not eliminate the deed. That which is done is done. This is not to say that it can never be undone at all, but few men can ever succeed in wholly accomplishing such an undoing. Incidentally, this is one of the chief differences between the permitted and the forbidden. The wrong action in the realm of the permitted can be set right, whereas the wrong action in the realm of the forbidden is beyond repair—for instance, unlawful coition, forbidden foods, or repellent thoughts.

On the other hand, the wasteful emission of semen, although connected with the three unclean shells, is a transgression which can, in essence, be repaired, because it has no consequences in terms of reality. It is written that whoever recites the "Shema" (Hear, O Israel, God is One) at bedtime, is like one who wields a two-edged sword to slay the "extraneous forces" that become garments for the unholy in the drops of semen. The shameful action may thus be wiped out. On the other hand, it is also written that the same transgression is incised into the structure of the world and leaves a hole or scar. It is an irreparable damage, no matter how much good one does afterwards. Nevertheless, it is noted that this sin of wasteful emission of semen is not mentioned specifically in the Torah.

The reason for this is that every transgression brings into being certain creatures, these so-called "extraneous forces." Just as every good deed creates an angel, the essence of every wrong action causes a similar essence to come into existence.

These evil products of sin, the many unnatural offspring of man, cry out to be recognized and supported as legitimate sons. They follow the person relentlessly, out of a sense of kinship and belonging, nurturing his remorse and exacting his punishment, unto death. Ordinarily a person cannot obliterate them. They exist in the worlds above and below ours, these angelic and demonic products of our deeds, and only repentance out of love can change the essence of the evil into good, the dark into light.

As for those terrible deeds whose consequences are irreparable and ineradicable—like conceiving a bastard or murdering a human being—there is no possible "Tikun" or correction for them. They are irreversible and ineradicable. The illegitimate child may become a great saint or Tzadik, but the evil is not thereby eliminated. The more a sin takes objective form, the more difficult it is to make reparation, which need not mean that sins of a physical nature are greater than those of a spiritual nature. A subtle, spiritual transgression can be even more profound and ugly, reaching right into the roots of life. Nevertheless, sins of the spirit are more easily given restoration and Tikun because they are less bound up with physical substance.

The point is that man is in a ceaseless state of conflict, suspended between the holy and the other side (Sitra Achra). He has to know where each is located, and mere adherence to the *Shulchan Aruch*, the code of law, is not enough. There are many areas and situations that require understanding and spiritual discrimination.

8

Concerning the Permitted and the Forbidden

A s we know, the definition of what is permitted and what is forbidden may be clear enough; and yet, the individual may easily err, for instance, by unwittingly eating prohibited food. Even if he has conducted himself properly, blessing the food and consuming it with the noblest of motives, there is no evading the objective reality of transgression. Once again, it is a question of the essential nature of holiness and of its opposite. The permitted and the forbidden are not subjective concepts related to one's personality, preferences, or opinions, but are derived from the fact of the existence of the holy and the profane. What is more, ignorance of the forbidden does not make it any less prohibited. The essence of the forbidden resides in the nature of the thing itself and is absolute, not relative. One may reach for beer in the refrigerator and draw forth a similar bottle of something which is in fact undrinkable: the fact that the intention was correct can have no influence on its disagreeable effects.

So it is with the sin of the individual who unknowingly does that which is forbidden. It makes no difference whether the act was performed in total ignorance, whether it was done under duress, whether it was a severe transgression of an injunction from the Torah or a trifling infringement of a rabbinical ruling. The fact that it is a forbidden act places it in the category of the three unclean shells, from which there is no simple and easy way back. In certain strange passages in the book *Tana d'vei Eliahu* dealing with the difference between ugly sins and transgressions that are not so repulsive, a parenthetical addition claims that the former are transgressions that are unsuited to Jews and can occur only through the agency of "alien" demons. Naturally, one can lust after all sorts of things, but there is nonetheless a distinction between normal and abnormal desires. When a person lives within the framework of a Jewish life, his struggles and misdemeanors are confined to the realm of the more or less permitted; and when he is attacked by desires that have their origin and quality in the absolutely forbidden, one says that they are not characteristically "Jewish."

The reason for the "Jewishness" of the demonic craving for the permissible is that this can be converted back to holiness. Anecdotes about the demons in yeshivot describe these impish creatures as quite well versed in Torah and adept at arguing issues of Halachic code. They are part of the Jewish domain of influence, and they assume the appropriate manners and language. We are able to converse with them, so to speak. Ultimately, our defeat at the hands of such an evil influence is never complete because there is something in us which says: "Well, so I've committed such and such a transgression, but I am really a good Jew. . . ." This saving factor consists of an inner hesitation or refusal to cut oneself off from one's Jewishness.

A story about two school friends, pupils of a certain famous rabbi in Russia, tells of their meeting again after many years. In the interim, one had become a Bolshevik commissar while the other had remained a simple God-fearing Jew. After their initial greetings, the pious disciple of the rabbi asked the commissar, "What have you retained of all that we once studied together?" The commissar answered: "I'll be frank with you, I remember practically nothing, but though I certainly sin without regret, I cannot enjoy it or even justify myself."

There is a question about the nature of these demons which

slip into our lives. It is difficult to answer because of the sly way in which they masquerade. In our imaginations, they are portrayed as only partly human and rather grotesque, so that we fail to identify them in the perfectly normal dress and features of passers-by or even of persons we know fairly well— those we meet, perhaps, twice a day. Another point is that we ourselves create demons in our lives, not in the form of a dybbuk who enters into us and causes trouble and consternation, but rather in the form of creatures to which our thoughts give birth. For every human being continually brings into existence a long line of spiritual offspring.

According to certain traditions, these demonic offspring can also multiply themselves. It is written in the Talmud that the first man, Adam, gave birth to the first demons and since then they have been our stepbrothers. Altogether, the relationship between good and evil, man and demon, is most complex. It is not a straightforward opposition of one against the other. It is more in the nature of a mutual dependence, or of a parasitical relationship, made up of compounded love and hate. The unclean does not only endeavor to destroy the holy, but also loves it because it is the source of its nourishment. There is a kind of attraction which becomes destructive upon contact but which nevertheless persists; the two forces strive to unite with one another in a process of exchange, of give and take.

It would seem that in this exchange of good and evil the demonic flourishes at the expense of the human. However, in certain instances it is otherwise, and this is the essence of Tikun, the process of repairing damage, of correcting wrong thoughts and actions. The difficulty in every attempt at Tikun, or making right the evil—and, perhaps, one of the central problems of repentance as a process and not as a decision—is the fact that when a person tries to return to the good by way of correcting the evil, he has to struggle with the evil, enter into it, and recall it. To feel remorse is to experience the curse and the pain of a sinful act. At the same time, it leads to temptation yet again, for dwelling on the evil act is itself a very involved and complex process, with love and attraction still alive behind the intention to overcome and abandon. The monster still loves and is loved, and there is a closeness, a kinship, which is

capable of drawing one back to that from which one is trying to
flee. Anyone who has sincerely worked at repentance will
know the complexity of the matter, that evil is capable of
breeding more evil in many ways, breeding itself independently of the good, and yet in such symbiotic association with
it that it becomes capable of destruction of that good without
intending or wishing to do so. Evil is a kind of parasite which
chokes the thing it lives on. This is one of the ways in which
"the sin lies in wait at the opening, and his desire is for you"
(Genesis 4:8). Sin wants you, lusts after you, not because you
are sinful and desire him, but because you are the substance
from which sin draws life.

Therefore, when a person lusts for that which is permitted,
he creates a Jewish sort of demon that is amenable to the
rectification process of Tikun. Although, to be sure, it is still
Sitra Achra and belongs to the shell. Let us take again the
example of eating whereby food instantaneously becomes part
of the individual. If the food is not holy, that is, not eaten with
proper *kavanah* for the sake of Heaven, then, at that moment of
partaking of the food, an opening is provided for the Sitra
Achra to enter. In the same way (and every metaphor has, of
course, a limited application), all harmful substances (such as
radiation), though they affect different people in different
ways, still have a cumulative effect of varying degree. So too,
a person can destroy himself with infinitesimal amounts of
uncleanness, even if he eats only according to what is permitted. If one adheres only to the external act of that which is
allowed by law, this can lead to a decline and fall.

The Talmud tells us that Jerusalem and the Second Temple
were destroyed because the people lived by the letter of the law
and not by its spirit. The danger in such a way of life is pride,
which can, without being noticed, carry the individual beyond
the limits of safety. Even the most decent and righteous
individual, almost every normal and good Jew, will experience
the absence of holiness in the passing of every day, even if only
for a few minutes. Therefore, the body must undergo the
purgatory of the grave, that is, death.

To be sure, there are the saintly ones, like Rabbi Yehudah
HaNasi, who, even though he lived in wealth and princely

splendor, was said never to have enjoyed the things of this world, not even to the minutest degree. When he died, it was declared that "holiness is nullified" in order to allow the Priests to bury him. For in contrast to ordinary mortals, the Tzadikim do not become impure, and their graves are not considered places of defilement. It is not the body itself which is unclean; it is the accumulation of unholiness throughout life which, when the soul departs, makes it a vessel of spiritual contamination.

Clearly, there is more to the Nogah Shell than the domain of permitted food and drink. A large variety of subtle and powerful forces are included in it, such as those which interfere with the capacity to concentrate on the study of Scripture. It is not only a matter of frustration and waste of time; neglect of Torah is also a serious sin.

To be sure, there are people who cannot study at all, and for them, the neglect of Torah has another connotation. Nevertheless, even for such as these, the transgression is just as real a fact, and correction or Tikun has to be made. Unlike the Tikun for wrong eating or drinking, where the damage is only potential since the food does serve to sustain the body for good deeds, any idle waste of time belongs almost entirely to the sins of the soul, and such a sin requires Tikun, or removal of the uncleanness, by "the hollow of a sling" (Talmud, Shabbat 152b, referring to I Samuel 25:29 which states: "The soul of my lord shall be bound in the bundle of life with the Lord your God, and the souls of thine enemies, them shall He sling out, as out of the hollow of a sling").

The expression "hollow of a sling" is connected with the "bundle of life" after death, and although the Bible hardly treats the subject (of life after death), the Sages have explained the "hollow of a sling" in unusual imagery. There are two angels at the opposite ends of the world, and between them they toss the soul from one end of the world to the other. The "hollow of a sling" is, thus, the experience of seeing life again; the sling itself is not Hell or purgatory, it is that which is experienced as a person goes back over his whole life and sees it all anew. True, this can be painful enough, for in life memory has a merciful way of not functioning; it is almost a necessity to forget the painfulness of pain. One recalls the fact that pain existed in certain situations and that an appropriate warning system was built up, but the pain itself can hardly be revived in memory.

The "hollow of a sling" is, in a certain sense, the transition and the purification of the soul. As happens in psychoanalysis with all recognition of the significant differences, when a patient is also put in the "hollow of a sling" in order to pass through an experience from its earliest beginnings to its later development or distortion. It is a process of elimination. The need for the "hollow of a sling" is limited perhaps to those who have something to get rid of. The person who has lived all his life in holiness and purity may not require it. To be sure, it does not involve actual punishment; it is more in the nature of purification from spiritual bondage, from a fascination for unworthy objects of desire. After all, an ordinary person can hardly be plunked down in Paradise; he probably wouldn't realize where he was, much less enjoy being there. A certain minimal preparation is needed. There are many stories about the world between worlds, the limbo where a person still imagines himself to be alive and continues to do what he was accustomed to do in his former existence.

According to one such story, a certain teamster, rough and unlearned, performed a great mitzvah, saving a soul from death. When he, himself, died and got to this in-between world, he was told that he would be granted whatever he wished. He asked for a wagon with six strong horses, and it is said that to this day he drives fast along a smooth and endless road fulfilling his heart's desire. In other words, most people cannot be given a free ticket to Paradise, just as they cannot all be expected to enjoy a special concert of classical music. Without the capacity to absorb the advantages of the higher world, a person has to recall this earthly world in the "hollow of a sling." He has to remain in limbo, in a world of formlessness. However, since we say that every soul in Israel has a spark of holiness, then after a period of time, the process of sloughing off ingrained habits and of gradual sensitization prepare the soul for a higher level of existence. True, the period of time required is indeterminate; it may take five hundred years, or it may take place while a person is still alive in body.

Thus, there are many areas of permitted action within which transgression can be repaired—like idle chatter to relieve the strain of intensive study of Torah. On the other hand, the indulgence in idle talk for its own enjoyment instead of study of the Torah or at the expense of Torah, is punishable in more severe terms than that meted out for laziness. There are two kinds of purgatory: that of fire and that of snow. In the Purgatory of Fire, a person is punished for that which he did too much of, for his excesses; and in the Purgatory of Snow, he suffers for his omissions.

The point is that idle speech derives from the domain of the emotions. Not that emotions cannot produce useful speech, but speech without wisdom or understanding or knowledge— without Chochmah, Binah, Daat—is essentially idle and useless even if it is still within the domain of the permitted. What is the soul doing during all this chatter? At least in its emotional aspect, if not at its higher levels, it is being contaminated by the Nogah Shell and can be redeemed only by Tikun.

Idle chatter may distract from Torah in one way; the study of science and mathematics or other profane (that is, not holy) subjects, distracts in a far more profound way. Therefore, "the hollow of a sling" principle is operative here too, to a more serious degree, and Tikun is far more difficult and complex. Concerning areas of wisdom that are not holy, the general directive is that a person may occupy himself with profane wisdom only if it is a matter of livelihood, like a craft or profession. As soon as a Jew relates to them as something other than a means of making a living, giving them the holiness and absolute surrender reserved only for Torah, he is on dangerous ground.

There is also the possibility of gaining from profane knowledge something that will help Torah study, like the Rambam's investigations in astronomy. Or the story told of a teacher and pupil who, when walking along a path, saw a worm and the teacher said he was surprised at the small-mindedness of the writer who maintained that only the sky reflected the glory of

God; after all, even a worm did so and, perhaps, showed the wonder of evolution in an even more subtle fashion. In short, the study of science and other nonsacred knowledge can be a means of approaching God and realizing the awe and love of God in such a convincing manner that it could only enhance the study of Torah. Indeed the adding of instruments of logic and examination can only sharpen the ability to study. Thus, if profane knowledge is indulged in for this purpose, it is like eating for the sake of Heaven; it becomes transformed into holiness.

All this is intended to delineate more clearly the nature of the Nogah Shell, where the good and the evil aspects touch and influence one another and form something which is given to Tikun, correction and transformation.

9

The Animal-Soul

Rabbi Schneur Zalman says: "The abode of the animal-soul is in the heart, in the left ventricle that is filled with blood. As it is written: '. . . for the blood is the nefesh.' "

The problem of the location of the soul is certainly not a matter of a dissectable place in the body. Nevertheless, it seems to be profoundly bound up with the heart, that is, with the feelings and emotions of man. This is not to say that the animal-soul is necessarily to be identified either with the crude passions or with the higher emotions, although they are quite evidently an integral part of it. Other parts do exist, even intellectual and abstract and moral parts in a certain way. Because the animal-soul is not necessarily bad or even dirty, although it is inextricably connected with the body, or at least with the image one has of the body.

Indeed, there are many forms to the animal-soul, some very subtle, having passed through a high degree of sublimation. But they can all be called the "blood." That is to say, one can view life as an instrument or as a means for something else, for reaching the Divine Soul; or one can see life as its own reason for being, whose ultimate truth is the fact that one is alive. In the latter case, the blood is the soul, and the soul is the blood; the "I" is the center of the being; everything comes from me and everything returns to me. To be sure this animal-soul may evolve into splendid forms, following on the development of personality. After all, the largeness and splendor of a personality do not necessarily depend on spiritual qualities—a saint can be quite an obscure figure, while the expressions of the animal-soul can produce extraordinary people. The important distinction seems to be the degree of emphasis on the self for its own sake.

Some passions, like anger and pride, are not exactly basic appetites. Nevertheless, there is no denying that anger can be enjoyed almost as a form of idolatry in the sense that a person makes a cult out of it. Vanity too can be a personal cult, a worshipful attitude towards oneself, while lust, or indulgence in any appetite, has another sort of function; it is the satisfaction of elemental desire. Pride and vanity are somewhat different, the first being a comparing of oneself with another, the second, simply a need for self-applause.

The passions are, thus, in the heart in the sense that their primary cause or drive comes from the factor we have called "the blood is the soul." They then spread throughout the whole body rising also to the head; and the function of the brain (in the head) is to think, to meditate on them, and to become "cunning in them."

It is not enough for a person to want something in order to get it done; one has to construct a whole mechanism to justify and direct one's action, and this is the task of the brain. In short, the brain receives an impulse from some other source by which means it proceeds to support the desired action. It is here likened to the fact that the blood, whose source is in the heart, spreads from the heart to all the organs of the body and also rises "to the brain in the head."

As we have mentioned previously, that which is here called "the brains in the head" is really the repository of the primary qualities of the intelligence—Chochmah (Wisdom), Binah (Understanding), and Daat (Knowledge)—or what we may term the "elements of consciousness." They constitute a sort of anchor, something by which the divine soul fastens itself to a person. It is not what one could call the "instinctive throb of life," but it is no less basic in determining the consciousness of the individual. This sense of awareness, however, is still not identifiable with Divine light. In a certain sense, the fundamental distinction between the ability of this consciousness to function as light, and between "the blood as the soul" lies in the quality of the heart. The heart lives its own life and can cause consciousness to deviate from its Divine source and express a mistaken form of surrender of the self. The mistake is a logical consistence based on ignorance of the Divine source. As soon as I exist for myself, then this becomes the Divine essence, and my entire worship consists in maintaining that I am Divine. In certain texts, there is an extensive description of the problem of the highest level of the ungodly, of blasphemy, which is the fiftieth gate of uncleanness and is known as "Pharoah" because Pharoah said: "Mine is the Nile, and I made myself." That is to say, "The river is mine, I made it just as I made myself." This is the closed circle of the shell, that I am the beginning and the end of all existence, and this is often viewed as the utmost blasphemy and uncleanness. On the other hand, the Divine consciousness in a person can be expressed by the highest level of holiness, which is called the "Chariot."

In this latter case, when a person becomes a vehicle (or chariot) of the Divine Will, not only the concept of "I made myself," but all words such as "I" and "mine" become meaningless. There is a custom, nowadays mostly among yeshivah students, that instead of writing, "This book belongs to so-and-so," they write, "The earth is the Lord's and the fullness thereof, and this book has been commended to the care of so-and-so."

The basic idea is that the source of individuality is in that power of consciousness which does not produce things but which absorbs them. Just as the power of wisdom is defined as the power of humility and self-nullification, the power to receive from above and the ability to open one's eyes and see. By the way, in contrast to certain old concepts about the eyes suddenly sending forth a flashing light, the Jewish idea of vision is totally passive. To be a wise man is like being a seer: Just as someone who sees does not send out light to the world

but receives the light from the world, so too he who is wise
does not send out his wisdom into things but is open to receive
that which he must receive.

This is only the aspect of intelligent awareness in the head.
There is also the aspect of the heart which, as we have
observed, is not at all a unified whole. Even in the domain of
the higher emotions, even in the right chamber of the heart
which is full of the love of God, there is also the fear of God and
all the various "feelings" one has about holiness.

The fact of the matter is that there is no essential difference
between the love of God and the love of man. But since love of
God is not described in numberless publications sold at corner
kiosks, with illustrations and cartoons, the matter seems to be
much more difficult. True, there is an intrinsic difficulty in that
love of God depends on one's ability to be aware of Him, not in
the sense of one's knowledge of what is written in this book or
another, but in terms of personal consciousness. That is to say,
one can love Him to the degree that one is able to be conscious
of Him or to feel Him. All that is necessary is to understand and
to sincerely inquire into one's knowledge of that which is
worthy of love, whereupon the natural impulse, the "other"
side of the personality, is awakened.

At the risk of oversimplification, we may start with the
existence of many fundamental emotions, love and fear, joy
and pity, enthusiasm and the like, which are generally combinations of several Divine attributes humanly manifested. That
which arouses these emotions varies, and the person whom
one loves may not arouse pity, and the one who is feared is not
usually the same as the one who is loved. We say, however,
that a person should love God and fear Him at the same time—
and it may well be asked, how can this be done? Is it not a
contradiction? The answer is that the relation to another person
is a relation to something finite and definite while the relation
to God is something that cannot be encompassed and which
changes from moment to moment, from situation to situation.
In one set of circumstances, a person can be full of awe and
trepidation, and, in another, full of love and longing. In this
way, the same thing—if it is infinite—can be the object of both
love and fear, depending on the viewpoint and on what one

sees as God. When consciousness is of a low level, a certain familiar pattern of crude reactions can be anticipated, except that a picture of Divine glory in the minds of children, for instance, can persist throughout life, with infantile images of the "grand old man" in the sky serving to obstruct the mature inquiry into the nature of the Divine. Indeed, the level of consciousness can be said to be the decisive factor in all the emotional relationships of a person. If a person remains at the level of consciousness of a 3-year-old, his emotional life will tend to remain at about the same level.

All of this is really a minor point in the line of thought stemming from the idea that "Two nations are in thy womb, and two kinds of people shall be separated from thy bowels; and the one people shall be stronger than the other people; and the elder shall serve the younger" (Genesis 25:23).

This verse relates to the Bible story of the twins in Rebecca's womb – Jacob and Esau – who were already then in conflict and causing Rebecca such trouble that she had to ask God about it. She was told that two personalities, two nations, were to be born out of the one seed and that each would go his separate way. The essence of the matter is that every human being contains not two sides to one being but two separate souls. No ordinary person can be so sure of himself that he will know exactly where he is going; he is always open to some other force within himself that may reorient him. There is a constant struggle between the two souls of a man, and one of the most enduring aspects of a human personality is its changeability, its tendency to flip and to be something else. Thus, most men strive and hope to reach some level of decency, goodness, or even holiness; but frequently there is a sudden turn for the worse, an unexpected upheaval in which the person looks at himself with shame and horror. A trifle may often upset a virtuous enterprise, a trifle that, as we now know, expresses deep layers of ignominy in a man.

It is a constant struggle, if somewhat concealed, and does not permit life to pursue an even course. True, a righteous individual or saintly Tzadik may indeed be far more securely in possession of one soul, to the extent that it may be said of him that he is single-hearted, of one integral mind or being. Such a

person may have other problems, but he will not be easily
turned inside out by some inexplicable wind of fortune. As for
the ordinary man, though the many books of ethics and the
Scriptures and other writings tell him how to behave, he may
sometimes feel that he does not, or is not able, to respond
properly. This is an intrinsic part of the way. As it is described
in *Messilat Yesharim* (*The Path of the Just*) by Chaim Luzatto, the
way has to be pursued with care and agility; but no matter how
alert and careful one may be in avoiding certain visible dangers,
one can easily fall into unseen pitfalls of another sort.

Outside of a chosen few, the doubleness of soul is the
destiny of every human being. One is never able to get rid of it,
even though, to be sure, it may assume more subtle forms and
become part of a cultural pattern that has its own moral
advantages and beauty. As it is said in *Pirkei Avot* by Rabbi
Yannai: "We do not possess either the insensitive composure of
the wicked or the anguished composure of the just." He who is
neither saintly nor wicked, the common individual, will never
know peace. In any case, not in this world. It is not given to a
man to be completely at rest and tranquil; at best, there can be
a temporary armistice, but never an inner wholeness. The
conflict between the two souls in him is unending, and his task
is to emerge from it as best he can. But even if the happiness of
the tranquil life is not granted to one, this does not signify that
the life struggle is in vain. All that one does within the struggle
is significant and contributes to the forward movement, to the
progress of the soul.

The question is asked: What about the aspiration for peace of
mind and heart? Of course, this is a universal longing, and
there are those who do reach a high degree of tranquility. It is
mentioned elsewhere in the *Tanya* that God weighs every
person differently; some are judged according to their achievements and others by their failures. No one is weighed in the
balance by the peace of mind he attained but rather by the
nature of his struggle and what was won in the battle.
Sometimes, by virtue of discipline and constant exercise, a
person can achieve a certain level of tranquility and even avoid
painful falls and moral turbulence. But it is more significant if
he can multiply goodness and make it a way of life, consciously

and habitually. The two souls in conflict within his being may then experience a relatively lasting peace.

The body, called "a small city," and all its organs, including heart and brain, are neutral in the struggle because, in contrast to considerable prejudice in this respect, the body is not the expression of the evil impulse. Neither is the body the degenerate part of the person, nor is the soul necessarily the expression of ingrained superiority. The body is the neutral territory; it is also the vehicle and the means. When the animal-soul sees it as the aim or end and not the means, it becomes a vessel of uncleanness. But this is not because it is a physical body, but because it has been converted from a means or an instrument into an end or a value in itself.

The Divine Soul, however, always sees the body as an instrument, a means which can serve the ends both of the unclean and of the holy. According to the Jewish concept of things, any physical thing is not necessarily of a lower order; the spiritual is not of itself something better. An object can be material or spiritual without qualifying it as having any more or less value. It can be good or bad without these necessarily being identical with its spiritual or material aspect. Much of Judaism rests on the practical mitzvot, which are quite simply actions performed in a certain way in the material world. Mitzvot are not necessarily intended to be used as a means to gain Divine love or spiritual enlightenment for oneself; they do not have any specific objective besides, perhaps, a union with God which, as explained elsewhere, is neither a spiritual nor a physical consummation. Indeed, both the spiritual and the physical are at the same distance from the Divine so that the question may legitimately be asked: What does it matter to God whether one blesses a piece of bread or whether one smokes on the Sabbath? Similarly, one may ask: What harm can it do God to deny Him or to hate Him? In terms of the Infinite, it is all on the same level of the inconsequential. The human struggle is for the body and the use of the body. What is one utilizing the body for? Is our physical neutral territory being lived in for the sake of God, and is the body mechanism expressing the yearning for God? There is so much the body can perform— indeed, it is said that only through the body, in any of a great many various modes of expression, can the genuinely spiritual be achieved.

To further clarify the above it may be appropriate to make a certain discrimination between "Devekut" (Divine Union) itself, and the feeling of "Devekut." They are not necessarily identical; and they can even be very far apart.

Devekut is something of fundamental essence: I cling to God; I am existentially in a state of Divine Union. At the same time, I may also be unaware of anything of the sort. But the test of the truth of the experience cannot be one's subjective feelings, for if I determine my own emotions and enjoyments, this makes me Divine; good or bad depends on my personal relation to it. Indeed, the whole matter of Divine Union becomes a function of the animal-soul.

Such feelings of perfection in an exalted situation are often misinterpreted as "Devekut"; the sages have called it "Klipah Yaffah" or Beautiful Shell. After all, every fruit has its shell; some are thrown away as useless, others are kept and used; still others are valued for some aesthetic quality or other, such as their fragrance or beauty. The point is that one's feelings or subjective reactions are the shell and cannot be the criterion of Divine Union.

True Devekut, therefore, is not always keenly felt as such— even if it has the ring of absolute truth and certainty. An example of the kind of emotion it arouses may be taken from the phrase in the "Song of Songs," a poem of Devekut, in which the beloved is called "my sister, my spouse." What is the difference in these titles of affection? The relationship to the wife is one that must constantly be renewed. The love of spouse is, therefore, far more intensive and sharp. No man loves his sister with the same fierce passion he has for his bride; and yet this fraternal love has the advantage of being beyond question. Since the love between a man and a woman is one of choice, it can always be taken away. It can collapse or wither, while the love of brother and sister, which may be without strong feeling and even cool in outer form, can never be dismantled or taken apart. No matter how difficult the relations between them, there is a Devekut or union beyond choice which does not depend on sentimental expression.

There is a story of one of the Chasidim who was very poor and yet somehow acquired a set of fine ritual utensils for the Passover *seder*. With his whole soul uplifted, he arranged each of the objects and happily performed the *seder* ceremony, giving it the utmost feeling and devotion and, indeed, experiencing a feeling that he was transported into higher spheres. The *seder* continued late into the night. The next day he was barely able to rest and prepare himself to perform the second seder. He was so rushed and preoccupied that he felt none of the enthusiasm of the previous day and was afterwards quite depressed. Some days later he went to the rabbi who looked at him pointedly and told him: "At Pesach one of my disciples had a heavenly feeling on the evening of the first *seder*; nu, so he felt uplifted, so what? But the second *seder*, that was very, very good."

In other words, the feeling of great happiness or sublimity is not in itself of any consequence. One may or may not experience it in Devekut. There is, however, something else that may be considered crucial. And a person cannot always be in a position to determine the level of the love and devotion of his performances. To be sure, in the essence of a genuine action, whether one prepares oneself or not, the innermost of one's being will manifest somehow in the spontaneity of the doing, even if it is less impressive or less satisfying than usual. Devekut or Divine Union is thus often hidden from view, being essentially an inner experience of great depth. One is deluded by the desire of the animal-soul to control both the physical and Divine aspects of life completely.

What the Divine Soul wants is that all the ten Attributes of the soul, from Wisdom to Kingdom (Malchut), in thought, speech and action, and all the forces and organs of the body, should be a vehicle of the expression of holiness. Evidently, the animal-soul and the Divine Soul desire the very opposite thing, and each wants the whole of a person. The question is: Who will rule the "little city" which is the outer person?

The two chambers of the heart represent the two aspects of the fundamental nature of the soul—the right-hand chamber, which is the repository of holiness, and the left-hand chamber, which is the place of the animal-soul. The truth of the matter is, however, that if a person's love of God is great enough, it overflows, spills over from the right chamber into the left chamber of the heart, inundating it, subduing the lusts of the outer shell and changing its orientation from the pleasures of this world to the joys of Divine essence. But, as we are only too well aware, the process of attaining "abundant love" is not at all simple. For it is not a question of will. There is a vast difference between what a person can accomplish by compelling his "other side" and what can be done by transforming it.

Over the centuries, a certain amount of knowledge has accumulated about this latter process of transformation; if one wishes to use modern terminology, a certain technique has been developed. It varies from person to person, of course, but there is a pattern which, in general terms, can be charted. The first stage is attained by contemplation and conscious awareness. This awareness stirs the potential love in the heart and focuses it so that it rises up like flames of passion thirsting for God. When this happens, it necessarily so influences the person that he cannot remain divided in himself any longer. He reaches out for the abundant love which is the delight of God and discovers that there are two expressions of this love which seem to be contradictory. One is like a burning flame, the other like cool water. And though each of them is equally concerned with achieving greater contact with the Beloved, there is a profound difference in the manner of doing it.

The love which is like fire is a desire for that which is lacking; and, like a flame, the more it feeds the desire, the more intense it becomes. It also grows with deprivation, becoming a passion that is nourished on thoughts of the object of its desire. For this reason, it remains forever in the domain of longing, of yearning for fulfillment. One of the strangest elements in the structure of this flamelike love is the fact that inwardly, for all its passion for the other, it is still essentially a love of self. It is ultimately for one's own satisfaction. I love flowers so I pick them in the fields. I love fish, not necessarily for the sake of the creature itself, but because I enjoy eating it. In a different way, this is true of the love between human beings, between a man and a woman, between parent and child. (Incidentally, the Yiddish expression for a couple in love is: they love themselves—*zei haben sich lieb.)* In a certain sense, every love is a love of oneself—no matter what the object of desire may be—whether it is a thing or a person or God. It is an expression of an insatiable lust for that which is lacking in oneself. Sometimes the love is quite straightforward in its grossness (like the love of fish), but very often it is a subtle need for that which does not exist in any graspable form, like the complement to the fear of God. This is why, incidentally, in fulfilling the double command to love and fear God, it is often easier to fear Him first, because fear is so much more impersonal, demanding so much less of the self. Sometimes, too, this love is a means of channeling love of oneself through the outer object. The result is a strange frustration and tragedy: The more one approaches the Beloved, the more one feels the distance; the more one loves, the more alluring does the object of love become.

There can be no denying, however, that often enough people do love each other with a love that is not a function of anything beyond the lovers themselves. Love of this sort, even if it is flamelike in its insatiability, can rise to very great heights of self-denial and beauty of expression. It does not have to be a burden or an imposition; on the contrary, it can be the most genuine and free manifestation of feeling.

The other kind of love is the love of delight, the taste of other-worldly bliss. When the self ceases to be the most important thing in the world and one's yearnings and desires no longer torment the soul, it becomes possible to love the object of adoration for its own sake and not for the satisfaction of any cravings. So long as one wants anything or anyone for oneself, the greater the anguished feeling of not being able to possess it. In the love of desire, the beloved must be mine; in the love of delight, the beloved is loved without any connection to myself; he is simply the object of my love and the more I occupy myself with the beloved, the more this satisfies me because I demand nothing more than that. I do not wish to possess the beloved, to own or control or have any greater intimacy with the one so favored.

In the development of one's relation to God, the direction is from one kind of love to the other. The same feeling that is so immensely full of torment and longing can change into the delight in God, the exquisite feeling that it is not dependent on possessing or having anything, being itself a union or, at least, a joyful contact. There is the oft repeated metaphor of Jacob and Rachel which declares that he loved her so much that the seven years he worked for her passed like so many days. From our human experience, we are cognizant of the opposite: When we want something badly, the period of time until we get it passes with excruciating slowness. The difference lies in the kind of love with which one seeks to unite with the object of one's love. When the self is involved, when it is a matter of satisfying one's need or demand for something, the days of waiting are long and full of yearning; the lack makes the time unendurable. By contrast, if the love is not selfish, if one is not pressed to fulfill some need or to possess the beloved, then seven years of waiting can pass like a few days—in the radiance of a feeling that is not affected by distance or parting.

The latter love is here called the love of delight, if for no other reason than that its opposite, the love of desire, of the burning flame, is not a delight, being more akin to pain and anguish. Of course, there are aspects of pain that have a strange fascination, beauty, and delight. But on the whole, the more one loves with an earthly love, the more vulnerable one is to pain, whereas the love of delight is more like the next world in its experience of a higher level of existence, beyond desire and the need for anything.

Just as there is a consciousness that can bring a sense of longing, of desire that causes discomfort, so is there another kind of consciousness that can contemplate things without desiring them and, in fact, can cause an ever-increasing happiness. When a person reaches such a consciousness of a love of delight, then nothing further is desired. It would seem to be the ultimate solution to the problem of lust of any and all kinds. Thus, when a person attains to this love, the love itself becomes a source of great satisfaction; and the more he dwells on it, the greater the level of delight. Everything else that may once have given pleasure, the joys of the world, now seem to be poor substitutes for the real thing which he is experiencing. Indeed, all the other burning desires can maintain themselves in flamelike intensity so long as one has not experienced the source of all happiness. Only when one has experienced the true source of happiness can the substitutes be seen for what they are, at one or two removes from the real thing; and it is clear that one wanted something only because it appeared to be that which would satisfy the fundamental need for the Divine. Without the love of God, one begins to love all sorts of other things, often the weirdest and most unlikely of objects. When one does attain the love of delight, however, then all the other pleasures and loves are automatically seen for what they are— substitutes.

To be sure, this is all a somewhat ideal, if not simplified, version of the way of man to happiness: contemplation of the Divine Reality, leading to a desire and passion for God, which in turn is realized by the love of delight. The fact is, each of these three stages may well last for a long time, and the whole may be a matter of many years of hard work on oneself. What is more, in real life there are a multitude of inner contradictions. For instance, the burning and flamelike love of God is supposed to consume the separate self of the lover and make it less of an obstacle to union, but it so happens that only too often passion feeds the ego, the self grows stronger and is made more capable of desire of all kinds.

So prevalent is this obstinacy of the self that the sages have claimed that the only safe way to Divine love, the love of delight, is through fear of God; that is to say, a person can nullify himself, obliterate the obstacle to Divine Union, only by renouncing his desire. So long as one continues to yearn and wish for anything, so long as something seems to be lacking, even if it is the one thing more that is needed for fulfillment, the fulfillment is postponed. Indeed, it is said that one has to renounce love itself—the very structure of desire has to collapse. There is the story of the Chasid who reached the next world and was asked what he wanted. "Now," he said, "all I want is to enjoy being with God." And he was granted his wish, but nothing much came of it. Whereas if he had been a real Tzadik, he would have said, "I wish for nothing more than to be nullified in God, to become nothing in Him." Had he renounced his wish for the personal enjoyment of endless bliss, he would have been raised to a higher level of being. Altogether then, the chart of human progress is not at all simple. Besides the contradictions barely hinted at here, there are processes of cyclic formation, to and fro movements of development, and inner and outer metaphysical systems with great power to influence personality and transform it. What is more, situations exist when a person is confronted with another sort of dilemma entirely, when the only thing to be done is to turn the situation inside out as one pulls open a glove.

At the highest level, a person does not only cease to occupy himself with the things of this world, he no longer desires them. One has to distinguish between the driving force behind a desire and the particular form or disguise something assumes to become an object of desire. Since the garments of desire are often soiled or distorted versions of something, one has to change — not the essence of the forces operating in the soul, but the object of those forces, what it is they strive to attain. In a way, this is a process of education, not a sublimation of desire, but an education of desire. After all, the whole problem of education is to guide desire in a certain direction, not to repress the appetites and innate force behind it.

In nature itself, there is no visible alternative to the objects of the physical world; one does not see anything else upon which to fasten one's desires. Nevertheless, people are always getting excited about things that have no genuine relation to their physical existence — like the useless joys and disappointments accompanying a football game. One is constantly confronted with the contradiction of so-called self-centered persons getting highly involved in matters completely outside themselves, whether related to football or politics. Evidently then, it is possible and eminently worthwhile to educate the desires in the direction of the abstract and towards things that do not provide any personal satisfaction in the narrow, physical sense. The expansion of a person's capacity to enjoy objects and situations of great variety is one of the achievements of education as a whole. In terms of the spiritual life, it is described as the ability to change one's soiled clothes at will, the garments being the modes of contact with the pleasures of the world. Indeed, the very same forces that bring a person to the lowest level of being can serve to bring him to the highest levels of self-sacrifice, conceptualization, and devotion.

This is accomplished by unifying all the faculties of the person, speech, thought, and action, around the Divine Soul. Everything that one thinks and does should be in connection with Torah, just as all one's speech should be sincere and single-minded. The Divine Soul wishes no more than this. The animal-soul, however, wishes the very opposite.

Without entering into the details of the antitheses between them, it is clear that human life generally proceeds in a state of coexistence if not peace, a dynamic détente at best, with each of the two souls seeming to agree to the existence of the other. There can be no real compromise, however, not because of any abysmal difference, but because neither of them can relinquish the smallest part of its ambition to gain control over the whole of the human being. This may be one of the most difficult aspects of the spiritual life to accept. Most people don't mind giving up a couple of hours each day to the Divine, being left to do as they please for the rest. A decent compromise is what the majority of mankind would prefer, namely, to live and let live. But, as it has been said, it is difficult to be a Jew because one cannot simply go to the synagogue and pray and then go about one's affairs with a purified mind and soul. The whole crux of Jewish life lies in what takes place during the busy hours of one's affairs as well as in the hours of prayer. One cannot reside in two worlds at once. There cannot be any pretense of having done one's spiritual duty at some other time or place. In the Jewish way of life, the challenge is constant. Although, as said, it is not simply an unending struggle between the animal-soul and the Divine Soul. For example, life provides many aesthetic and philosophical situations affording opportunities to enjoy the Divine through music, literature, scriptural commentary, and so forth. God can even become a respectable hobby. The problem then becomes apparent, and one finds it there where the center of a human being is located. Beyond what one *does* is the question of *where* one is. As one of the Sages said: "When Satan steals the heart of Truth from a person, he leaves him all his superfluities to play with; if a person wants to pray, then by all means let him pray; if he wants to act the pious Chasid, then let him do so with conviction." For man is flesh and blood, an animal creature, and he needs amusement; one person goes to a concert, another to the synagogue, a third to a football game; it's all a matter of education.

Evidently then, life is not a pure dualism—holiness against pollution—for both the two souls of man are the children of God. In fact, the animal-soul wishes, with the deepest sources of its being, to be like the Divine, and eventually to have the Divine Soul dominate it. Its reason for existence, however, is to be open to the opposite, to be tempted by evil. This temptation is the essential challenge to life which in turn enables the Divine Soul to rise to a higher level.

In other words, a pure human soul, undivided and static, does not—and perhaps cannot—exist. Without anything to struggle against, without any resistance, there is no progress. As the Chasidim used to say, "If God wanted man to be like that, He would have done better to create a few million more angels." But it seems that the angels are limited; they are static and each is eternally the same. The fact that the human soul needs to be challenged by the animal-soul is, therefore, for the sake of the individual's growth, and it is not fair to call the animal-soul evil because it merely does its duty. Its duty is to tempt: its deepest hope is that the person is not tempted. In the famous story in the Zohar, the king hired a courtesan to lure his son into evil ways, wishing she might fail. The dilemma of the courtesan, the animal-soul, is thus obvious.

The daily prayer book of the Baal HaTanya contains a rather surprising commentary that says—there are souls who have descended to earth only to suffer for seventy years; and God has no other need of them but that—neither their Torah learning, nor their good deeds, nor anything else but their suffering for His sake. This seems cruel, but its intention is really to ease the pressure, to tell us that it is not a matter of accomplishments: How many pages of Gemara have you learned? How many mitzvot have you performed? The central issue of life is thus clearly defined as the victory of the soul over itself, the overcoming "in spite of." After all, people are human in their weakness, and God knows what each person is. Is it not said that God never imposes a test on a man that the man cannot successfully pass and that the greater the man, the more severe the test?

10

Varieties of Sainthood

Although the passage in the Torah "And thou shalt purge the evil from amongst you" pertains to the collective House of Israel, it is here concerned with the individual. When an individual manages to purge the evil from within him but cannot transform the evil to good he is then called "Tzadik shelo Gamur" (an imperfect Tzadik) or, as Jewish ethics has so often felt it necessary to point out, a suffering Tzadik (Tzadik vera lo), one who is still beset by evil. The problem of such a person is not only that he is troubled by evil but that the evil is his own; it comes from within him. True, there is the opposite case of the wicked man who is happy (Rasha vetov lo) who still has enough good in him to keep him content even though this good is dominated by the evil.

What is the difference between a complete Tzadik and an incomplete one? It is clearly nothing external; not by thought, word, or deed is a real Tzadik distinguished from a Benoni (Intermediate) who is an incomplete Tzadik. It is an internal difference, quite imperceptible to the external gaze, and often invisible even to the interior eye. All we know is that the Tzadik is one who has definitely overcome the animal-soul. Thus, many altogether admirable persons, who are great and even

68

holy in their own way, are not Tzadikim because they have not completely vanquished the source of evil in themselves. One can even acquire considerable merit in terms of the next world, as well as power and influence in this one, and still not be a Tzadik.

Briefly, the Tzadik is in control of life, having gained final dominance over the inimical forces. And he remains a Tzadik, for he cannot slide back as can an incomplete Tzadik. This does not mean that he makes no mistakes—for a Tzadik too is still a creature of flesh and blood and is correspondingly limited in his capacities. Simply, he no longer has to contend, he is no longer subject to the inner conflict of two souls. It would, therefore, not be an exaggeration to state that the complete Tzadik is one who has nothing in him of the evil inclination, whether in terms of temptation or whether in terms of unwitting actions. It may be appropriate here to recollect that this description of the Tzadik was addressed in the late eighteenth century to readers who were already at a very high spiritual level. Prospective pupils, for example, were supposed to be thoroughly versed in Talmud, completely at home with Kabbalah and familiar with the *musar* (ethics) literature and Jewish philosophy of the Middle Ages. Continued discipleship demanded extraordinary spiritual and intellectual qualities that cannot be listed. In short, there was no lack of men of stature, of men who were quite well aware of their own worth and able to ask of themselves and others around them, in all sincerity, whether they were Tzadikim. The question was not a theoretical one.

It may be wondered whether pride entered in. But the point is that "Tzadik" is not just a title given to some impressive person who seems to be close to God. Not only can one never know for certain who is close to God, who is more favored in His eyes, and who is less so; *all* human standards are inadequate and questionable. To be sure, there are moments when a person at a low level of spiritual life makes such a tremendous effort that he rises higher than a holy person who is fixed at a relatively high level. Therefore, should a person sometimes say of himself that he rose to the heights of Tzadik, it may be difficult to prove, but neither can it be denied. It is also possible to approach this negatively: If a person who thinks or does evil or who doesn't ever repent in his heart cannot be a Tzadik, then, in the same way, someone can say of himself, without pride, that he does not know sin and therefore, to all intents and purposes, is a Tzadik. There is a story of the Chasid who somehow found himself on his death bed away from home and was asked to confess his sins. He said he couldn't think of any offhand, so he was handed the prayer book wherein appears a list of possible transgressions. He read each of these aloud and, after a moment's reflection on each one, shook his head and continued until he reached "we have mocked." At that point he admitted that he had once indeed mocked the Mitnagdim (those who opposed Chasidism), but he could not bring himself to be sorry for that. Thus we see that even in the seriousness of death these men were genuinely aware of their own worth. In those days too, the community was an intimate affair, no house was locked, no curtains hung at the windows to hide what was going on within. Life was shared from the earliest years, and everyone knew, or seemed to know, what everyone else was up to, so that there was scarcely a gap between what a person thought of himself and what others thought of him.

Nevertheless, how can the Tzadik be certain that he has indeed reached the level from which he will not fall? An incomplete Tzadik may think he has rid himself of the evil because he has reached a state of mastery, of control. However, if in truth there was absolutely no evil left in him then something more drastic would have occurred. All the evil (that was once in him) would have been transformed into genuine good. Something more than overcoming and control would have resulted. The holy vanquishing the unholy is more than a negative overcoming of the power of the animal-soul; it is a total transformation of self so that even that which was animal-soul is made over into Divine Soul. If a person does not make such a transformation of his very essence, it means that he is still within the restricted realm of the suffering saint, the incomplete Tzadik.

As explained elsewhere, it seems that evil is that which results from the flow of unruly powers into and through that which is not holy. This is connected with the idea of the primordial shattering of the vessels according to which the forces of chaos sow the seeds of evil because they cannot enter the fixed world of order and sanctity. Being thus deprived of expression, they burst into realms where the powers of intelligence and consciousness are not in control; they give themselves over to primordial forces of the unconscious. So long as man balances the two sides of his soul, he directs these elemental forces; he compels them to follow a desired course, and the result, even if it involves intimidating and oppressing the chaotic elements, is the normal balance of life. These few men, however, who have truly conquered the animal side of the soul and don't have an alternate channel for those forces of chaos, have only one possible way of expressing themselves. The result is a multiplication of the powers of good.

What is involved here is similar to the process of the separation of the good from its shell, based on the idea of the nature of shadow or untruth; that is to say, there is no shadow without light, no lie that does not contain some truth. Absolute darkness or an absolute lie cannot exist; they need some measure, even the smallest, of light or truth to sustain them. When this measure of light or truth is extended and grows to such an extent that it changes the shadow into luminosity or the lie into truth, then we have a situation in which the evil is transformed into the good. When a person passes the stage of the heroic or the incomplete Tzadik and becomes a genuine Tzadik, this is what occurs, and all that was once potential good (or repressed evil) is now expressed freely. As Rabbi Tzadok HaCohen once wrote: There are two kinds of Tzadikim; there is the Tzadik who does the will of God, and there is the Tzadik whose every deed, all that he does, is the will of God. For, as we have said, the limitations of humanity adhere to a person only so long as he is an ordinary man. There is the story of the rabbi who found his Chasidim playing checkers and asked them whether they indeed understood the rules of the game: at the beginning, one may advance only forward; one may move only one step at a time; and only when one reaches the last row can one go in any direction whatsoever.

To be sure, the Tzadik has his limitations precisely because he does choose, and every choice is a possible error. Even the Tzadik can make the wrong choice or err in his judgment. What is worse, no matter what he does, he may somehow be wrong, whether in terms of absolute ethics or of relative human needs. For example, regarding the commentary on the sin of anger for which Moses paid such a dear penalty, it is said that he really chose to strike the rock in anger because otherwise, if the dumb rock should think that it could obey the command of God without being compelled to do so, then the people of Israel would have been put to unbearable shame. Nevertheless, beating the rock was a sinful expression of anger, even if, to this day, an enormous positive response is aroused by the image of Moses striking the rock and making water gush forth. What, on one hand, is sin and error, can, from another viewpoint, be good and necessary. The Tzadik can do something which, from his dependence on the world as it is, leaves him no alternative.

This may help to explain many of the transgressions of the saintly or the wise. Had the great personalities of the Bible been perfect, there would have been no human history to speak of. Can we judge them in any other way than to admit that their wrong actions made our correct actions possible? The problem exists; its solution lies beyond any rational determination of right and wrong. At any event, we ourselves cannot always be sure about it. A person may perform a meritorious deed that would have been better left undone, and he may transgress and do something that has the most blessed results. As the Rambam said, we cannot make the final reckoning between mitzvah and transgression; we do not have the wisdom to judge between the ultimate worth of anything, whether good or wicked. Concerning the statement that a Tzadik becomes complete when he transforms the evil in himself to good, we may question how a Tzadik can have any evil in him altogether. In truth, there were such people, though our present generation has lost touch with personalities of such saintly character that even physical pleasure for its own sake was quite unknown to them. For the Tzadik, the very idea of enjoying food because it was tasty was gross and unthinkable. Many Jews, not necessarily Tzadikim, were not abstemious or ascetic; they had simply gone so far beyond the vulgarity of "enjoying oneself" that anything less than doing something for the "sake of Heaven" was not even considered worthy of their attention. What is more, if one's heart is not whole then even one's hatred (of evil) is not complete. The capacity to be disgusted depends on one's wholeheartedness in loving. Thus, the incomplete Tzadik is one who is somehow not entirely repelled by evil.

Indeed, every human being has his own range of tolerance between the utterly obscene or repulsive and the unthinkably wonderful. In every culture, things are either within or outside the compass of temptation, so that an individual person has to struggle only with that which is possible in terms of his scale of values. The rather terrible actions of people of other times and places cause us to feel profound disgust and even hatred. The whole matter lies in the range of tolerance—how generous one is in permitting certain thoughts to enter one's mind; even though many crimes will certainly not be committed by most good people, the fact that people can read about such crimes with complacence is itself an indication of a certain murkiness of soul.

The complete Tzadik is absolutely incapable of conceiving certain thoughts and actions. He cannot understand how other people can do so. The incomplete Tzadik, however, is one who can understand the souls of those who are tempted by evil, even though he himself is not. It is thus that the incomplete Tzadik suffers; he is closer to humanity, being still capable of containing their weaknesses. As for the complete Tzadik, his purity of mind may place him in the unenviable position of one who repents for sins he has never committed in order to learn to sympathize with the world of sinners.

An incomplete Tzadik is thus one who is outwardly indistinguishable from a complete Tzadik, having, like him, gone beyond the doubts and conflicts of the inner life. But he has not yet transformed the evil in him into good. He is, therefore, limited in his capacity for serving God to the powers of only one part of his soul, while the other part is still held by the Sitra Achra. That is, the incomplete Tzadik has succeeded in bringing this negative part of his soul under control, but he has not yet transformed it, so that he still cannot be said to love God with the entirety of his being.

An incomplete Tzadik is not at one single level, nor is he a single essence; he is at several levels at the same time because of the evil that is left in him. In order for the evil, or the unclean, to be nullified, it has to become relatively minute, no more than a sixtieth part (or in extreme cases, one in a thousand) as the Halachah has determined. The difference, which in Halachah may not be decisive, is very important for each individual person. It is a matter of how closely a person approaches the utmost of his own capacity, the pinnacle of his being.

Is there then no gradual development from Benoni to Tzadik? The fact of the matter is that the two—Benoni and Tzadik—are not the same person at all. True, the Tzadik at first travels a similar path, but he reaches a point far beyond that which the Benoni attains, and he then continues his own way until he reaches the level of a complete Tzadik. In any event, it seems fairly evident that there are very few such Tzadikim in every generation. They are called "superior men" by the sages because they have gone beyond the stage of having to control evil; they are on the level of raising evil to good, of transforming the very essence of their soul into holiness. They are the ones who convert the darkness into light, the bitter into sweetness. The complete Tzadik has thus effected a total transformation of his being; he is now at one with the Divine in all parts of his personality. He is considered a superior man also because he is no longer in need of the personal satisfaction of the mitzvah or the correct action; whatever he does is done for the sake of Heaven. This is illustrated by the story of two Chasidim who met after having once, long before, studied together with the same teacher. One asked another: "Why was a man created?" The other answered: "A man was created in order to correct himself, to make himself whole." To which the first said: "Have you forgotten what we learned—that man was created to raise the Heavens?" Such a posing of the issue emphasizes the difference between the two types of men: the one who strives to reach God by improving himself and the one who strives to raise the Heavens, that is, to realize a union of God and His Shechinah without thinking of his own craving for union.

To better comprehend this latter point it may be important to recall that devotion and self-sacrifice can comprise more than offering up one's life for something. When a person is prepared to die for a cause, it proves a certain physical devotion; when a person is prepared to renounce his very soul for the sake of Heaven, this is spiritual devotion. That is to say, the readiness for spiritual self-sacrifice is a far greater thing than physical martyrdom. Among the truly holy men, this conscious submission of one's spiritual well-being is a more profound sacramental offering than the death of the body. This is exemplified by leaders like Moses who sacrificed the joys and blessings of Divine Union in order to take care of the weak and sick, that is, to deal with the petty problems of the ordinary man. One sees it quite clearly in the reluctance shown by such men to assume tasks of leadership. Naturally enough, men like Moses want to remain in the state of blissful Divine Union and have no desire to bother with stubborn Pharoahs or to deal with a complaining slave people and their petty grievances, their fears and their faithlessness. Therefore, when Moses does assume the task, it is a true act of self-sacrifice; he descends from his real greatness and the height of the spirit which he had attained. Indeed, it is said that any genuine leader is one who has to be compelled to abandon his inner peace and glory for the thankless task of caring for ordinary people. The Tzadik of his generation thus becomes the leader of his generation by sacrificing himself for the sake of Heaven.

There is an apparent contradiction here, namely, that for the perfect Tzadik, who can transform darkness into light, being himself so full of light, the world remains a problematic factor full of pain and temptation. To be sure, since most men never achieve that higher level of being, it is not a pressing question. Nevertheless, what is apparent from traditional experience is that at the level of the Tzadik, there is no strong feeling of a gap between above and below, between the physical and the spiritual. The true Tzadik has no sense of a separation between worlds: He can pray to God and also eat and talk to common people with the same unvarying keenness of interest and total participation. This, as we have seen, is only one aspect of that higher level of being; another aspect of this same level is that the perfect Tzadik does the work of God without any thought of self, and, in fact, renounces himself in the doing. The human and the Divine somehow merge into a single type by a continuous process of refinement, or a sifting of the good out of the Nogah Shell. This process is also known as the uncovering of "feminine waters" causing "supernal union" and the bringing down of "masculine waters" to facilitate the flow of Divine goodness.

In a certain sense, most of the Divine worship of the religious person through works of Torah and mitzvot consists largely of such a filtering out, or separating the inner substance from the Nogah Shell and raising it to holiness. For example, consider the act of taking a coin and giving it to charity. The coin itself is of the Nogah Shell; it is the mitzvah of charity that extricates and lifts up the essential good in it and brings it to holiness. This raising up of the holy from below is called the elevation of feminine waters. The raising up of the level of the world, thereby responding to an influence from above called the masculine waters, makes possible a supernal union which results in a downflow of Divine plenty. Thus, the holy union of God and the Shechinah, which characterizes every mitzvah, is a merging of forces from above and below, and almost all that man does in prayer and Torah consists of such an uncovering of feminine waters, which in turn awakens the higher forces. The more genuine and sincere one's thoughts and actions, the more this hastens the Divine Union. That is the difference between an ordinary person and a Tzadik, and especially a complete Tzadik who transforms darkness to light, bitter to sweet. With every step he takes in his life, the Tzadik elevates something into holiness and binds the worlds. His whole existence becomes such a dedication; and naturally, he will tend to isolate himself from the common world and responsibilities of man in order to better perform his destiny and fulfill his obligation to God.

There is a story about a conscientious rabbi who fell ill and was unable to perform his various duties properly. He consulted one of the famous Tzadikim and was told to hold a feast in which the main course should consist of cheese. The reason for this was that the rabbi had always had a distaste for cheese and had never eaten any, and, since according to Chasidic doctrine, eating is a process of raising food to holiness, cheese had remained neglected by the rabbi and demanded to be redeemed. Indeed, all the fussiness about food is a kind of defiance of God's abundant goodness, and a Tzadik has to bless and be grateful equally for all that is given. The task of transforming darkness into light and the bitter into sweet is a kind of self-sacrifice: The Tzadik does not have to do it; he is actually out of it; he himself doesn't suffer the darkness or the bitterness; he does it for the sake of Heaven, to allow His Blessed Divinity to flow from above downward, to be clothed in those who live in the lower worlds.

11

The Wicked Man Who Prospers

T he "wicked man who prospers" is antithetical to the "righteous man who suffers." The wicked is wicked only because the shell controls him in spite of the fact that he has much good in him. Just as there can be a Tzadik who suffers because of greater or lesser remnants of evil in himself, so there can be a wicked man with more or less good in himself. Apparently, most men can only rarely be completely evil, that is, with their good side totally submerged.

A person who is wicked and prospers is usually temporarily under the control of evil as a result of circumstances, and he is not at one with himself in this situation. There is a trespassing which men can enjoy, at least during the act itself, and another stage of evildoing which is accompanied by a painful reluctance—all dependent on the degree of control exercised by the evil. It is a matter of delicate balance.

Altogether, the category of the wicked one who prospers can include the most respectable people, those who only occasionally lose control and whose trespasses are not necessarily premeditated acts. Take the story of Rav Huna, whose phylactery strap was accidentally turned inside out over his arm and who, in order to atone for this "severe" trespass, fasted forty days. It is a matter of feeling the sense of wrong, a feeling that one has destroyed the world, and often has no relation to the degree of harm to oneself or to others. It is a sensitivity to wrongdoing that only increases as one becomes more pure in goodness. As Rabbi Elimelech said: "The more thin and sharp a thing, the more it pierces and wounds." The higher one's level of awareness, the more sensitive to failings and imperfections.

For instance, in speech that borders on slander, in scoffing and in many unconsidered actions unaccompanied by a wish to do harm, the fact of the matter is that one is still at a level of wickedness. Because there exists an absolute distinction between the side of holiness and all else. It does not matter how far or how close one is to the border, one is still on the other side. To be sure, there are distinctions concerning the kinds of transgressions and their punishments. There are also instances when a person crosses over from holiness and is then totally on the side of the unclean, so that even if it be a slight wrongdoing, it has the nature of a betrayal and deserves corresponding punishment.

All of this concerns the person in whom evil plays a very feeble role and who quickly restores the control of the good in himself, feeling remorse for his straying and ready to plead for forgiveness. He is, nevertheless, considered wicked in contrast to the Benoni—the Benoni being someone who is unable to be wicked at any time. Thus, there seems to be a contradiction in the nature of the wicked who prospers. He is a person who is generally decent and law-abiding but whose goodness is not spontaneous or "creative." Moreover, he does not possess a permanent control over the evil in himself. He is merely in a state of balance that can be disturbed at any moment, and, therefore, he is called wicked in spite of the fact that he manages to be at his best behavior practically all of the time. It may be that he was simply never confronted by situations that put him to the test. Sin is a complex thing, made up of circumstances as well as personality. There are thieves who are not tempted by petty cash and who will remain models of honesty in the world as long as they are not tempted by a real haul.

In other words, it is not at all a simple matter of outer actions. There can be a devout scholar who is inwardly just as wicked as any, but because he has no other strong impulse but the intellectual urge, he will be considered a saint; and yet he can never correct anything in himself because he has never gained any knowledge of his evil potential. In this way, the wicked who prosper may include those who have never, in fact, really transgressed. Obviously, however, the position of one who doesn't sin through lack of opportunity is not the same as the one who struggles with temptation and overcomes it.

Then too there are the wicked who are full of genuine regrets but continue to perform their habitual deeds. This is, at least, an indication of an inner struggle; although the thoughts of repentance seldom go further. In fact, most men can be said to belong to this category of the wicked who are happy, of those who never really manage to overcome their evil inclinations and continue to oscillate between sin and regret.

To be sure, it all depends on the structure of one's life, on the dominant quality of one's thoughts. There are those who go about full of genuine regrets but never get around to changing anything. And there are those who never have any regrets at all. These latter may be called the "wicked who are unhappy" (even if they are not aware of their wretchedness) on account of the evil that controls them and the absence of active good. Nevertheless, even in this instance, a person cannot cast out the Divine Soul in oneself altogether. Just as one can never really get rid of the animal-soul; at best one can repress it to fit into the condition of a "Tzadik who is unhappy," or one can just sublimate its force some other way.

This brings us to an examination of a situation which is rather asymmetrical. The soul of man is not really a single level of being; according to tradition it consists of five layers: Nefesh (Vital Soul), Ruach (Spirit), Neshamah (Higher Soul), Chayah (Higher Spirit), and Yechidah (Divine Union). In general, only one of these, that which is lowest, namely the vital soul, is consciously operative. The higher levels of spiritual being are usually beyond the direct perception of most of humanity. As it will be explained later, the essence of human growth and progress is the augmentation of consciousness and its rise in the levels of the soul until it becomes completely aware of itself. When a person reaches this highest level of consciousness, the soul becomes fundamentally identical with the Divine in a state of what is called "Union." At no level can the soul root out God or evade Him. At worst, one can try to cast feelings of God out of oneself or at least refuse to acknowledge His presence in consciousness. Even in such a case, when the Divine Soul stands apart or is not manifest in consciousness, it is still there. The circumstance of His being hidden simply enables a person to do all kinds of things that he would otherwise be unable to do.

An interesting sideline to this idea concerns the fate of these unknown layers of thought and feeling lodged in the subconscious. As Rabbi Tzadok HaCohen of Lublin wrote, there are various levels of holiness among the Tzadikim. There is the one who is a Tzadik in all his conscious thoughts and actions but who is unable to be a Tzadik in his dreams; and there are those very rare and exceptional men who are Tzadikim even in their dreams. He also went on to say that the clarity of a dream is not in itself proof of anything; nevertheless, most of the men who become complete Tzadikim are often able to proceed easily from the dream state to the vision of the wakeful trance. This is the sort of thing that has been described concerning several of the biblical prophets. The prophetic trance can rarely be entered directly from the usual state of consciousness; indeed, there is some indication that this was possible only by Moses, who could speak "mouth to mouth" with God. What is true of many ordinary men, however, is the relatively wakeful awareness of the higher soul in oneself and its manifestation only in dreams—which is obviously not enough to make any difference in life itself.

Within this scale of values a completely wicked person is a contradiction of terms because anything that is totally of the Sitra Achra is only an intellectual abstraction; like a total lie, it cannot exist in reality. One can perpetrate a lie, small or large, but it is quite impossible for a total lie to exist without the support of some increment, small or large, of fact. Similarly, total wickedness can only be a concept about which one speaks—anyone who even came near to personifying it would not be able to maintain any hold on life and would die. In a way, this is one of the kinds of death that a person could bring on himself, not only in spiritual terms but on every level of being. The essence of the Sitra Achra is entirely negative, and it forces everything to a zero point of its being, a nullification. Therefore, even the very wicked person, if he is not totally evil and is still alive, can theoretically be saved; he can repent in any number of ways, even if it is unlikely that he will himself take the initiative because he has long since lost all conscious control. Nevertheless, circumstances may exert pressure on him and as long as he is still alive, he can choose. Of course, like his complete opposite, the Tzadik, he is rather limited in his choice by firmly entrenched habits of thought. A person who has always been thinking in a certain selfish way and has hardly practiced anything but evil in his actions cannot be expected to change all at once, although there are many instances when such a person is thrust into a situation that compels him to perform some extraordinary act of grace.

However, it can be said that wherever ten Jews stand together the Shechinah rests on them—and it makes no difference who the ten are, whether they are Tzadikim or whether they are weak and ordinary men, or even wicked ones. Even if the ten are engaged in mundane tasks, they constitute a potentially holy community. A play on words deals with the contradiction: "Over every ten of Israel the Shechinah hovers"—since the Shechinah is above and not necessarily within the ten, it cannot be easily disposed of. This also intimates that over every cinema and coffee house in Israel, where ten or more congregate, there too holiness hovers. The evidence points to the sad fact that few, if any, are aware of this. As it has been said, the difference between the saint and the sinner lies in their degree of openness. There is the story of the disciple who asked, "Where is God?" And his fellows answered, "He is everywhere, of course," while the rabbi said, "He is in every place where He is allowed to enter." In practice, therefore, or rather, in terms of consciousness, He can be within the soul of a person or He can surround the soul. The latter case, where God is absent from the soul, where He is forced out and has to be above and around the soul, is called "the wicked who suffers." A complete Tzadik cannot feel evil as evil in the external sense because he is not open to it. In order to relate to anything as bad and to suffer it, one must be in the position of a victim to begin with. The person who has gone beyond that position is oblivious to the suffering aspect of hardship; even if he does see evil, he is not affected by it. There is a description of Rabbi Elazar, son of Shimon bar Yochai, who used to tell the sufferings to leave him every morning so that he could get something useful done during the day; and in the evening, he would let them return to torment him all night. His wife, as may be surmised, couldn't bear this indifferent attitude to suffering and ran away. In a sense, the complete Tzadik cannot feel bad no matter what the circumstances.

Following the same logic, as we have hinted, the thoroughly wicked person cannot feel good. He is, therefore, called the "wicked who suffers," not necessarily because he can never be satisfied with himself, but because he can never enjoy any of the things he so desperately desires. There seems to be a point of satiation where, in order to enjoy something, one has to be in a minimal state of compliance, prepared to accept that which is offered as good. And the one who has driven the good from himself has also driven out all chance of enjoying the fruits of his wickedness. At this level, there appears to be a certain correlation between the wickedness of the wicked and his being closed to goodness and the goodness of the Tzadik and his being closed to evil. After all, there aren't so many things that are objectively good; most of the good things require a certain preparation of the mind, a recognition that there is value to them. Otherwise, life can be a round of monotonous sameness, if not of actual torment. Only too clearly, one can witness the perversion that results from the wild efforts and artificial constructions aimed at saving some vestige of the enjoyment of life. Indeed, this horror of the abyss created by evil, by the lack of good as a base for enjoyment, has forced many people to extremes of all sorts, from frantic repentance to wild, self-destructive accumulation of money, power, or whatever. One can find any number of parallels between the dynamics of the Tzadik and of the wicked, but there is not much point in making them. The fact is that most people are neither one nor the other; and the Benoni, the intermediate man, is much more of a possible ideal.

By now, it should be evident that the Benoni is the highest possibility of development open to the normal individual. To be a potential Tzadik is not given to most people – one has to be born a Tzadik, or one has to be exceptional to an extraordinary degree of spiritual power. Whereas everyone can become a Benoni; it is that which is possible as a result of a certain effort.

12

Limitations of the Benoni

The Benoni is he on whom evil never attains enough power to capture the "small city," which is the body, and make it sin. In short, the Benoni is a person who never does anything sinful whether in thought or action. He is wholly involved in mitzvot, doing only good. And if in the past he ever did transgress, he has completely repented, and the evil is no longer operative in his life. This means that even the sinful person can become a Benoni if he puts all sin behind him saying, "The one who I now am could never conceivably have done these abominable deeds." Indeed, everyone has such an experience of outgrowing childish things and being unable to relate to them, even being unable to remember that they were once so intimately part of oneself.

Now, if a Benoni is always doing and thinking good, why is he not a Tzadik? He remains an "intermediate" because in essence he is precisely that, not half a Tzadik and half a wicked person, but something special in himself that belongs to another category of good and evil. He is in a state of constant conflict between the two, and the good is in control only because he has struggled to make it so. Holiness rules his soul, but his soul is not yet holy. The tension is almost never relaxed, and complete rest is unknown.

The true Tzadik, on the other hand, doesn't have to strive to be good. Everything in him is centered and unified; there is no need to keep an anxious watch on the borders of his being. Admittedly, there is a realm outside that is not of the Tzadik; but it does not constitute a threat in any way.

The Benoni, however, is never allowed to know more than a momentary peace, a transient armistice within a permanent struggle. For him, the danger of collapse can never be over-come or eliminated, and the tension is relentless. Unlike the wicked person who experiences constant invasion of evil in the "small city" of his consciousness, or the Tzadik who doesn't even have to guard his walls, the Benoni is in control but must maintain a vigilant watch on his ramparts.

The basic structure of the souls of the Tzadik and the Benoni are thus very different, even though they operate on the same level and do the very same things. In terms of behavior, the Benoni is outwardly—and even inwardly—a wholly integrated individual on a very high plane of being. He can, therefore, become a great man and a saint, but the incessant struggle still remains.

Evidently then, the way of the Tzadik and the way of the Benoni do not extend from the same trunk; they branch out from different trees and a Benoni cannot usually become a Tzadik. If it does happen, it is not a process of natural growth, for they pursue different lines of development. And this is, after all, the importance of the message of the *Tanya*: The Benoni is a realistic goal for all, and it is not the same as the very special grace from on High that is given to a few holy souls. Inner tranquility and peace is given to those whom God chooses, whereas the effort to attain it is given to all, and the eventual reward may be greater. True, a Benoni does attain a state of peace on his borders, a relatively quiet and contented condition, without soul-storms and struggle. But it may well be the illusory state of a cold war, for the Benoni, like all ordinary men, has to remain alert to the task of worshipping God all his life. He is a person with an ideal, and the ideal includes assuming his responsibility in the struggle against the evil impulse. If, therefore, he succeeds in controlling his thoughts, speech, and action, so that only good emerges, he is not yet at peace; it is no indication of anything more than that he is a Benoni and not a Tzadik.

True, the Benoni can attain a height where he feels like a Tzadik, but this is almost always at times of uplift when he is engaged in an act of holiness and worship. The difference perhaps lies in the fact that the Tzadik never bothers to think about it. The Benoni can pray fervently and rise to heights; but, on return, he has to steady himself lest he make a wrong move and lose everything. The Benoni is a level available to every person; and it is even demanded of every individual, difficult though this may be.

13
Truth and Sincerity in Divine Service

According to what has been said about the Tzadik, one may gather that he is so vastly superior to an ordinary mortal that he can be compared to what the cinema has called a superman. However, the chief concern here is with the Benoni, the "intermediate" person. True, the *Tanya* was written for people who were superior to the ordinary man and were even considered Tzadikim by their contemporaries. Nevertheless, the ideal that is being offered to us, the ideal toward which we should all aspire, is the Benoni—and not the Tzadik who is born a saint. Because the Benoni is a human type that can be achieved by effort and practice. The Benoni is one who has reached a level in which the love of God streams forth out of him, and he is often and easily in a state of ecstasy, such as during the time of prayer. To be sure, the animal-soul does emerge to dominate the individual soon after these periods of Divine union, and the ecstasy gives way to the afflictions of the external life.

This prospect may well bring one to the edge of despair: If all one's efforts and successes in holiness cannot prevent the onslaught of shameful thoughts, if life is a constant swing from one to the other, from the Divine Soul to the animal-soul, there can be no peace. Nevertheless, when the holiness prevails, one does not feel the other side, nor does one seek it out; on the other hand, when the animal-soul takes over, the person strives to restore contact with his Divine part, at least through his understanding. And in this he has the help of the fundamental structure of things as well as Divine grace.

According to the chart of the Sefirot, there are three vertical lines: The one on the right goes from Chochmah (Wisdom) to Chesed (Love) to Netzach (Victory). The left proceeds from Binah (Understanding) to Gevurah (Severity or Strength) to Hod (Splendor); the central line goes from Keter (Crown) through Daat (Knowledge) to Tiferet (Beauty, Harmony, or Truth), Yesod (Foundation), and Malchut (Kingdom). In other words, the way to overcome the difficulties of the attribute of Gevurah is through Binah, by comprehending the dynamics of what is happening to one by getting at the source of the trouble. To be sure, this effort to correct the difficulty at its source is not a consistent Chabad method; as often as not the Chabad will counsel one to deal vigorously with symptoms and to let the soul correct itself. Nevertheless, there is this more fundamental way, the way of concentrating one's attention on Binah because this leads directly to Gevurah and right action.

Thus the Benoni meditates on Binah precisely because of the need to get to the root of the matter. Meditation on Chochmah, according to the same logic, would lead to Chesed and an abundance of love; but this would only leave the Benoni more exposed to the powers of the Sitra Achra. Because in the ecstasy of love he is like someone asleep, and the animal-soul is free to do as it wishes. To be sure, when at prayer, the Benoni does give himself to the bliss of Divine love, but then he is also protected. However, afterwards he is vulnerable again, and he must resort to his understanding, to a disciplined life of study and good deeds. Therefore, too, many a holy rabbi who seemed to be such a pure Tzadik, devoting himself entirely to Torah and mitzvot, was really a Benoni who was fighting relentlessly by never exposing himself to the forces of the animal-soul. What is characteristic of many of these men is their utmost humility, their incisive knowledge of themselves, as exemplified by Rabbi Yizhak Isaac of Kallo, who was among

those who brought Chasidism to Hungary. A leader of more
than forty congregations, and a writer and poet of renown, he
insisted that upon his tombstone should be inscribed the fact
that "the person lying here was a devout Jew who knew how
to study Gemara (Talmud) according to the order of the pages."
Nothing else seemed truthful to say about himself.

True, one can immerse oneself in Torah and become so full of
love and sublime thoughts while doing it that it feels like a
Divine revelation. The moment after, however, is the real test,
when most men are bitten by the primordial snake crawling
unseen at their feet. There is the story of the Gaon of Vilna,
who was one of the greatest saints and scholars of the age.
Upon urging the Maggid of Dubnow to admonish him, as the
Maggid was in the habit of reproving the people of his
generation, the Gaon was told: "Rebbe, you keep yourself holy
in candlelight behind the closed shutters of your windows;
could you be as much of a Tzadik if you went out into the
marketplace?" The Gaon accepted this in good faith and quoted
from the Talmud in corroboration. "As the Rabbi of Kobrin
used to sing: 'Angel, O angel, you have no wife or children, no
worries about livelihood or health; therefore, you can be a holy
angel.' "

This does not deny the fact of the experience of Divine love of
the Benoni while in prayer. What is questioned is the truth of
the experience. After all, if a love is not constant, can it be
called true? This does not mean that the devout person is
deluding himself; but if the bliss of Divine Unity passes so easily
after prayer, should its authenticity not be questioned? In
Hebrew, just as there are constant or reliable streams (*nachal
eitan*), which flow all the year round, there are also inconstant
streams, which are called "false" or "disappointing" (*nachal
achzav*), because they dry up for a certain part of the year.

On the other hand, is this not too harsh a definition of Truth.
After all, it is in the nature of all things in the world to change,
and as the Rambam pointed out, only God is true in the sense
of absolute reliability. We still continue to recognize the sincerity of worship of the Benoni, knowing that every human
being has his own utmost Truth, and that it is different for each
person. What is more, this too is not absolute; what was true
one day can be something else another day. Sincere worship of

God, however, is of another category; it is by nature dynamic and changing and has its own relation to truth; that is, although there is one undeviating and eternal Absolute, there are also innumerable specific situations, each with its own right relation to this Absolute.

The love of the Benoni is true not only because it has the power to overcome falsehood, but also because it can always return to itself and even rise to higher levels. This is not an easy conclusion to arrive at in terms of scientific thinking. By scientific thought we mean the experimental approach, the ability to repeat the same thing and get the same results. However, in spite of the obvious difficulties in this respect, it is maintained that a person can come back to a high level of sincerity in worship, even if he falls away from it. If he does not, one can then begin to question the authenticity of the experience. But, for the most part, the fact that every time he prays the Benoni does return to a level of Divine love is as valid a sign of its Truth as we can have.

To be sure, there is a factor here which we have not emphasized: A considerable amount of preparation and practice is required for anyone who is not a Tzadik to rise to this level of prayer. The Benoni sometimes reaches it only after hours of study and meditation. Not every school of Chasidism was of the same opinion on this. The school of Kotzk, for example, went to such extremes in their concentration on sincerity, that it led to a great flexibility in the times of prayer and the duration of each service. As the Rabbi of Kotzk once explained it, the time spent in sharpening the ax is as important as the time spent in chopping the tree. In order to pray with truth and effectiveness, we have to prepare ourselves properly.

Truth itself cannot be flexible, of course. The central line of the Sefirot, proceeding from Crown through Knowledge to Beauty and down to Foundation and Kingdom, is known as the "middle bolt (or rod) which secures everything from end to end." For Truth is the attribute of Jacob (Beauty, the middle Sefirah), and it is an "unbounded inheritance, which has no limit upwards to the highest degrees, while all lower gradations and degrees are as nothing compared with those that are superior to them." Truth is thus the middle line from infinity to all that is below in the world, and everything has its point of contact with it. All that exists has to possess its kernel of truth in order to be what it is. This heart of Truth is the attribute of Jacob—Tiferet (Beauty, Harmony, and Justice), which has no measure; that is, there cannot be too much of it. At the same time, it is a vertical line, not a point, and at every level of being a man can say that all I did previously was not Truth. It is a progressive Truth; at each level, it is perfect in its own terms and related to the Infinite at a definite point along the line; but when seen from a higher level, this same point is seen as lacking; it is a lesser truth. If I now say this is a table, my words will have to be corrected in a hundred years to say that it has become something else; if I say this is a sun, the same correction will have to be made in billions of light years, and so on. All truths have their limitations, and as one gains more knowledge, one's previous understanding is seen to have been only partial truth, if not actually false. Every point of contact with Truth is thus incomplete and temporary. The Benoni is therefore enjoined to remember that his worship is indeed imperfect, even though his thoughts and feelings of exaltation are true.

There is the story of the sage who did not want to go to the synagogue on Yom Kippur (Day of Atonement), saying: "Last year I claimed to be penitent and to return to God, but since this has proved to be false I do not desire to repeat it." The others consoled him by telling him to say: "Lord God, this time I speak truly, with all the sincerity of my heart." That is to say, a person can promise something with all his heart, and if it turns out that he is unable to carry it out, it only means that the promise lacks the truth of eternity; it does not repudiate the truth of the present, this moment of life, and this level of one's inner being.

For there is a general law to the effect that the lower degree of a higher level is a little higher than the highest degree of a lower level. And this is true of all the stages and degrees of being. All that was previously true may become untrue as a person rises. What was yesterday my heaven has to become my earth today. And tomorrow there will be higher heavens and truths which are today beyond my grasp.

14

The Struggle against Evil

The Tzadik is born to be a Tzadik, and only a very few people can achieve this level of sanctity. It is said that before birth every infant is sworn to strive for sainthood—is told "to be Tzadik and not a wicked one." But what is the point of it if almost everyone chooses the life of wickedness? The answer is that to be a Tzadik is not something that depends on one's own choice. What is granted is the choice between being a Tzadik if you can and, if not, then at least not being wicked.

To the injunction "Turn from evil and do good," the Sages have added: "And there is no good except for Torah and the study of Torah as against them all." The phrase "study of Torah" being something that is weighed against all else, has a double meaning: Firstly, it means the actual learning of Torah; and secondly, it refers to the broad context of Torah and the relation to it. That is to say, a person actually has no time for doing good, he can barely fulfill his obligations to God by performing the required mitzvot for the day. Bialik described it as binding and unwinding and kissing *tefillin*, praying and blessing and orienting oneself, all before even beginning to eat in the morning; and then, when one has nothing else of great

93

urgency to do during the day, one has to sit down and study. The idea here is that "doing good" is not a specific set of actions that one can complete and then feel that now one has time for oneself.

The language of the oath enjoins a person, even before he is born, to strive to be a Tzadik or, at the very least, to refrain from wickedness; it seems to indicate that a person does not have any way of knowing beforehand whether he is to be a Tzadik or a Benoni. It is not written on the forehead; and the difference is apparent only after great effort and struggle. The child who is born a Tzadik is not born complete with wisdom or the inability to sin; he is only a potential Tzadik with the possibility of developing along certain lines. If he does not develop in this way he may even make the wrong use of his potential and become a wicked person; there is no assurance or compulsion. Thus, only the Tzadik has the freedom to choose to be a Tzadik, and still he has to make the choice. From this it may be gathered that the contents of the oath sworn by the unborn infant is in the nature of a directive, indicating how one should aspire to live. Indeed, later in the course of the reasoning, this point is again brought up as a possible conversion or mutation, a transformation open to man, enabling him to become a Tzadik. True, there is only a remote possibility of such a transformation, but it is not to be rejected. And, in any case, the injunction administered remains valid—to be as complete a Tzadik as you can and, at least, not to be wicked. This statement of double purpose fits the category of Benoni, he who has risen by his efforts beyond wickedness even though he is not a Tzadik. It is also said that this oath gives the unborn soul strength to deal with whatever he has to overcome in life.

One of the main distinctions between the Tzadik and the Benoni is the way they relate to evil. Of course, neither of them could ever do any evil; and, even in thought, the Benoni may not fall far behind the Tzadik and, like him, the Benoni may be quite unable to think evil. Thus, the Benoni could be constantly immersed in holy thoughts and never dwell on anything else; he could even be a great man in the world and a saint in his inner life. The rest of mankind may consider him a Tzadik, there being no reason for them to believe otherwise; yet the Benoni himself knows that he is not a Tzadik. The difference is that he does not abhor evil as the Tzadik does; he understands it, even if he is not attracted to it; he knows its power and the hold it can have over man.

The Tzadik, however, has no point of contact with evil; he is repelled by it as something entirely different and alien to him. As one Tzadik put it: "I constantly thank God for prohibiting pride, because were it commanded that pride be a mitzvah, I would be at a loss; what could I be proud of?" The problem for such saintly persons is their ignorance of evil for they do not know pride or envy, greed and the like. And, for many of the truly great Tzadikim, this proved such a weakness that they could not be the leaders they should have been. Without knowing what the poor really craved and desired, they were forever apart, unable to share what they could only perceive as the oddities of the ordinary man. It was not a matter of comprehending the heart of a simple person; it was an inability to take seriously the evil imagination of men, never having experienced such a fascination personally. It is like the inability of a sane person to grasp the antics of the mad. The Benoni on the other hand could, if he made the effort, find the evil existing somewhere in himself. He would have the power to sympathize with transgression in a way that is beyond the Tzadik.

In their relation to good or the higher experiences of consciousness, the Benoni and the Tzadik do not differ much. The Tzadik enjoys the bliss of the Shechinah, which is called love in all its delight; but the Benoni, and even the lesser man, can know such joys in a life of Torah and mitzvot. It should not be forgotten that the Benoni is capable of extreme sensitivity and great spiritual power, so that when he performs a mitzvah it raises him to a level as high as that of the Tzadik. However, he must bring himself to performing the mitzvah, and this is not necessarily a matter of doing anything but what he desires to do. Thus, in terms of the good, the difference here is not at all apparent. It is in relation to evil that the disparity between the Tzadik and the Benoni is decisive: No matter how hard he tries, the Benoni cannot rid himself of the roots of evil. There is absolutely no hypocrisy involved, nor even a lack of whole-ness. And the fact that, after many years of struggle and devotion to Torah, a person does not reach perfection and peace of mind is no proof that there is something wrong with him. It is only a sign that he is a Benoni and not a Tzadik, which is more a lack of good fortune than a disability.

Although the Benoni does not abhor evil by nature, he should at least simulate this abhorrence by an effort of imagi-nation. It is known that a person can bring himself to a state of mind in which certain desirable things become utterly repel-lent, for the quality of desirability is the product of a one-sided perspective; for example, a many-sided view of an attractive woman would make it difficult for her to remain desirable. One can even carry this to an extreme, transforming that which is coveted into an object of repulsion. For all lust depends on the way one sees an object. Indeed, if someone is unable to cut loose from such binding image, he suffers from mental illness. The one-sided picture generally becomes an obsession.

To be sure, such a severely prejudiced analysis of the delights of this world—reducing them to their ultimate rot and filth—has its own weakness. Life itself is then misconceived as the corrupting process of death, and one loses a certain sense of proportion. What is more, even when one does manage to recoil from the temptations of the flesh, by concentrating on its corruptibility and watching out for signs of one's own greed or lust, the ability to recoil is usually effective only for a short while. One forgets all too rapidly.

What is preferred, therefore, is the positive approach, that is to rejoice in God by reflecting on His infinite blessings. But, just as the abhorrence of evil is largely a matter of imagination, as is evident from the fact that it is forgotten so easily, the attraction to Divine goodness may also be illusory. What is the true stance then? Should it not be something that does not need crutches or outside support of any kind? A person needs to feel that his reactions are stable and based on truth, that whatever he claims to be genuine has something of the absolute and the eternal. Merely to be aware of the delusory nature of physical pleasures does not express the essential need of one's soul. One returns to the oath administered at the very beginning of life, "to be a Tzadik," and the complementary saying, "and God will do as He sees fit." This appears to be the one certainty that is granted—one cannot know whether it is possible to be a Tzadik; all one can know is that one has to strive to be one and, at least, to turn away from evil. The rest is up to the Divine. He who struggles greatly with himself also has to contend with imagination, something which is not so easy to do. Every fragment of thought and imagination has its own force, whether in the world of substance or of spirit. Just as the smallest trickle of water can make a deep impression, even on stone, over a long period of time, so do thoughts affect the soul. If a person entertains certain imaginations over a consistent period of time, they will become part of him, whether he wishes it or not. Just as diplomats are not retained for any considerable number of years in any ambassadorial post because they tend to become identified with their surroundings, so it is not healthy for any person to let his thoughts range over any of the realms of evil in casual imagination or even disputation. Therefore, we have the recommendation to dwell on the greatness and goodness of God. Even if this fulfills its purpose for only a moment or two, and one quickly returns to a normal state of forgetfulness, it may, by repetition, acquire the cumulative influence of habit.

Furthermore, as we know, habit can become second nature—which explains the emphasis on prayer—for when a person can make a meaningful move from below, it arouses a similar action from above. As the Baal Shem Tov said, "God is your shadow," and whatever you do He will copy; lift your hand and He raises His; give charity and He will be charitable with you; do something ugly and He will perform a similar action on you. The more significant and soul-stirring the action from below, the higher the plane on which one receives the life force. Hence, even if one is not a Tzadik, it is possible to merit something of the spirit that is rooted in some Tzadik or other. The Kabbalah mentions this possibility as "Ibur," the partial incarnation of one soul into another—which is not quite the same as what is known as a dybbuk in folklore. A dybbuk is a soul that invades another person's soul, either intermittently or permanently, and acts on it as an alien force. Someone suffering in this way is under a strange influence. (Incidentally, one is reminded that Rabbi Kook, who is considered a modern, twentieth-century sage, had occasion to expel a dybbuk, so that the phenomenon is not necessarily confined to folklore.) In any case, what is casually indicated here as a remote possibility is "Ibur," the receiving, in whole or in part, of an additional soul which is not alien to one's own soul. It is another soul that in some way belongs to one; and it can merge into the consciousness of the receiver so completely that in the passage of more or less time it becomes a part of the intrinsic whole. The difference is not only in terms of value or level of the occurrence; it is also in the quality of the manifestation. If the soul of a Tzadik is lodged in one, it is not felt as a foreign influence. Jewish tradition does not have many descriptions of the phenomenon, not because of its scarcity, but because of the general reluctance to put it into words and the scrupulous concern lest it be misconstrued.

From the little written evidence we do possess, it may be gathered that the "Ibur" generally occurs without the person being in any way prepared for it. There is no particular relation to time or place or events. The result is a sensation of having grown suddenly, of being able to act far more cogently, and of being able to see and feel and experience things that were previously beyond one's powers. It may be a transient state or a more lasting one, characterized by the sense of having changed, grown, and matured greatly. On the other hand, it may be felt as a complete transformation, a fact, obvious to everyone, that the person has become someone else.

Jewish tradition is familiar with several different kinds of such sudden growth or change, in addition to this one of being visited by a higher soul. For example, there is the rarely mentioned instance of a revelation of a high level of soul, such as that of "Chayah," and there is the better-known phenomenon of martyrdom (Kiddush HaShem) when there is a bursting out of an inner spiritual force.

The reason for this digression into the subject of Ibur is to further explain the capacity of the Benoni to receive such a visitation of soul-power from a Tzadik, thereby becoming a Tzadik himself. In other words, he becomes another person, not necessarily because of the visitation as an external influence, but because the visitation comes as a climax to an internal growth process. Hence, the urge to know the exact identity of the one whose soul has entered the being is of no consequence, even if it is revealed.

The result of such a visitation is the great joy and bliss known only to the Tzadik. Thus, even though a Benoni will most likely never become a Tzadik and will, at best, do no more than unequivocally remove himself from evil, nevertheless, he should strive, as he is enjoined to do, to imitate the deeds of the Patriarchs—Abraham, Isaac, and Jacob. This means that he has to stand forever on tiptoe, stretching out his arms and trying to receive, if only for a moment, that which is beyond his reach. Even if he never touches anything at all, the effort is not in vain. For there are invisible processes at work on the soul, changing it and bringing the person closer to a higher state. After a certain period of time, the problems of the Benoni become less severe, even if more compounded in the spiritual sense. He is supported and soothed by the force of habit and the stability of a structure of life that may not be able to resolve his problems but can mitigate their effect on him. He can bring himself to consider his position with some detachment. This is the result of exercise and work on himself as though he were a Tzadik, even though he knows he is not. It is like teaching a person to swim by telling him to imagine that he is a fish. Although he will certainly never be a fish, it will help him to swim like a man.

15

The Need for Conflict

It has been emphasized that one of the chief characteristics of the Benoni is his persistence in Divine worship, the fact that there is no respite. His work is never done: He is forever poised between the two commandments, to be a Tzadik and not to be wicked; and although he knows he will never be a Tzadik, he has no choice but to maintain the tension.

With this in mind, the biblical saying (Malachi 3:18), "Then shall ye again discern between the righteous man and the wicked, between him who serves God and him who serves Him not," directs our attention to the different levels of righteousness. The Tzadik, however, is beyond these categories. While the Benoni is still one who serves God, the Tzadik's whole life has been given to God. He is no longer striving to do anything for God; he is already totally an instrument of Divine Will. It may be compared to the difference between a wage laborer, whose efforts will determine his compensation, and of a slave, or a king, whose efforts do not in any way affect their status. The Tzadik, too, has already reached his place—what he does will not make any difference. Consider the effort to learn something: Once the learning is done, it becomes superfluous;

there is no point in repeating the lesson. So too, the Tzadik does not need to struggle anymore between good and evil, and he is free to advance further in the worship of God. It is only in this sense that the Tzadik does not rest; he is forging ahead, beyond the basic lessons or conflicts of ordinary men.

To be sure, there is also a doubtful realm, even for the Tzadik, concerning that which is not known to be evil. But it belongs to another dimension. The Tzadik is not immune to error; he can make mistakes. What he does possess, however, is a powerful instinct for the good. This may be illustrated by the story of the holy man (Baal Chidushei HaRim) who never ate anything questionable. Once, there was some slight confusion in the kitchen, and he was presented with a dish which, although kosher, he firmly rejected. After some further inquiry, something not quite up to his standards was discovered, and he was asked how he had been able to detect it. He answered that it was obvious. All a person needed to do was to decide with resolute heart that he would never swallow any food that was not absolutely pure and he would be preserved from error.

To be sure, there are those who, for entirely different reasons, do not struggle against evil. These are personalities who can hardly be considered to be devoted servants of God— they just continue to perform their good deeds as a matter of routine, studying, praying, and doing mitzvot. There is no inner conflict because they are motivated only by their intrinsic Jewishness, not by any particular passion for God. Habit thus becomes second nature. Even when there are genuine achievements, moral as well as intellectual, this does not necessarily entitle a person to be called a true servant of God. It is a matter of balance and inertia. A stone lying on the ground is inert and is making no progress; when lifted to the roof of a building and left there, it is still making no progress, even if it is on a higher level. So too, those persons who are not constantly aspiring and striving can hardly be called servants of God; their second nature on the higher level is not much different from their original nature on the ground.

Thus, the question of habit is crucial. To get used to studying for one hour a day is easy; the problem is the incessant effort, the constant increment of Divine love. And it does not matter what the content of the routine is, whether religious or otherwise, habit can change service into something else than what it is supposed to be.

The danger for a Benoni, therefore, resides in his continuing to do worthy actions out of habit and, at the same time, ceasing to be a servant of God. True, such a one may still be preferred to the wicked, but it is a different category of Benoni. As it is said in the Talmud, a person should know whether or not he is a Tzadik. If he isn't, and yet feels that he has reached a degree of perfect serenity, it is a sign that he has fallen from his level.

It follows that in order to overcome lethargy and habit—the evil impulse in the left side of the heart—it is necessary to hold before one's gaze the unattainable greatness of God and to feel in one's heart the passionate love of God. At the very least, one should arouse the hidden love, which is not that of habit, that stirs up a renewal of the inner struggle.

This suggests that there are two ways of serving God; the first is contemplating the greatness of the Divine and thereby attaining a love of God which evokes a simple and pure worship. If this is not granted to a person, it is possible to take the second way, to awaken the hidden love—a love which is not necessarily anything new, but rather a product of will power—and to make it a desire to move ahead and not to remain fixed at any habitual feeling. The inner emotions of this second way may not be as uplifting as those evoked in a simple and innocent worship; but it allows for a person to be in spiritual conflict with himself. A person may also manage to exploit this hidden love; that is to say, if one cannot, in all innocence, rise to a higher level of experience, the constant renewal of the human aspiration for God can reinforce the sense of one's self as a person and result in creative action of a meaningful nature.

However, if there is no conflict, this hidden love can hardly be considered service. True, absence of conflict does not point to transgression, but it does indicate a cessation of the intense concern with God, and this a Benoni cannot permit to happen. He has no choice but to carry on an endless contest with himself, forever adding new difficulties, so that the defeat of old habits only makes it possible to engage in new struggle. Only then may one be considered a servant of God.

16

The Never-Ending Work of the Benoni

What is the driving force that enables us to persevere in Divine worship? Is it simply to follow the heart, to rely on the natural love of God, which is not the product of intellectual effort, or is it to continue to consciously make ever renewed efforts and to proceed from intellectual awareness to feeling and from feeling to action? The latter would indeed be the more complete course, for it would be the worship of God with the entirety of one's being.

Only too often, however, the religious life is a matter involving only a certain part of the personality. When eating, for example, the relation to the Divine varies—before partaking of food only half the person is thinking of God; the other half is straying toward the menu. It is during the meal that there may be said to be a certain unity of all the parts of the being. The physical, the aesthetic, the ethical, and the spiritual are all integrated in the act of eating. The nature of this unity may be made more apparent if we imagine the reaction to the same meal if all the courses were mixed together, the ingredients all chopped up and served in one bowl. Not only would the aesthetic part rebel, but the physical appetite would, most likely, also shrink; and the integral unity of the act of eating would be greatly disrupted, even though the very same food is being consumed. A similar reaction occurs when a person performs a religious act as though he were eating without appetite, only because he has to eat, that is, without the eager participation of the soul.

Thus, in order for Divine worship to be whole, a certain degree of participation is required from all the aspects of the being. If only one part is active, the act tends to be shaky and vulnerable. And it is the intellectual awareness that can best accomplish such an amalgamation of the inner spiritual aspects and the outer rational aspects of the personality, thereby raising the act to its proper level of Divine "love and fear." Such, in any case, is the way of the Benoni, using his consciousness to combine the awakened soul with the awakened will in the heart, in the act of doing the mitzvah.

If a person cannot reach this degree of love of God in mind and heart, it is usually the result of an inability to discern certain things. To be sure, it is not simply a visual deficiency; it is a profound incapacity that exists in the inner being of many people, whether intellectually gifted or not. Many of them strive in vain to imagine a spiritual reality to which they can relate in all sincerity. There are others who are unable to do more than play with a number of key words in a desperate attempt to retrieve their abstract meaning. The inability to crystallize a convincing framework of coherence for oneself, in any field, whether aesthetic or intellectual or spiritual, combined with a lack of receptivity to the inarticulate, makes it difficult to genuinely experience the love of God. Without a doubt, however, this is a fault which can be corrected, albeit with very great effort; and there have been those who, with proper motivation and concentration over a longer or shorter period of time, have been able to do so.

A person who has achieved an intellectual, nonvisual image that is so convincing to his soul that it arouses the love and fear of God in him has already proceeded far in the direction of this goal. Many people, however, will suffice with words or arguments that seem to persuade, even though they admit the impossibility of delineating what it is that is so persuasive. Reciting the Simchat Torah prayers in the synagogue or the verse: "This is our God for whom we have been hoping"—even the devotion of a lifetime—may take one no further than this point, which is already a serious step forward. Because it is the stage where no theological explanations or descriptions are needed, one simply points and says, "This" as a self-understood act of knowing. To be sure, not everyone can achieve this stage where the heart is so full of eagerness for God's presence that it overcomes the actual lack of possession (of God) and finds its own rapturous gratification.

All of this is a digression from our main idea concerning the hidden love of God, which is sometimes so hidden away that even the person himself will not sense its existence. And even when one is able to make intellectual assertions proving the greatness of God and His omnipresence, the experience itself is denied to him, and all he feels is the hiddenness. His heart cannot even say with conviction "This" (is our God), although his mind understands that God is the source of all and should be loved with the wholeness of his being.

This kind of experience is not confined only to the love of God; many emotions are not truly experienced in the heart and remain in the realm of mental conceptions, as a sense of obligation or as adherence to social patterns of behavior. Of course, it often works in the same way as the genuine experience; there are people who are very decent, kind, and affectionate, and they live most, if not all, their lives without knowing love or hate. What is important is to be aware of the difference, to discriminate between a genuine live emotion and an emotion, which even though it is not counterfeit, is not on the same level as Truth. The Benoni in particular has to discriminate between the various ways of experiencing the intrinsic love of God. He should not delude himself into thinking that he can love like a Tzadik, nor should he fall into depression because it is beyond his powers.

That is to say, the capacity to create persuasive abstract images of spiritual reality is limited, even for the Benoni. True, he can build up a framework of experiences that are genuine enough, but they still would not touch that level of intensity which would be more inward. Because, if the Benoni had the spiritual facility, in one form or another, to perceive God standing over him all the time, he would become a Tzadik. As has been said elsewhere, the Torah was forced on the people like a mountain tumbling on their heads—when God Himself reveals His irresistible love, He compels one like a mountain, and all of the human being's freedom of choice evaporates. As in life, any acute emotion—extreme fear, grief, passion—can undermine self-control and eliminate the illusion of freedom of choice. Even when one chooses the situation himself, even if it is to enter the lion's den, the confrontation with the hungry lion will usually restrict one's thoughts considerably.

The problem is: What does one do when God is no longer standing over him, the moment after experiencing the sublimity of His presence? And here the way one comes to God is crucial. He who has arrived the long and hard way, by continual effort, has had his courage fortified; he knows. He who has not made this effort will be subjected to a trying ordeal. As it is told in the Song of Songs: "Listen, my beloved knocks. . . . How shall I put on the robe that I have taken off; how shall I soil my feet. . . ." One hesitates to leap out of a warm comfortable bed to open the door, to meet the Beloved at last. So that it often happens: "My love had turned and gone past. . . . I sought him but did not find him." And indeed, a person may keep running about and searching all his life without being able to restore the opportune moment of a meeting with the Divine.

A story from the Midrash tells that when God wanted to reveal His face to Moses (at the burning bush), Moses was not ready and did not want it; then when Moses matured and asked for it, God did not want to reveal His face. So it is for many people. One is afraid to look and thus hides his face before God; then when he is able to see, it turns out that God has turned away. Hence it is written that were the soul liberated from the body and from the senses, the capacity to realize God from the abstract knowledge we have of Him would perhaps be possible. The very structure of our existence, however, thinking as we do through our physical brains and limited bodies, emphasizes the truth of the statement: "And no man shall see Me and live." The other side of reality is barred.

Nevertheless, one does grasp the reality of the King, by

means, at least, of the Torah and mitzvot. In that way, one does embrace the Divine essence, even, perhaps, without ever being sure of what it is that one is embracing, for the action of consciousness at its highest level is enough to overcome that which may be lacking in emotional terms. That is to say, even if one cannot love God with the same purity and holiness of a Tzadik, one can arouse one's soul to an experience of the Divine essence by conscious fulfillment of the mitzvot. And this is the way of the Benoni. By working at it, my immeasurably painstaking effort, he performs acts of devotion which are different from those of the Tzadik, but which have their own splendor and holiness. The Benoni must make use of his limitations and not merely refuse to reconcile himself to them; he cannot allow himself to suffice with a perfection of habit and routine. He has to keep the understanding of both the heart and the mind awake, for all things, great and small, compel his thoughts and urge him to contemplate on them. Only by continual alertness will he reach a level that corresponds to the level attained by a Tzadik.

17

Concerning the Intrinsic Love of God

It is axiomatic that one of the most important ways of experiencing the love and awe of God is through meditation on the Divine. But not everyone has the capacity for abstract conceptualization. A certain amount of knowledge and learning is needed, for it is difficult to meditate on the greatness of God without a minimal grasp of the laws of nature and the immensity of the cosmos. What is more important, an emotional maturity is needed in order to integrate the understanding into one's being, to convert the meditation from an intellectual truth to a power for living.

But as we know, there is no straight channel between mind and heart; there are any number of "pressure points" which greatly influence the proper flow of thoughts, feelings, and actions. In particular, the narrow passage of the throat, which, altogether, is so decisive in the circuit of human energy, is connected with emotions and lusts of the body. Thus, a person can reach a very high level of truly understanding the greatness and goodness of God, but it can remain theoretical. The understanding may not be able to get through the narrow passage in order to affect the rest of the person, and this block will be a constant threat to health and well-being.

In Jewish tradition, this blocked state of being is given any number of symbolic names, like Pharoah or Amalek, the stubborn ones who resist God, either with self-will or with doubt. Amalek is the eternal enemy of Israel; he is that in all of us which suggests: "and perhaps it is not so?" Indeed, the basis of all evil can be seen as a certain unyieldingness; and the power given to oppose it is that which has become symbolized by a stiff-necked people, a holy stubbornness, as distinct from a stubbornness of the outer "Klipah" or shell. In any case, the central problem of an intellectual person is that of the narrow passage, the transformation of correct thought into emotionally integrated living.

Thus, it frequently happens that one is unable to experience the love and fear of God properly, either as a profound feeling in the heart or even in the realm of the intellect and understanding. At the same time, the surface thought can almost always grasp something of the essence of this experience. What is more, it is possible for all men to study Torah and practice the mitzvot. For the mitzvot are practical actions that can be carried out in a definite time and place. And this, in turn, fills all that is lacking in a person. As a part of this, one can cultivate the well-tried habit of using all of one's free time to study Torah. As it is written, Talmud Torah, the study of Torah, is weighed against all the other commandments in that it fills all the empty and unoccupied places, and it does not allow a person to be in a vacuum. For there is no neutral territory. Either one is in the domain of the holy or one is abandoned to Sitra Achra. Even when one is idle, walking in the fields or whatever, the mind and heart are occupied with something or other, and this can be connected with Torah or things of the spirit as well as it can be a surrender to temptation.

The point of it all, however, is that one does not use the powers of Divine worship (God's work in life) for oneself; one aspires to the "highest" levels of such Divine worship only in order to get to the deepest truth of oneself. The Sages have often issued a sharp warning against imaginary experiences and illusion of all sorts. And to make sure that one remains sincere, it is necessary to draw upon the essence of the inherited tradition within the soul, that which, on one hand, is not entirely under one's control and, on the other, is strong enough to nourish one's life and the life of the people as a whole. This is the faith of the simple Jew, which does not come from an intellectual understanding and fear of the Divine but from an intrinsic love of God. And this love, as said, is strong enough to nourish the life of the nation. What is more, every Jew is given such a root, or source, of power in his soul, which can be drawn upon endlessly. A human energy source, so to speak. After one has exhausted the external sources, one penetrates into the abyss of oneself and draws forth the passion and power that are hidden there. Sometimes this passion bursts forth of itself, and it can be very destructive. Sometimes, such a bursting occurs in a moment of crisis, such as that offered by martyrdom. It is a potential, however, that can be utilized for ordinary purposes as well. Recognizing this vast potential, for good or for bad, one can tap it and make it serve the purposes of daily life. But how is this to be done?

How can one use this power, which is in one and yet beyond one, which is so terrifying that one spends a lifetime trying to keep it within bounds? How can one dole it out in controllable portions and live with it? The Chabad way is that of constant exhortation to make the intellectual effort to maintain control over oneself and to develop consciousness; and, on the other hand, there is this admission that the source of all power and effectiveness is in the unconscious depths.

One is reminded that in certain other schools of Chasidism, the emphasis was placed almost entirely on inner sincerity. The Chasidim of Kotzk, for example, claimed that developed souls could permit themselves to act without intellectual control; they could rely completely on their inner sanctity, on their spiritual spontaneity. In other words, the mature soul was not only a source of energy; it could be put in charge of life and be relied upon to act responsibly. It did not even have to rise to outer consciousness.

Thus, one can depend on intrinsic love of God inherited from the Patriarchs, even though there is a certain opposition between this and the fear of God, which presupposes a distance between oneself and the Divine. One seems to be torn between a profound attraction to God, beyond one's comprehension, and an equally profound thrust away from the Divine through dread of encroaching on holiness.

To better comprehend this legacy of Divine love, it may be useful to recall that the Patriarchs, from whom we have received our Divine Souls, with all that this signifies, constitute the Chariot. The Chariot is here distinguished from the dimension of prophecy. The prophet is still on a level of being human, a very high level indeed, and while he prophesies, he is a vehicle of the Shechinah, and the Shechinah speaks in his throat. The essence of the Chariot, however, is a total opposite to the level of the human. When the Patriarchs are said to be the components of the Chariot, they are being viewed as part of the pure structure of the system of holiness of the World of Emanation (Atzilut). They are parts of this structure, not only by virtue of any particular capacity or power, but because of their entire essence. That is to say, the Patriarchs cease to be human in the usual duality of being: good and evil, body and soul, and the like; they become whole as only the Chariot is whole, and in this way, as Divine emanation, are parts of the structure of the Divine manifestation.

Consequently, it is a new humanity of which we speak. The human nature that has been in existence prior to this is full of problems; what the Patriarchs do by becoming a Chariot is a total transformation and the creation of a new species of humanity, whose chief characteristic is a Divine Soul. The old humanity has life force or life-soul and mind-soul, which is the capacity to reach the highest levels of organization and intellect (like Aristotle, as the Rambam put it). Whereas the Jewish inheritance from the Fathers, this holy spark, or Divine Soul, is not dependent on any level of intelligence or any physical or vital factor. One may be good or bad, near or far from God, and the inheritance from the Patriarchs remains an essential, unchanging spark of the Divine in every Jew.

Another illustration of the nature of the Chariot may be obtained from the tradition of the Seven Shepherds—Abraham, Isaac, Jacob, Moses, Aaron, Joseph, and David. A complex hierarchy of relations is here symbolized, none of it simple and unequivocal. Thus, in a certain way, Moses is higher than all the others; but in spite of the fact that the Shechinah speaks through him, he himself is not part of the Chariot. Just as Aaron or Joseph are not parts of the Chariot. The paradox is that David is the fourth wheel of the Chariot, the other three being the Patriarchs, Abraham, Isaac, and Jacob. The question is: What is the biological transformation required to effect the change to a new humanity? What makes a man part of that power which creates the new species of man? To be sure, such ideas seem to contain certain unsavory elements of physical or racial superiority which are very non-Jewish.

To clarify this, it may be pertinent to point to a few important basic Jewish concepts which have become obscured as a result of the long controversy with Christianity and the defensive measures which had to be taken. For example, in ancient times, the Talmid Chacham, or scholar of the Torah, was not just an ordinary person with a gift for intellectual matters; he was considered a sort of repository of holiness. The implication of such an idea was that the Talmid Chacham is like a temple or an altar to which one offer gifts; and therefore, to support and sustain him is a religious duty. Thus, too, the idea that the Patriarchs are the Chariot implies that they unite, almost physically, with the essence of the Divine so that holiness passes through them biologically, strange as this may seem. This means that the Divine spark is transferred to their descendants, irrespective of other facts.

A Jew, therefore, was one who had this holiness in him; and if he decided to convert, it was a sign that he wasn't really a Jew in essence, even though he may have been born of Jewish parents. Similarly, a Gentile who became a proselyte was really a Jew in essence, even though he may not have been born of Jewish parents. The definition of who is a Jew is thus clearly beyond biology; it is simply one who has the holy spark. And, according to the *Tanya*, the confirmation of this definition resides in the fact that in the last resort when faced with some ultimate decision such as martyrdom, the Jew will offer himself to God.

Souls have their own hierarchy. Naturally, it has nothing to do with the position of a person in the world. A great soul can be hidden in a simple and obscure individual, and a person highly respected for his wisdom or social eminence can have a small soul of no significance. The greatness of a soul depends on the relation to the Divine holiness in terms of essence, instinctively, so to speak. There are individuals in every nation and culture who, by virtue of their spiritual efforts, can attain some contact with God. This does not necessarily mean that they possess great souls. A great soul does not even have to make these mighty efforts. The soul of a person, like a Tzadik, for example, is a flame that rises of itself to the Divine. And every Jew, no matter who he may be, has something of a spark of Divine sanctity in him. His soul is a holy soul, irrespective of who his parents were. Even those of double nature, who have criminal tendencies as well as noble aspirations, can have great souls in them. Here, one makes a distinction between the innately wicked and the socially delinquent. Because it can happen that a person becomes a delinquent precisely because the soul demands certain extreme actions in order to resolve something.

Even if the parents are of the most worthless and lowliest sort, they still bequeath to their child a soul that is holy. The potential of Israel is passed on in all circumstances. True, the soul can be small and without much power; but it is holy. This implies a certain optimism, a hope based on the fact that even the smallest and lowliest of souls can be the beginning of great things, bearing as it does the holiness of the Chariot itself. Everyone contains at least the "Wisdom of Action."

In other words, God creates the world in Wisdom (Chochmah). Wisdom is the Sefirah which stands between consciousness and that which is higher than consciousness. It is this ultimate in the manifested universe beyond which there is the nothingness of transcendence, since it is the Divine spark which transmits the holiness; it is a point without dimension containing all the potential of being. And since this Wisdom, even as a "point," exists in every soul, every Jew is inwardly, at least, a part of the Divine. True, this may be manifested only in rare or crucial moments, when the connection with the Divine, which lies at the limit of consciousness, bursts into consciousness. It is a more profound force than the biological will to live which explodes into power when threatened by death. Therefore, it is the basis of martyrdom of all sorts, although it does not necessarily follow that the person will know or understand what he is doing.

In short, throughout one's life, a person can be confined to the body; one may even be a sinner and an unbeliever, but, at a crucial moment, it can all change and the Divine Soul can express itself. This does not mean that the person changes, or that the immoral and wicked aspects are suddenly wiped out of existence. There is merely a totally inexplicable bursting forth of the point—the point of Wisdom in the soul.

This implies that even the one born with relatively poor genetic qualities can grow and become a great soul. To digress, there is something mentioned of another order of being—the fact that souls can also transmigrate. There are souls and beings which are suspended in the twilight realm between holiness and abomination. They cannot be born as children to holy parents because there is no point of contact; so that they have to come into the world on the edge of the Sitra Achra. In Jewish tradition, this has been reflected in the strange antecedents of the Messiah himself, such as the stories of Judah and Tamar, Boaz and Ruth the Moabite, David and Batsheva, Solomon and Naama the Ammonite, among others. That is to say, in order to get to the soul of the Messiah, the holiest of human souls, there has to be a certain coupling of doubtful holiness, if not of one that is actually prohibited.

18

On Faith and Martyrdom

It has been said that every Jewish person, no matter what sort he may be, has in him something of the Divine; he possesses it as an essential part of the soul which is inherited from the Patriarchs. And in this respect, even the lowliest of Israel transmits this legacy, for the essential holiness of the Jewish soul is passed on regardless of the level of the parents. Nevertheless, this holiness may be focused at only one point, in the Sefirah of Wisdom (Chochmah) in the soul. At this point it is clothed or wrapped, as in a sheath, level upon level, until the highest level. In order to better grasp this process, it should be recalled that Chochmah is the source of intelligence and comprehension, and it is above Binah (Understanding), which is intellectual in nature.

Wisdom is the flash of immediate comprehension, while understanding is the intellectual grasp which gradually develops from this first flash or origin of comprehension. Wisdom is thus the transmission point between the source of understanding and understanding itself; it makes it possible for Divine intelligence to penetrate one personally and thus to become useful as a power of reasoning and intellect. We think, and our thinking consists of a certain process of joining and

116

analysis, discrimination and integration. It is a process that is effective or coherent only if there is an idea present that can somehow or other be manipulated, that is, given to intelligent reasoning. The question of where this idea comes from hardly arises; and, indeed, the rapid steps of intellection as a whole are usually never made conscious. Whenever there is some slowing down of the process, however, it is possible to catch a glimpse of the action as a whole. The original idea is then seen as a kernel, which has to grow and develop, undergo gestation and birth. Wisdom is the original lightning flash of thought, the kernel of enlightenment that brings forth an idea. Afterwards, one has to understand what he has perceived, and this is a process that may take time. Usually it is broken up into small fragments of reasoning, for each idea has to be grasped fully before going further. At the very moment light breaks into the darkness of a problem, however, it is impossible to know what it is that has been apprehended. Wisdom is thus only the beginning, the point of departure; it is not yet comprehension. It is still unintellectualized intelligence. From this, it may be gathered that Wisdom is the source of all understanding and should not be identified with it.

If the Hebrew letters of the word "Chochmah" (wisdom) are broken down into its two component syllables, as Koach and Mah, the resultant meaning is power *(koach)*, which is not yet existent, a potential force or, rather, a hardly graspable reality — the word Mah being an expression, in a certain context, of "something not worth bothering about," of that which is on the border of being nothing. Of course, the word Mah can also be interpreted in its usual meaning of a question — "What?" As a Kabbalistic work expresses it, the question of Chochmah (Wisdom) is "Mah?" (What?), and the question of Binah (Understanding) is "Mi?" (Who?). The logic here is based on the idea that the preliminary problem is "what is it all about?" and only then, having realized that there is something there, the question "who?" becomes valid.

The Kabbalah has also played with the letter-numbers of the two words and has thereby evoked many further possibilities. "Mi" in gematria is fifty, which is associated with the fifty gates of Binah and the name of God, "Elokim," the letters of which can be separated and recombined into "Mi" (who) and "Eleh" (those).

"Wisdom is the power of that which is not comprehended and understood or grasped intellectually; consequently, there is vested in it the light of the Infinite—the Ain Sof—Blessed be He, who can in no way be comprehended by any thought." God being infinite cannot be grasped by the mind, and whatever is grasped by the mind is certainly not God. What the mind can experience, however, is Wisdom, that Sefirah which is not yet given to understanding. And it is in Wisdom that the light of the Infinite is vested.

There is an anecdote which, however crude, expresses an aspect of this idea. When the Rabbi of Kotzk was asked to explain why God did this or that, he answered in his own blunt fashion: "A God whom any stinking human can understand is not worth worshipping." In other words, if reason is satisfied concerning the Divine, it has not attained anything consequential. Nevertheless, there is a higher, if hidden, grasping of the Divine, which is given to every person to understand, even the unlearned. This is expressed in a faith that is itself enlightenment. In Proverbs 14:15, we find: "The simple (man) believeth everything, but the prudent man understandeth." Faith is, thus, not a matter of simple believing but of that special quality which goes beyond the mind, which is of wisdom—that is to say, it is an experience directly connected with the Divine and not with knowing this or that about Him. Therefore, the fact that a person is unlearned or even lacking in intellectual capacity makes no difference. One's faith is not nourished by the mind but by wisdom of the soul; so that faith is available to all men, irrespective of their mental abilities.

On the other hand, it has been maintained by tradition that faith needs to be supported by study and contemplation. Evidently, the contemplation prescribed is not aimed at achieving visualization of the Divine; it is rather intended as a way of making God present for oneself. The simple believer, not having anything definite before him, does not really know what it is he believes in. And this is too perilously close to the uncritical belief of the sinner, the thief who naively prays to God for success before every unsavory adventure.

Therefore, it is, alas, true that in order for faith to have consistent influence on behavior, the work of the mind, study and contemplation, are almost always essential. A firm connection has to be established between Chochmah and Binah, between faith as sudden illumination and understanding of all that this implies. Nevertheless, faith is not the product of comprehension; it exists independently of it and separate from it. The comprehension is that which makes contact with understanding; but the faith of the fool, like the faith of the Sage, comes from the inner part of the soul and not from the mind; it comes from Chochmah and not from Binah.

To say that the man of simple faith is like the fool who believes everything seems to suggest an attitude of scorn; and if this simple faith is so ineffectual, why use it as a model for anything? The answer lies in the fact that before God, all men are like fools in this respect. In other areas of mental behavior, simplemindedness can well be a critical impediment to the ability to understand; but in this area of thought, which is beyond intellectual comprehension, there is no difference between the fool and the wise man. Before the Infinite, there is no large or small, stupid or clever; all are of the same category. Hence, there is no significant distinction between any one person and another in terms of grasping the Divine.

Faith is essentially simple in that the acknowledgment of the holiness of the Divine is not a function of the qualities of one's comprehension; it is rather a part of every person of Israel, as something beyond comprehension. As a result, in the majority of cases, even the most worthless of Israel are ready to sacrifice their lives for the sanctity of God's name. This, incidentally, points to an aspect of the Jewish soul which is rather original. In the book *The Kuzari*, by Rabbi Yehudah HaLevi, there is a declaration to the effect: who amongst the nations of the world has such prophets, such patriarchs, such men of mind and spirit as those who are described in the Scriptures and the Talmud? The statement being made here concerning the Jewish readiness for martyrdom says something else: Who amongst the nations of the world has such fools and thieves and simple folk who are prepared to sacrifice their lives for the sanctity of God? This proves the existence of an inner relation to the holy that is beyond intellect and contemplation and even morals.

The mechanism involved is the confrontation with an urgent need to decide whether or not to cut oneself off from holiness. At this moment, a hidden factor operates, as always in supreme danger, compelling a person out of himself and enabling him to perform that which was previously unthinkable. He is given over to the power of the wisdom in his soul and, as legend has it, transcends all suffering and pain. Thus, even the common and ordinary man, even one who was never taught the meaning of holiness, can achieve the highest degree of self-sacrifice and devotion because "the one God" illuminates and animates the entire soul, clothed in its faculty of "Chochmah" which is beyond any graspable and understood knowledge or intelligence. When a person touches this point in his soul, this inner point which is wisdom, he is capable of acting in an entirely different way from the ordinary course of his life.

All of this is intended to emphasize the possibility of self-development in every person, that is, of the capacity of sacrificing himself in life and not only in death. It is a matter of using this intrinsic potential for martyrdom as a constant drive in living. This is made available by a proper relation to the mitzvah—the chance is given to choose God, at every confrontation with the opportunity of performing or refusing to perform the commandment.

The reason for the failure to choose correctly in life is usually a spirit of folly. The trouble is that the person who so lightly transgresses is convinced that he is still connected to the Divine, that his transgression is really of no consequence. It is only when he realizes that it is a matter of a test, a trial of his very being, that the same force that impels a person to renounce his life for God in martyrdom will operate to impel him to renounce the impulse to transgress. The difficulty, of course, lies in being able to persist, day after day. Not everyone can retain a steady hold on the impulse for martyrdom, giving himself up in self-sacrifice to God, not only for a single moment of glory but for all of the hours and days of living.

19

On the Difference between Holiness and the Other Side

To help us appreciate the rather inexplicable phenomenon of martyrdom as an emphatic and extreme response to the threat of being cut off from one's roots, consider the image of the soul of man as a candle of God (Proverbs 20:27). One of the possible explanations of this many-sided allegory is that it is actually the flame that is the soul, and that the candle (or, rather, the lamp) is the body, while the oil itself, which feeds the flame, corresponds to "Torah and mitzvot," the actions of serving God. In order for the lamp to give light, it has to enable the fuel of Torah and good deeds to nourish the flame of the soul. The body itself is a dark vessel, useless and dispensable; its function is to contain the burning wick and the fuel which feeds the flame. If the oil, as a constant source of burning, is not available, the body of the lamp dies even if the soul is still connected with the wick. The reason for this is, perhaps, that body and soul are not a natural and mutually sustaining combination. They are really opposites, and in order for them to combine, great forces have to be put into operation. If these forces are not exercised constantly, the unification of the two cannot be sustained. The soul tends to go one way and the body another. It is, in a way, the

121

relationship of God to the world. And Israel, by its work of Divine worship, helps to maintain the contact between the Creator and the world.

Thus, the lamp of God burns within a Jew; it is the flame-soul seeking to convert all that is material substance to light, aspiring to escape from the confines of the body, leaping from the wick toward God. If there is any tampering with the arrangement, if there is an obstacle to block the oil of Torah and mitzvot, then the flame is in jeopardy, as in martyrdom, liable to cut itself off and become burning fire, consuming all that it touches.

This point of martyrdom, when one decides to sever oneself from the wick of life, offering oneself to the Divine, is different for every person. It is usually a result of a decisive recognition of having reached one's limit, of saying to oneself, "This is it." The candle can no longer continue to subsist in the threatening conditions of a particular situation; the flame cuts itself off and, in the self-extinguishing, realizes its union with God. With some Jews, the extreme point may be reached in adherence to the rules of the Sabbath; with others, it may be conversion or, as in the case of some apostates who were ready enough to sell their own Jewish souls, it can be in a refusal to help convict other Jews. No matter how far apart these points may be from individual to individual, when it is reached, the decision is final, and one ceases to be whatever one was and becomes something entirely other.

To be sure, this allegory of the soul as the candle of God is only a partial delineation of the human situation. It is also based on the ancient premise that four basic elements, earth, water, air, and fire, constitute the layers of reality, with fire at the top. Each element is drawn toward its source—solids and liquids down toward the earth, air and fire up toward the sky. This aspiration of the flame toward the source of the fire in the sun is like the yearning of the soul for God.

Hence, we have this apparent irrationality and unnaturalness of the soul, the law of nature being that of gravity and inertia and survival of self. Unlike the stone, which in falling unites with its source, the earth, the flame of the soul, in rising to God, eliminates itself as a separate existence. It does not alter its shape and become something else; it loses itself completely. There is a double self-renunciation here, an abandonment not only of separate selfhood but of any and all separate existence. It is in life that the soul wishes to nullify itself, as a return to the source of life, or the life of life. But it is not a "natural" drive.

This incidentally brings us to the concept of nature (in Hebrew, Teva), a word which does not appear in the Bible. From a certain point of view, the word indicates an inexplicable and even illogical phenomenon—the nature of things. It lies outside the realm of explanation, for a rational elucidation is not the same as "knowing" the nature of something. We can only describe and analyze nature, but it remains baffling to our reasoning intelligence. Subsequently, even the word nature itself has been endlessly abused. It has become the excuse for anything inexplicable, from the spiritual nature of the Divine to the "natural" wickedness of "human nature." The Hebrew word is derived from the same root letters as the word *to impress*, to give a thing its stamp or shape. The idea is that natural objects are impressed with their form, beyond human reason, and whatever reasoning is afterward applied to these forms only describes them; it does not really affect them.

Concerning the soul too, any statement made about its nature does not serve to explain anything. Nevertheless, in purely rational terms, the core of any coherent thought is the self, the existence of an "I" who thinks and feels in a certain way. Even the moral and responsible actions of a person in observing the mitzvot may be considered expressions of the soul in its effort to support and enhance the self. In fact, perhaps the whole striving of man toward God is such an effort of growth on the part of the self in order to exceed the physical limitations of the body. All of this is quite consistent and reasonable. What is not given to explanation is the phenomenon of martyrdom, the sanctification of the soul. To say that the Divine Soul strives, by its very essence, to consume itself in God is beyond our understanding. It is no longer consistent with the idea of self-interest.

The question is asked why martyrdom is known in Hebrew as "soul offering," or giving up of the soul, instead of "body offering." The answer is precisely that—the basis of martyrdom is not a sojourn of the soul in Paradise to change the physical garment for another; it is essentially a renunciation of the self. The Tzadik, as one who practices such total self-renunciation all the time, is more akin to the ecstatic or highest mystical personality than to the conventional image of the rational sage. It is related that the Baal HaTanya, who was accustomed to spend hours in prayer long after the congregation had dispersed, was once found in the streets far from the synagogue, completely immersed in prayer; he was still clutching a section of the banister, which surrounded the podium (where the Torah Scroll is read), for it had come apart in his hand without his even realizing it. Even if such excesses were naturally rare, they point to an essential singleness of love for the Divine, a longing for complete immersion, or obliteration of self, in Him. The personal problem for a Tzadik like the Baal HaTanya was not how to wake the soul, but how to prevent the awakened soul from abandoning itself to God. It may be pertinent here to indicate that the *Tanya* was written for an audience of highly developed Chasidim, many of whom were able to consider themselves, in all honesty, of the caliber of saints and sages. And one of the reasons for the discourses on the difference between Tzadikim and Benonim was to help these readers make the distinction for themselves—to enable each of them to realize that he was not a Tzadik and should not try to act like one; rather, he was, more likely, a Benoni, which the Baal HaTanya took pains to show was also a very high order of responsibility and achievement. The fact that this category also became an unrealizable ideal is one of the ironies of history.

Wisdom (Chochmah) is thus derived from God, and it is in this sense of not being a human contrivance that it is known as "nothing" (Ayin). A way of understanding this further is noting the critical relationship between wisdom and humility or self-nullification. As long as one is full of knowledge, or of the pride of knowledge (the arrogance of feeling that one knows), one cannot recognize anything new; anything that is not a part of what one knows, or thinks one knows, is not allowed entrance into consciousness. One plays with innumerable variations of the old material. In order to internalize something new, an hour is needed, a minute, even a moment, of self-nullification to allow new experiences of reality to penetrate. This is why children learn so much better and more quickly; this is why the more learned a person is the less likely he is to be able to absorb new wisdoms. For wisdom is the connection with what comes from outside, from another source. It has to be allowed to enter by giving it a vehicle, and that vehicle is the potential power, Koach Mah, the power of self-nullification that is required to absorb what is. Wisdom, which is the highest sanctity, can exist only because it is nullified in the reality of the Infinite light, and it is not something in itself.

Thus, Israel is holy because it is able to nullify itself in God, to sanctify its soul in martyrdom. Therefore, the essential question of the difference between holiness and the Sitra Achra (the other side) cannot be decided by any external distinction, appearances, or actions, but by the innermost essence of things, the source of the appearance or action, that is, for whom it is done. If it is for oneself, for the shell of being, it is of Sitra Achra. In this respect, all pride is idolatry; any self-centeredness that leaves the Divine out remains in the realm of the shell.

To be sure, there is no intention of idolatry—the shell, by its very nature, will tend to identify itself with the source, the cause of all causes. It will be inclined to think of itself as though it were God. There is a story about Satan, who really meant to do the best thing, showing that the primary root of evil is not its repulsiveness but rather the sanctimonious appearance behind the recognition of self, putting oneself forward as a separate reality. The shell is, therefore, the inability to nullify the illusion of an existing "I," making barking noises, as the Zohar puts it, asking for food and shelter and forgiveness. As long as things are built on the principle of "give me," then "I deserve it," and, finally, "I am the center of the world," the image of man as a barking creature who cannot be satisfied will continue to repeat itself. In this sense, the Sitra DiKedusha, the holy, is that which gives and continues to give, until everything is renounced, including one's very self, while the Sitra Achra, the other side, invests in something profitable, whether in this world or the next, with the intention of gaining from it always.

There is the expression in the Sayings of the Fathers about servants who serve not for the reward, and there is the story of the Maggid of Mezritch: When a voice from Heaven told him that he was unworthy of his portion in the world to come because he sighed with sorrow, he rejoiced saying, "Now I can serve God wholly without expecting anything in return."

Actually, there is a very thin line separating the holy from the other side. In their more extreme expressions, they are, of course, worlds apart; but at their source, when they are still close to their origins, it is sometimes difficult to distinguish between them. Thus, for example, there is a legend about the prophet Balaam who was said to be as great as his contemporary, Moses. What was the essential difference between them? It was the attribute of humility. Moses was said to be the humblest of men while Balaam was proud and disdainful. Thus, Balaam, with all his potential, remained part of the shell, and Moses became part of the holy. The sign of holiness is the diminishing of the self; the sign of the shell, the augmentation of the self. The difference, at least at the beginning of the process, is indistinct—it is only later, when success and greatness accumulate, that one can clearly see on what it rests.

To be something in oneself is, therefore, the essence of the shell. Wisdom is to be nothing—or rather, it is the point of contact between the nothing that is oneself and that something which is the other. The wicked are called dead for the same reason, for wisdom is also the source of life. Thus, the shells, or the wicked, are parasitically related to wisdom and the good as their source of life and vitality. Evil draws upon the good for its very capacity to keep alive, barking "Hav, Hav" in its hellish need to be nourished by the fountains of wisdom. It doesn't even know that it is dead and that it is dead because of a refusal, or inability, to nullify itself before the holy.

Another basic element of evil is idolatry, that is, the fashioning of a being that claims to be something in itself. To attach any kind of divinity to the sun, to a creature, or to oneself requires the acceptance that it has an independent life of its own, that it does not have to be subservient to the Divine Oneness.

The fiftieth gate of impurity is said to be Pharoah who says:

"Mine is the Nile, I made myself" (Ezekiel 29:3). Not only is the great river, the source of life, "mine," but also "I even created myself." The first spark of impurity, that I am something in myself, leads to the final abomination in which the Sitra Achra is triumphant: "I made all else."

The holy is thus based on the innate desire of the soul to nullify itself before God. It presumes the existence of a Divine spark in oneself, making this possible. If a person is great enough, the spark will carry him through a more intense and thorough nullification process, like the Patriarchs who become Chariots of the Shechinah, or Moses from whose throat the Divine Spirit spoke. If one is of a lesser capacity and the process is incomplete, there are all the manifold degrees of humanity. At the other end of the scale are those who, unable to nullify themselves at all, are wicked and evil in their lives. Even they, however, continue to possess the potential of such nullification, which is what keeps them alive; it is their fountain of life.

There is always the possibility, therefore, of an awakening to the source of life, and one can then decide whether one will belong to holiness or to the Sitra Achra.

We have said that every individual of Israel has a soul that is holy in the sense that it is a spark of the Divine. It is only partly revealed in ordinary persons; and in the case of the wicked, the potential power of Wisdom, called Chochmah, is not operative at all. It is the Sefirah of Wisdom that makes the connection between what is and the nothingness from which all is derived. Thus, unrighteousness is the result of the fact that the Wisdom in the soul is "in exile"; that is, it is not available or within reach. This does not mean that it is necessarily far away. On the contrary, it remains in the soul, but is unseen, wrapped up in its fold and still capable of being a vehicle for contact with the Divine. To say that it is in exile parallels the line of thought which asserts that the Shechinah is in exile; and, of course, in reality the Shechinah cannot be banished to another country; it simply exists in another way, within other factors than those proper to it; that is, it is hidden in the very substance and hardness of the shell, indeed of the evil itself. This is the secret of the exile of the Shechinah, that it goes with the soul into the place of exile, accompanying Israel to Babylon, to wherever the banished people may wander. The Shechinah is in exile simply because it is nowhere to be seen; the Divine light is hidden by that which is "other."

So too in the individual, the Shechinah can be in exile within one's own soul. As one of the Tzadikim said, there are three levels of the exile of the Shechinah: the exile of Israel among the nations; more difficult than this is the exile of Israel in Israel; and most unbearable of all is the exile of man within himself. In the context of our discourse on the *Tanya*, the exile of the Shechinah relates to the third level of exile, the one within a person's soul.

Hence the love of the Divine Soul is called the life of life. It is not the result of a particular sentiment or even an affinity; it is rather the self-experience of the Divine Soul in man; and it makes no difference who the soul is—it simply craves to return to its source—and this yearning-connection is called love. In other contexts, love is also described as a feeling with a vast diversity of expression. Here, love is a rather specific feeling, the immeasurable desire to be close to the beloved. All other forms of love may be considered secondary emotions derived from, or associated with, this basic attraction to the one object deserving of adoration. This clutching at the essence of life—the life of life—may be seen as the basic urge of the soul to be at one with God, or at least to cling to Him and adhere to the One of Whom it is an integral part. This desire is called "the hidden love, for it is concealed and swathed in the shell of the sinners of Israel." That is to say, the love of God is not revealed to the beholder; it is covered by the shell, like the allegorical image of Zechariah of the High Priest clothed in filthy garments.

Where does this filth come from? The answer is that "a person does not sin unless the spirit of folly has entered into him" (Sotah 3a). To be sure, this spirit of folly can take any number of forms besides those that are self-evident—like acting against one's own interests or inclinations. For the most part, this spirit of folly is more subtle, acting, as sin often does, disguised as something eminently desirable and yet somehow separating one from God. It is a feeling that what one wishes to do is not so terrible, a mere trifle, a product of fancy which the merciful Lord of the Universe, Who is easily conciliated, will surely overlook.

True, every person of Israel will emphatically confirm his unwillingness to cut himself off from God and, in crisis, will even show a certain readiness for martyrdom. However, when the spirit of folly enters into him, he will maintain that his action really does not matter so much, that it is only a tiny particle of universal reality, historically insignificant; after all, what really counts is the good and sound intention of the heart, and so on. There are all sorts of variations of this rationalization, more or less intellectual; its chief characteristic is the wrapping, the attractive packaging, enabling a person to carry on with his questionable way of life and its gradual departure from the Divine, in spite of the undoubted existence in him of the hidden love for God.

As against this folly, Wisdom gives a person life, and it is the source of joy. It spreads throughout the physical and spiritual being of a person and reveals itself accordingly. For the root of wisdom in the Divine Soul remains in the brain; it does not clothe itself in the shell, which is the left chamber of the heart, otherwise known as "exile." In the case of the wicked, it is, so to speak, dormant.

What then is the difference between "exile" and "sleep" in so far as the Shechinah is concerned? When the Shechinah is in exile, its Divine power continues to function; but it acts as though it were in captivity or enslaved to some other force which it has to serve. It does not act freely as it would for itself; it performs a role of subservience to another will and is perverted. That is to say, the soul's basic essence, love and devotion and so on, still exists, but its expressions are twisted and distorted, and its force is diverted into something else. Thus, the exile of the Shechinah may cause a soul to express itself in very strange and even antagonistic forms.

As an illustration, we note that the Jewish people has contributed a relatively large number of its best youth to the various revolutionary movements of the last century. In a way, this is an expression of Shechinah in exile. The relation to the Shechinah, or the Divine spark of freedom (or as someone

jokingly said, the "Messiah complex of the Jew"), not finding
an outlet in the worship of God, was manifested in an opposite
direction, in indifference or even in antagonism to God. Driven
by sincere love for humanity and a purity of purpose that was
not far from holiness, there was an ironic likeness between
these revolutionaries and their old-fashioned fathers who lived
exclusively according to the Torah. It was simply that with
them the Divine spark, the Shechinah, operated in an alien
environment, in Exile.

At the same time, there remains a certain aspect of the soul
that does not go into exile. It continues to exist unimpaired,
without submitting to an alien element. It may be said to be
that which is asleep when the rest of the soul is alienating itself.
As it is written, "I sleep, but my heart waketh" (Song of Songs
5:2).

This interpretation of the Exile views the situation as a dream
state. And when God effects the restoration of Zion to its land,
then it will become evident that we are asleep and dreaming.
For in sleep, life continues; the spark of holiness is present
even though it is unable to rise to conscious expression. Thus,
a person can feel that he is still a Jew in spite of the fact that all
his words and actions are anti-Jewish. Sometimes, out of an
excessive zeal for holiness, of whatever sort, a person commits
horrendous crimes; and this can be in a state of absence of the
Shechinah in which the Divine spark is asleep.

The certain aspect of the attribute of Wisdom is inactive, at
least in such a situation. What may be active are the forces of
the attributes of Knowledge and Understanding, channeled
into worldly cleverness, with each individual giving it his own
expression. When, and if, an individual comes to a totally
unprecedented and irrational situation, in which there is no
weighing of opinions but only a crisis of being, when one's
ideology is suddenly superfluous, then there may be a trial of
faith. This crucial point is surely different for every person;
everyone has his own subjective value system, with its intellectual priorities and emotional attachment. For one it may be
forced conversion, for another a relatively minor infringement
of Halachah. There are many instances of Jews, who were so

completely at the mercy of circumstances, that they could no longer be considered free to choose; they were so stripped of all spiritual inspiration that there was no return. And yet, even such persons can be confronted with a test of faith, and the result can be an eruption of unexpected and inexplicable truth. When God is thus revealed, nothing can withstand Him. The one who was a captive in the exile of the Shechinah had to follow a certain course; he was unable to act freely. Only now, in the new situation, he stands as if at Mount Sinai—also beyond his choice; but the dominion here is of a different nature; his enemies are destroyed before him, and suddenly what heretofore was a wall of outer compulsion and coercion falls down, and he is free to choose what is proffered. A person in such an extreme crisis does not become someone else; he responds to a sudden revelation of what he really is within himself.

Even when it is clear that the nature of the crisis is external, and even when it is not an obvious matter of faith, there can be such a genuine response of the soul. As an illustration, one can recall the many instances of Jews who refused, at the risk of their lives, to bow to an idol, although they were fully aware that it would be a meaningless gesture on their part, devoid of any intent. The point is that not every situation is a trial of essentials; there are very many that are relatively external and insignificant. Nevertheless, a Jew sometimes has to assert his destiny as a Jew, with all that may be awesome and terrible about it, even if all the circumstances do not necessarily demand it of him. In addition to the many examples of Jews who sacrificed so much, there is the case of the philosopher, Henri Bergson, who lived most of his life in an assimilated environment—even considering the desirability of baptism—until, in his last years, when the Nazis entered Paris and demanded all Jews to register, he was among the very first to do so. In the crisis of identity, he reacted without hesitation.

This is related to the precept to love and fear God. What has been described above as inexplicable, spontaneous acts of self-sacrifice do not seem to be expressions of love of God. They fall more into the category of a certain fear or dread. Of what? A fear of being cut off from a life source which, whether recognized or not, is Divine love. The fear is not a fear of punishment by God; it is a fear of being separated from God.

Of course, the Sages of Israel are in a different category. They are acutely conscious of their love for God and eager to prove it. The point in describing the martyrdom of those who do not know God is to show that even in them, this crux or core of the Jewish essence exists. That is what identifies a Jew as one who, at the ultimate moment of decision, will be able and ready to sanctify his soul.

Accordingly, every Jew should be repulsed by idolatry; the problem is to define idolatry properly. When there is a doubt, an ignorance of what idolatry is, many Jews may be led astray to bring themselves, to a greater or lesser extent, to idolatry. In a manner of speaking, all of the Torah, as a whole, is an explanation of the first two commandments: "I am . . ." and "Thou shalt have no other. . . ." All the positive mitzvot are modes of contact with the one "I am"; and the negative mitzvot, the prohibitions, can be considered as modes of avoiding severance from God. Seen in this way, all that is required in following the Torah is a single, total sanctification of one's soul.

It is as though one were to inquire of the loving soul: If you are so capable of spiritual self-sacrifice, why do you continue to deviate so much and get lost in far less important matters, which may bring about a severance from the loved one? There is a passionate reasoning here, urging one to accomplish the impossible. For most persons, the answer usually takes the form: "My soul is not ready for it," even though the same person has the capacity, as described, for offering up his soul in martyrdom. The important thing for everyone is to strive to remain connected. But it seems that to scrape together enough force to break a single small habit is more difficult than to die a martyr's death on the pyre.

Such is the challenge of Israel—the readiness to give oneself in small things as well as in big ones.

20

Concerning Divine Speech

The essence of being a man of Israel may be said to be expressed in the first two of the Ten Commandments: "I am the Lord thy God. . ." and "Thou shalt have no other gods besides me. . . ." These include all the mitzvot—the positive ones, which confirm the Divine by making contact with Him, and the negative prohibitions, which repudiate idolatry of any kind, great or small. Transgression is thus a kind of blasphemy. And sin is impossible for a Jew unless a spirit of folly enters and confuses him. It does not make any difference whether it is a serious offense or a light one. Forgetting the Divine spark in oneself, which makes it possible to transgress, is the essence of idolatry; it is subservience to strange gods and demons. Even putting oneself as the decisive factor in any action is idolatry. To say "I want this or that" is to deny that God has a will in the matter also.

The core of all denial of God is ignorance of the Divine Unity. The word "Unity" is most often used, rather than the terms "One" or "Single," both which, perhaps, more precisely define the uniqueness of God—there is nothing else. This is because Unity is more expressive of the concept of universality, of inclusiveness, while singleness suggests isolation and separation. Both terms, then, are needed in order to define this aspect of God, as it is stated in the prayer: "Thou wast the same ere the world was created; Thou hast been the same since the world hath been created. . . ."

This brings us back to the concept that God is one in the sense that there is nothing besides Him, both before and after the Creation. The universe does not make any difference as far as God is concerned. He remains forever the same without ever changing. Even though we may be conscious of a world apparently apart from God, this is only the ongoing act of Creation. The words that made the world are constantly being spoken anew, and nothing can exist unless it is sustained by them. If they were to cease being spoken, all would revert to emptiness and chaos.

There is a power, then, in the word spoken by God. It is a power that changes form and combines in a multitude of different combinations, such as the myriad species and individual manifestations of plants that continually come into being by virtue of the words, "Let the earth bring forth grass." Speech itself, or rather Divine speech, is creative. What, however, is the relation between speaking and the One Who speaks?

To illustrate: when a man utters a word, it is as nothing in comparison with the man himself—all that he is, and so forth. Speech is only the "middle garment" of the soul, between thought and action. In itself it does not have much meaning. It is thought which creates speech and gives it meaning. On the other hand, there is often a gap between thought and speech. This discrepancy points to the essential fault in human communication, its inability to be a proper vehicle for Wisdom (Chochmah) or to make proper contact between the Ten Sefirot. Because the contents of thought are determined by the inner relations of a man with himself, words are only the outward communication devices. Even a prophet is one who listens to God speaking to Himself. In biblical Hebrew, the reflexive form is often used to express this. The process of thinking, then, which is physical only in that it is done with the material brain and nervous system, is essentially spiritual in that it is a way of "speaking with oneself."

To go deeper into the process, we may consider what precedes thought, namely, an impulse or a desire. The next step is to become aware of this desire. Upon becoming conscious of it, one defines it in words. In short, first there is an attraction or impulse which is the potential thought, and only afterwards, when this becomes conscious, can we say that there is a thought. It does not matter whether it is a desire for an apple or for the Divine, the process is similar. On the other hand, in order to want something there has to be an awareness that it is in some way desirable. This is the function of education. For men surrender to their evil impulses and desires out of wrong consciousness of the object of their desires. As soon as a person becomes enlightened about the nature of holiness, his whole desire system will react accordingly.

Of course, there are serious obstacles to the smooth flow between head and heart. One can admit that something is good and beautiful, and yet fail to see that it relates to oneself in any way. Desire is a universal, nonpersonal, phenonemon. Hunger and lust are common to all men. There has to be a certain differentiation, a particularization and defining before a person can say, "I want this." In short, there is a great distance to be traversed before speech expresses thought and takes on meaning. It is not a simple, mechanical translation; there are any number of inner communication factors between the Sefirot, such as those between Chochmah and Binah, that can effect a transmutation. For these varied paths, generally unnoticed by consciousness, determine the content and the quality of the inner life and, subsequently, of thought. And at every stage, there is a certain addition or processing, an infusion of something new.

Thus, if we endeavor to find out the relation between isolated speech and the power of speech, between the power of speech and the sources of this power, stage by stage, we get to the Primal Wisdom (Chochmah), and we discover that there is an abyss between any one stage and another. Sometimes, there is no resemblance or visible connection between stages.

What we are trying to explain is the relationship between the Divine speech and the Divine essence. In life, the relationship between one's own speaking and one's experience is not necessary or significant. Insofar as God is concerned, this absence of relation is more difficult to grasp. God keeps giving Himself to the world when He creates it; He is not an intrinsic part of it. There is a distance. Even to call Him the King of kings is to diminish Him in some way; the uniqueness and the oneness of God are beyond whatever I can say. Moreover, my expressions have their own existence; as soon as they are spoken, they are no longer me. So is God related to the world—to an infinitely greater extent—and the gap becomes the basis for Torah and mitzvot and the seeking for unity. But eventually, only God Himself can provide the means to overcome the gap and reach Him. Thus, the two basic formulations—"I am. . ." and "Thou shalt have no other. . ."—become the bridgeheads on which to build and cross over.

Therefore, too, as soon as one severs the contact and asks, "What does all this mean to me?" one falls into the abyss of nothingness; and no human being can afford to lose touch with the Divine, no matter how faint or ambiguous this contact may be.

21

Hiddenness as a Part of Unity

One of the many points of difference between man and God is the nature of speech. Human speech, which is basically communication, becomes something else than the "I" who speaks. As soon as it goes out from the speaker's mouth, it cannot be taken back; it has a life of its own and is no longer in need of the thought or vital thrust of its origins. Divine speech, however, is never separated from God, not only because there is nothing that is not God, but because Divine speech is by its very essence united with God in a singleness of being, like thought. As it is written, "For my thoughts are not like unto your thoughts" (Isaiah 55:8). What is common to them both is the functional aspect, the use of speech as a means of expression and communication; what distinguishes them is the substantiality of human speech in terms of definite elements of sound or sight.

Divine speech is always creative and is a part of that which it creates. True, human speech may also be creative in that it can constitute a revelation of some new level of being. Although it does not alter the essential fact that it is immediately transformed into something exterior to, and independent of, the speaker. Thus, the Hebrew root of *speech* is *davar*, which also means *thing* and points to the same quality of being exterior and independent. The root word also refers to *one who leads* (the flock of sheep). Another root, following the same sort of transformation, is *NGD, to oppose*. From this root, several nouns have sprung, with various meanings, such as *leader* or *teller* of tales, and *speaker* of wisdom *(maggid)*. From this, it may be surmised that the basic definition of speech, in the present context, is the transfer, or relegation, of something from one level of being to another, such as from the hidden to the manifest. It is a creative process like that involved in the creation of the world.

In this sense, the Bible is the same thing as the world—a Divine revelation. One is physical existence, the other is the word, and the only difference between them is in the manner and degree of expressiveness. Human speech is like the arrow shot from the bow—it goes forth with an irretrievable force of its own. Divine speech, however, is not separate from God. True, there seems to be an identification between what a man says and what he is, but this is because he is altogether so small that the distance is often imperceptible. Altogether, the distance between human thought and action is limited, but it exists—for example, the gap between the intention and the end of the matter. Whereas in terms of whatever we can conceive of the Divine, there is no outer or inner, no separation between one aspect of God and another, in spite of the immeasurable distance between a specific Divine saying and the essence of the Creator.

The contact between man and God is not a two-way, but a one-way, communication. We are dependent on Him; He is not dependent on us. He sees us; we do not see Him. We are products of His speech, and with difficulty, we can even make out something of this speech. Anything else is out of our domain. When do we grasp Divine speech? Only when we ourselves speak of the Shechinah (as the Zohar says, the Shechinah is Divine speech or manifestation). When man reaches a level where he can feel the immanence of the Divine, this is as far as he can go. The essence of God is infinitely beyond this—but when one relates to Divine speech and seems to understand something, there is contact.

To be sure, any metaphor is grossly inadequate. Let us suppose that I am talking to a young child. I understand what I am saying just as he presumably understands what I am saying; we understand one another on the level of certain words that are uttered. Beyond that he cannot go. But within the range of what is spoken between us, there is something of my being, a part of me, that he grasps. But only a part. One may even say that the child is, in most respects, cut off from the essence of me, the speaker; and, thus, much of me is left to his imagination. If the speaker happens to be an exceptional person, a wise man, the difference is all the greater. In that case, the speaker has had to descend even further, going to considerable lengths to make himself understood. So too, God may be said to have made the immeasurable descent, the enormous contraction of light and energy in order to come into contact with us. If we do perceive something, no matter how little, it becomes the great achievement of our being. Because we recognize the incalculable and unbridgeable distance between the Divine speaker and the human listener. However, when I say in prayer, "Oh God, cure me of my ache and trouble," it is with the irrational certainty that God had nothing better to do than to listen to my complaints, as though I were putting the fate of galaxies and my own needs on the same level.

This may help to explain why the great Tzadikim in Heaven do not pray for the community. They can no longer relate seriously to the frivolous requests of men. God, however, who is Infinite, makes no such distinction; He hears all men equally. What is more, there is no before or after in God, no distinction of time or place, size or value. This means that causality, as men know it, does not necessarily correspond to the true process and cycles of existence.

This then is the meaning of the Divine contraction and descent. The contraction was necessary to create a world, a reality, that is not nullified in God's all-embracing existence. The creatures of God could not exist as separate entities within the presence of God unless there was a veil of ignorance, a contraction of Divine effulgence allowing room for free play. Man needs the world to be what it is—something that conceals

God, something that prevents one from "seeing the Divine, eye to eye," for such ecstasy is given to man only at the End of Days. Even the very word *world (olam)* contains the root *to conceal*.

Thus, in order for the world to exist as a coherent entity, one has to have a philosophical awareness of the fact that there is both a universe and a Creator of the universe. In order to function realistically, one has to assume a world which is not God, for if everything is the One God, there is no other (human) reality. Indeed, God has had to descend to us, and to talk in words that are comprehensible to us in order to avoid being too far away. It is like the children's game of hide-and-seek. God pretends to hide, and we look for Him; and then we think that He looks for us; and all the while, it is a game the Divine Omniscience plays with us for our sakes.

This may be likened to the caterpillar and the cocoon it spins; both the insect and that which wraps him up are the same. Manifest nature, law, God's concealment, and God's essence are one. Just as the riddle is a mystery only to the one who is questioned; and the one who asks knows both the answer and the riddle. In other words, concealment can be part of an essential unity in the dynamics of speech; the speaker knows what is being spoken, and the one on the other side of speech, the listener, tries to penetrate the "mystery" and to understand.

22

Divine Word and Its Manifestation

The Torah from God necessarily speaks in the language of men; yet as men, we are limited by our inability to comprehend it properly. If a certain concept is precise, it is almost certainly beyond us, and we will probably fail to get its meaning. If we do think we understand something, it is probably because it is not precise. For everything in Torah has more than one level of meaning in terms of symbol and application to reality, by virtue of the descent and flow of the life-force to the lower planes.

Necessarily, this process includes movement through various levels and even certain leaps. What is more, every transition from the transcendent (beyond comprehension) to the immanent (or knowable) involves reduction or contraction of sorts. From this, it is evident that "Tzimtzum," or contraction of Divine light, is much more than a one-dimensional cause-and-effect relationship; it is essentially a passage to another medium or dimension, something that involves transformation.

But before trying to understand this process of "transformation," it may be worthwhile to review the action of speech within a single dimension of common life. Here, the contraction from thought to action may be considered a double contraction, with speech in between. And we can appreciate the fact that, even in the simplest passage from thought or speech to action, there is a certain loss of breadth and profundity.

As a rule, speech expresses only the lower or outer periphery of thought. It does not render the whole thought, but only that portion which is given to verbalization by a particular speaker; the rest is not expressed at all, although, occasionally, it may be felt as the unutterable truth behind what is spoken. To be sure, there are also things that cannot even be thought, that cannot be brought to the light of consciousness. For the mind is filled with so much that remains in darkness, without a vehicle of some kind to bring it to our attention.

It is the flash of Wisdom that brings about the sudden illumination of a whole new semblance of reality. To comprehend and to communicate this primal flash of Wisdom requires giving it a formal intellectual word order, even if doing so causes a considerable "blowing up" and artificial expansion of the picture. There is no way of reproducing the original flash. There have been people, and many great men among them, whose entire lives have been expressions of only one such flash, source of all their ideas and originality.

Of course, there can also be instances when speech is more significant than thought, and action exceeds anything that can be conceived by the mind. Even then, they remain essentially an instrument or a result of something else, such as deeper unconscious layers of the mind. In such instances, speech is said to flow, as if from itself; just as action can be seen to emerge of itself, from its own inner necessity. And often, this is considered creativity of a higher order than that which is produced with the aid of conscious thought.

There is a commentary on this which uses the metaphor of horse and rider. The letters are the horse (speech), and they have the power to carry their rider (thought), even against the rider's will—but as it is written: It is not the might of the horse that He (the Lord) wishes. He wishes to receive the love and collaboration that springs from the essence of the relationship to the Divine; He does not desire the energy that accompanies the words, much less the words themselves.

What is more, there is a certain ambivalence between thought and word—a contraction or distortion of the abstract thought as it takes expression. There may also be an expansion or elaboration of the thought from the words. This is similar to what is known in the Kabbalah as the direct light and the reflected light; the latter is the interaction of human consciousness with a Divine manifestation or even with any higher consciousness, as when a person observes something he himself has said and wonders how he could ever have said it. The answer is that the source is not from the person himself; it came from outside him. But it takes wisdom to discern even that. Not everyone is wise enough to hear what he is saying.

In any case, all this is meant as an illustration. We are using the model of speech to explain the distance or gap, the necessary contraction, which is so essential a part of the act of creation. As we have seen, the contractions may be many and varied—in size, in power, in essence—each of them constituting a transition from the Unity to the multiplicity, from the utmost good and the perfect to the makeshift nature of reality.

Indeed, the contraction reaches such a point that the Divine countenance is hidden, and we are confronted with a paradox—the fact that man no longer perceives God, the very source and meaning of his being. As it has been said, the incredible greatness of the Creator lies not in the immense worlds He made, but in the fact that among His creations are men who can repudiate His existence. In a way that is the most extraordinary formation of all—creatures who can deny the Creator.

This confronts us with the fact that besides the mystery of the upper worlds and the manifestations of Divine omnipotence, there is also the Divine hiddenness and the paradox of the shells, those outer, unspiritual coverings that are part of the Sitra Achra, the other side of the Divine which gets its power from God and yet, in some very clear way, is not God.

As a ramification of this paradox, the question is asked: What is the difference between human creativity and Divine creation? The human creation, it is explained, is the manufacture of implements that have their own existence; they can continue to exist independently of the one who made them. The Divine creation, however, is continuous; God keeps sustaining and developing what He makes by re-creating every particle of existence in endless succession.

This, then, is the wonder of the Divine hiddenness: The holiness and the life-force, which are the expression of Divine power, give life to the world, including the evil and the blasphemous. As it is written in certain prayers: God creates and fashions men, and even though they rebel against Him and disown Him, he continues to create them.

There is a Chasidic chant: "Thou art a hidden God," which, in contrast to what one would expect, is a joyful song. Because, as the Baal Shem Tov said, the Divine hiddenness ceases to be significant as soon as one knows that it is a matter of His hiding Himself and not that He isn't there. As long as I am not sure of His existence, I am in a state of darkness; as soon as I am convinced that He does exist, that He is merely concealing Himself, I have every reason for joy. The hiding of the Divine countenance is terrible only because it makes it so difficult to see God—and that is the whole tragedy of the concealment.

There is the anecdote of the grandson of a famous rabbi who, while playing hide-and-seek with the other children, hid himself. The others forgot about him somehow, and after some time, the little boy ran weeping to the rabbi. "Grandfather," he cried, "I hid myself and no one looked for me!" Whereupon the rabbi was deeply moved and answered, "Why, that is the very same thing that God is saying all the time."

In a certain way, the very purpose of the Tzimtzum (contraction), or withdrawal of God, is to reveal something beyond the withdrawal. It is not an aim in itself. It is a part of the process of Creation, but it is a part that, like in the game of hide-and-seek, has to be broken through at some time. And if the Divine hiddenness is not overcome, if one fails to see the Divine light that sustains one, then the conditions ripen for the growth of outer shells that not only conceal the Truth but cause a profound confusion in the mind, so that the genuine and the holy are mixed up with the products of the Sitra Achra.

23
Torah as God's Will

The significance of a mitzvah
lies in its function as a vehicle for God's will. The hand that
distributes charity is, in one way or another, the hand of God,
an instrument of His power. And if all the life of a person is
devoted to carrying out the commandments, that person may
be said to become a vehicle of the Shechinah.

It should be emphasized that when a person's hand or
speech becomes an instrument of God's will, it does not mean
that it is the organ itself that is thus being used; God is acting
through the person as a whole. However, when a person
studies Torah, with mouth and mind, he reaches a deeper and
more internalized relation with God. Because there is a certain
difference between the mitzvah and Torah study. The performance of the mitzvah is a means of expressing and fulfilling
whatever God wishes to happen in the world. When my hand
gives alms, it means that God desires to sustain this needy
person. I am only a means of accomplishing this. If God wishes
someone to wear *tefillin,* my hand and head serve to realize
this; if He wants the Chanukah candles lit at a certain moment,
my performance of the mitzvah assures that His will is done.

However, when a person studies Torah, there is a more profound factor involved, for the Torah itself is God's will.

Thus, for instance, when one studies a Halachah, the way of Torah, about the performance of a ritual, such as the lighting of the Chanukah candles, and it becomes apparent (through study) that a source of flame that is fed like a bonfire is not a proper Chanukah candle, one is taking part in the idea behind the ritual as well as performing it. One is identifying with the Divine Will in the matter and not only obeying it. By becoming involved in the reasons for the action and the correct way of doing it, one is raised to a higher level of functioning, like one who reads the plans for a building under construction and does not merely lay the bricks.

In other words, the range of Torah is much wider than what is outlined by human action. One is connected with the Divine Will through the idea; if, for instance, one studies a passage concerning a hypothetical circumstance, something that could never happen, the Halachic conclusion helps us to know the Divine preference in any such situation. In Torah study, one is engaged in the planning process; in action, one is carrying out the idea. It is in the planning or conceptualizing that there is a greater degree of participation in God. What is more, by creating something new, man is able to expand this participation and to manifest His will.

Indeed, it is the very letters of the Bible, and not only the sentences, that reveal God's will. This is one of the characteristics of the Bible, making it the unique basis of Torah Scriptures and differentiating it from other sacred works like the Mishnah. The holiness of the Bible is in the very letters of the text. Naturally, this makes for a difference in relation to the study of these books, as tradition has shown. Every letter and sign in the Bible is pored over as a Divine mystery waiting to be revealed; the combinations of the letters in words and sentences are, of course, the manner in which their meaning is communicated to us; but it may well be a secondary meaning. One may make all sorts of combinations, on a variety of levels, and obtain 600,000 possible revelations. As the Ramban said, all of the Torah spells out the names of God; it is a list of His names, very little of which has any meaning for us. It is like a secret code with an infinite number of possible interpretations, a tale within a tale within a tale. Each one is equally valid and holy.

What can be inferred from this concerning the difference between Torah and the world? After all, the world does not function entirely in accordance with the Divine Will; there is a certain amount of independence—such as the play of free choice given to each individual—whereas the Torah is completely an expression of God's will. Evidently, this expression may not be altogether understood, but, at least, one has the reliable foundation of the letters of the Torah to fall back on. If one is sincere in the search for the source of faith, one can get beyond any single level of comprehension. As it is said: Even if one studies Torah without knowledge of its esoteric meanings, but does so "for the sake of Heaven," all the various levels of the Torah are revealed. And in Torah, there is no distortion or artificiality, there is only a contraction of holiness into various molds.

Thus, if Scripture declares that when an ox gores another man's ox, such-and-such should be the indemnity payment, this may be interpreted in any number of ways according to one's point of departure. In the physical world, it is fairly straightforward commonsense justice, not necessarily a reflection of the Torah as a whole. For all images of Torah are vehicles of expressing something definite; every level of expression has meaning on its own level. There is that which is of spiritual value and that which is of physical value, each with its own validity. Therefore, when a person is engaged in Torah without ulterior motive, he may be said to be united with the Divine Will. He is thinking God's thoughts concerning God's world. And there is no essential difference between the one who studies with the highest esoteric comprehension and the one who merely reads the written words correctly. In order to help illuminate this point, consider a complex electrical device. Although one may not understand how it works, it may be easily operated by pushing certain buttons. One simply has to be aware of the consequences of pressing the wrong one. Although one may be limited in one's comprehension, there is no relation to the rightness or wrongness of what one does or to the benefit one gets from it. So too with Torah and Halachah—one may grasp more or less of the inner meaning and rise to higher levels according to one's ability. This does not influence the degree of correctness of the action or the advantages of a proper relation to Scripture.

This, incidentally, is one of the problems of studying Torah. It cannot be required of every person to learn all of the Torah or even to understand all of what is learned. All that can be required is that whatever one does learn should be correct Truth—not more or less or probable truth—but the kind of truth that will enable a person to be sure about which buttons he has to press and those which he has to avoid in an incompletely comprehended world. It is not a matter of how much one knows but of how reliable and integral the knowledge is, no matter on what level.

After all, in every system of faith and religion, the mystical union with God is the ultimate aspiration. And even though we may say: "Blessed are those who experience such a mystical union," actual union with the Divine may not be experienced blissfully as a mystical union. Instead, what is experienced is simply the tranquil joy of being wholly engaged in Torah. The privately felt blissfulness may or may not accompany the action; and it is in no case a measure of the depth or meaning of the action. Just as any creative act may be performed with more or less enthusiasm and inspiration without this affecting the final product, which stands by itself. The blissfulness is a free gift to the person involved in Torah or creativity. The intensity of the subjective relation to Torah may be expressed in many ways—even by saying the *alef-bet*, as the Baal Shem Tov did when all his knowledge failed him. Whatever the spiritual quality and level of this expression, it belongs to a subjective world with its own values and meanings. It should not be confused with the contents of Torah which is the word of God.

To be sure, all that exists, including the upper worlds, receive their vital essence from the light of the Shechinah, but the one who is engaged in Torah becomes a part of the Shechinah itself. He is higher even than the creative light that is active in the world, being connected with the Divine Will, which is beyond the world. Therefore, when one is thus united with God in Torah, one is far beyond anything that is of the world, which is no more than a vessel for His will.

Even if a person does not feel this connection, his soul, the source of his being, does feel it. In ancient times, awe and terror would often overwhelm a person without his knowing what it was that affected him so; and he would have to do something to escape from the situation. So too, with someone studying Torah – his soul reacts even if his outer consciousness does not. Perhaps, this simply makes it possible for a person to be engaged in Torah; for if one were aware of its awesome power, it would hardly be possible to focus one's attention. Man's dull-wittedness is often his protection, enabling him to relate to sacred texts without being consumed by them.

There is a tale which may illustrate this. A great king ordered the manufacture of a special crown, providing for this purpose extremely valuable jewels and ornaments. The master jeweler prepared the frame, but when it came to setting the priceless jewels in their place, he found his hands trembling with anxiety lest something go wrong. He called a local rustic, who had no idea of the value of the jewels, to put them in place, and the task was done simply, without any excitement. In this way too, an ordinary person who does not appreciate the terrible holiness of what he is doing may read Torah and even determine Halachic procedure and ritual.

There seems to be an odd paradox here. The physical being of man, notwithstanding all its innate evil impulses and limited comprehension, is what makes it possible for him to engage in Torah. In certain respects, it may be likened to the special protective mask that welders wear to avoid being blinded by the intense flame.

This is why the Sages have said that Torah is the most eminent of the mitzvot, even greater than prayer. And prayer is considered powerful enough to make "combinations" that can influence the forces in the higher worlds. On the other hand, Halachah dictates that even if one is studying Torah one has to stop for prayer. But after all, if one is engaged with the Divine word itself, why does one have to be compelled to speak with God on a possibly lower level? The answer is that the Halachic ruling is for those who do not study all the time, for those who do other things besides study. It is not for those who, like Rav Yehudah, ceased studying Torah only once a month to pray.

At such a level of conscious enjoyment in Torah, a person can begin to comprehend the awe, the exultation, and the sublimity of what he is doing. It also sheds light on the ultimate human question: "What am I doing here?" The definition of one's task on earth, in itself, raises the problem of lower and higher obligations, Torah being one of the higher obligations, higher than other mitzvot. On the other hand, the basic mitzvot are not to be easily pushed aside in favor of study. There is a complex relationship between them and it involves a proper evaluation of what a person is capable of accomplishing.

As we have seen, Torah is the way of man with God: "He who is thirsty, go to the water. And there is no water besides Torah." In other words, he who is thirsty for God, let him go to Torah, for nothing else will quench his thirst. And even if the words of Torah may seem to deal with mundane things, they will serve to satisfy one's soul.

The study of Torah is thus considered the greatest mitzvah, greater even than prayer, because it enables one to be identified with the will of God, with the act of Divine creation itself. One is thereby engaged in the very thoughts of God, participating in the structuring of the universe.

What is important to realize is that this is true at all levels of study. Although, to be sure, it is not altogether true when there is distortion; when one introduces one's own personal ideas and preferences into the Torah, one is very liable to sever the contact, for one is no longer thinking God's thoughts. On the other hand, one may make a mistake, such as a technical one, and still continue to think God's thoughts.

Moreover, because thought is a dialectic process, full of many possible extenuations, one's explanations may be only approximate truths. It is as though Torah were the blueprint of the world, and in order to construct one's own building, one would have to draw one's own extensions to the master plan, creating a private version of Creation with all the inevitable errors, erasures, and corrections.

One of the most frequently misunderstood points about Torah study is the fact that intellectual achievement is not the purpose. It does not matter how much or on what level one studies, whether it is mastery of all of the Talmud or reading a single psalm. What matters is the purity of the relationship to the text and not the degree of intellectual comprehension, that is, the capacity to become a vessel of Torah. After all, irrespective of how much one may claim to comprehend God's wisdom, there is always far more that is beyond one's comprehension. The best that one can do—besides endeavoring to understand—is to be in resonance with this wisdom. To let the Torah provide the answers.

To be sure, this kind of relationship to knowledge exists in other fields of experience as well. There are many people today, and there certainly were many more in the past, who have a kind of instinctive comprehension of certain problems—be it building, with stone, wood, or iron, or working, with people, animals, machines, or plants. There are huge structures still standing, like cathedrals, which were built by people who did not know how to read or write and certainly had none of the mathematical expertise so essential today for putting up buildings of that size. Those who built such structures, however, had this inner comprehension of the material they used; they knew how much stress a wall could take and how it would stand up to time. Even when mistakes are made by such inner understanding, it is not a matter of miscalculation, nor of introducing personal wishes into the matter. So too is the study of Torah. If one introduces the egotistical self into the study of Torah, it ceases to be the Torah of God and becomes one's own Torah. This, of course, is quite worthless—no matter how much intellect or brilliance is poured into it—it tends to become mere speculation.

This brings us to the only requisite stance to be taken before the study of Torah—awe—which comes from realizing its Divine essence, that it is beyond anything else in the world. Of this particular awe it has been said, "Without wisdom, there is no awe (fear) of God." On the other hand, it has also been said, "Without awe, there is no wisdom." The point is that without a certain amount of fear and trembling before its sanctity, it is impossible to study Torah. If one approaches it any other way, it is no longer Torah. Whereas only if one does study Torah, no matter on what level, is one able to acquire wisdom. And upon the acquisition of a degree of wisdom comes a higher level of awe, the fear and trembling of a person who knows enough to be afraid of Torah.

There is the story told of the Chasid who said: "We have studied Torah with the Baal Shem Tov, with thunder and lightning and the sound of trumpets, because, as he told us, 'the receiving of the Torah on Mount Sinai has never ceased; it is a permanent stance—just as the Creation itself is unceasing.' " Similarly, the blessing which is recited on the occasion of reading from the Torah Scrolls ". . .who gives us the Torah," is in the present tense, *gives*, not the past, *gave*. This idea has developed from the attitude that the Torah itself is always forming and expanding; it is a constant growth. The event at Mount Sinai is an ongoing Revelation which repeats itself whenever one studies Torah. One may not be aware of standing before the Holy Mountain, but God is still uttering the Ten Commandments. Even if one does not hear them, the standing itself, in awe and terror, is enough to establish the correct relationship to Torah. The realization of this is, in turn, something acquired by study.

The above notwithstanding, not every person is able to relate in this way, in awe and terror, to the Torah. There are many degrees of sensitivity to the holy, and truly spiritual souls are those with a special aptitude for the sacred. This sensitivity is not necessarily a function of the intellect; a very learned and clever person can well have a lesser soul, while a simple man can have a great soul. It may be likened to other talents, a musical ear, for instance, with the entire range of differences that this suggests. Thus, there are many excellent people who are somewhat immune to awe, who cannot feel the particular subtle fearfulness of God's presence. Regrettable as this may be, the study of Torah will still bring about a union with God's will—even if one does not experience it as such. Indeed, a person can experience such an influx of this Divine Wisdom that one is sure that the Shechinah is speaking in his throat; and yet he himself, poor fellow, may be unaware of anything extraordinary. Just as a person can perform a mitzvah without feeling any holiness in the action. For the experience of the numinous and the sacred event are two different realms of experience. To be sure, happy is he who feels as though he were standing at Mount Sinai every time he is engaged in Torah. The point is that irrespective of one's feelings about it, the contact with Divinity is established, and it exists in every such situation. One can be great in the eyes of the world and even full of real accomplishment and still not know what is meant by this. It does not diminish the value or the importance of the person's accomplishments. Such practical theology does not presume to analyze the experience of union with God. It simply proclaims the fact that there is no such thing as a small or a great act of devotion; each is equally capable of establishing the connection with holiness. Every Jew has the capacity within himself to decide, at least, whether he is for or against the contact. The difficulty lies in the tendency to diminish, by some intellectual reasoning, the transcendental meaning of Torah and mitzvot. But when a person does reach an awareness of this meaning, his approach will change. This actually is the purpose of education.

In the same way, there is no essential difference between a minor trespass and an act of idolatry, for everything done in opposition to God's will may be considered idolatry. Furthermore, all transgression is a movement into the domain of nothingness. There is no neutral territory, no no-man's-land, between what is of God and what is not of God. It can even be said that the Sitra Achra has two sides—its own otherness and the otherness of holiness—and there is no inbetween. Everything has to belong to one side or the other, so that any transgression contains the elements of rebellion and betrayal.

Thus, when a person transgresses against one of the laws of Torah, he becomes worse than the shell, or than that which does not worship God. For the shell does not, of itself, produce new forms, and no kind of idolatry can be truly creative. Even death and the devil are instruments in the hand of God; they do not have the power of independent action. It is the servants of the devil, those who worship idolatrously, who are unsympathetic creatures. In the Book of Job, when all the sons of God come before the Lord, with Satan among them, it is the latter's readiness to do the "dirty work" that makes him different. Actually, he is only fulfilling his duty—like all the angels. However, the man who binds himself to Satan is another matter; he is voluntarily undertaking to act against God. The person who sells his soul to the devil is worse than the devil; the one who gives himself to the shell is much worse than the shell itself, for the shell is only being what it has to be, while the person is choosing to be something other than what God wishes him to be.

One of the most daring of the allegories of the Baal Shem Tov, as noted down by his disciple, Rabbi Yaakov Yoseph, is an attempt to explain the nature of evil. It tells of a great king who wishes to test the loyalty of his subjects. He takes one of his slaves, dresses him in splendid garments, and orders him to organize a rebellious coup against him. Upon hearing of the coup, those who are wickedly inclined will promptly join the rebellion, while others, who are righteous and wise, will defy the slave and tell him to his face that he has no authority of his own. The fact is that the shell, which carries the evil, has its source in God and cannot really claim any authority or real power on its own. The person who joins the forces of evil, however, is as base and low as can be. As Yaakov Yoseph said elsewhere, the most unclean worm, crawling on the ground, is not as foul as the human being who transgresses, because the worm is guiltless of wrongdoing; it is simply impure as food, whereas the man who sins is far below that.

Even the idolatrous believe in God in that they know of the existence of a higher essence which is above all else. Their error lies in removing themselves from this all-embracing Divine light, where they feel dependent on it, and in placing themselves in a position of shadow, where they "make believe" that the light does not exist for them. In this state of exile of the Shechinah, even if the Shechinah continues to sustain man's life, he feels free and relatively independent, as though he himself is God. To be sure, there are those, like Balaam in the Bible story, who do continue to realize their dependence on that higher essence, even when they do not bend their will to it. For the fact is that the false gods of idolatry can never really stand up in opposition to God. The problem of idolaters is their pride, their feeling that they are self-sufficient, even in the face of their acknowledged limitations.

At the same time, the true believer who transgresses denies God more profoundly than the idolater. Having once admitted the truth of his dependence on the Divine, his fall may be considered an act of rebellion.

The evil in our world is not only the shell; it is the very lowest state of being. The world we live in is itself the lowest of the worlds, and it is the only world in which not only evil can exist, but even willful evil, rebelliously and freely chosen. Thus, it is not the bacteria of cholera that are evil; it is man who makes it so. The destructive bacteria are part of an independent system which can be one thing or another, but they are ultimately performing the Divine Will. The person who transgresses is lower than this natural evil. This is why it may be said that, with so much transgression, the world is almost entirely evil and, at best, is given to correction.

In other words, what is being said here is not the same as what the philosopher Leibniz said, that this world of ours is the best of all possible worlds; it is more like what Voltaire maintained, that it is the depth of corruption. What is being added in the present context is that our world is the worst of all worlds in which correction (Tikun) is still possible. Our world is still balanced, albeit rather precariously, on the edge of the abyss of evil, but it can still rise up and extricate itself. Were it only a little worse, it would be a world without hope of redemption. That is to say, were a world worse than ours to exist, it would no longer be a world—it would be Hell. From this, we recognize that the final verdict is optimistic, that although this dark and evil world may not be so wonderful, there is still hope for it.

As an illustration of the possibility of correction, consider the case of an adulterous woman. Were she put to the test of performing a clearly idolatrous action, she would most likely do what many other Jewish women before her did—be ready to die a martyr's death at the stake. And yet, it is easier to overcome the evil impulse in oneself than to die at the stake. Why then does this woman let herself be tempted? The answer, as given by the Sages, is that a spirit of folly enters the soul, overthrowing the judgment concerning the worth and consequence of an action. It is as though this spirit of folly were to say: "Go ahead, yield to temptation; you will remain a Jew after all, with the soul of God alive in you." The folly lies in not thinking further to the consequences of the act, in clinging to the root of one's life without realizing that the transgression tears at these roots and cuts one off in the same way as denying God would do.

And yet, in every Jewish soul there is a point of conjunction that, directly or indirectly, puts one in contact with the life of the Infinite, with the Divine Holiness. The one who touches this point will experience something altogether different from anything else in life; he will begin to become someone he had not previously known.

24
On Transgression

As we have said, every mitzvah is, in fact, a contact with the Divine Unity, and every transgression is a form of idolatry, of alienation from God. To be sure, a person does not transgress unless he is invaded by the spirit of folly, or, to be more specific, unless he is deluded into thinking the transgression will not really cut him off from God. For there is a certain lack of awareness at the core of any sinful action. The very same person who is ready to give his life in martyrdom for God does not realize that by some trivial wrongdoing he is severing that very connection with God for which he was willing to die.

What is more, the person who opposes God's will by transgression is worse than the Klipah, because the shell is part of a great structure of reality; by contrast, a person who commits a transgression is not a part of reality; he is a contradiction to the reality of Divine holiness. This is explained by the fact that just as the entire framework of reality includes angels and seraphs and various other holy creations, it also includes demons and evildoers. But so long as they are left alone to themselves, the latter remain instruments of the framework. They serve to keep the framework intact, be-

157

coming bad only when man becomes involved with them. To make a rather unsatisfactory analogy, a policeman is usually a rather undistinguished presence, but as soon as one commits a crime, he stands out as an object of fear, a vehicle of justice and punishment.

Clearly the role of the shell is not simply like that of the policeman. The shell is, in fact, the incarnation of the evil impulse (the within), the satanic power (the without), and the angel of death (the beyond). In this way, the task of the shell, at a certain level, is threefold; and it is not only hostile, because to maintain the universal harmony, a certain division of labor is necessary.

There is an inexplicable attraction between the evil impulse and man. Indeed, this is the very source of life for evil and makes possible its growth. On the other hand, the contact—even when it is full of love—is destructive. For the evil impulse is a spiritual parasite, incapable of independent existence; it has to live off some living creature. As it grows, sapping strength and holiness, it destroys the human being who feeds it, and thereby undermines its own existence.

Consequently, it is said that the Divine seems to go out of His way to provoke scholars and saints. One who is superior to his fellows has to suffer more from the provocations of the evil impulse. The more pure and holy the man, the more he is prey to the parasitic forces of evil. Thus, in him, evil, of whatever scale, becomes a significant factor, drawing on his very greatness of soul. Also, the punishment is proportionately severe, the self-punishment of the righteous. The ironic thing is that, in itself, the evil impulse is quite impotent; it cannot really do much harm, being nothing more than a negation, a zero, devoid of real being of its own.

It may be noted that a weak and impoverished society generally has a relatively smaller share of evildoers, thieves, and criminals. They do not have enough to thrive on. At the other extreme, a completely parasitic society, made up of wicked and corrupt elements, soon arrives at the outer limits of its existence and must seek nourishment from outside. Almost any host society provides plenty of opportunities for the parasitic forces to take hold—the merchants who buy stolen goods, the lawyers who defend criminals in court, the social theoreticians who thwart the natural defenses of the society, among others.

Among the many symbols for evil, the image of the mosquito or gnat designates the lowest form. Because this creature takes and does not give, while the holiness is that which offers, influences, and creates. The obscure ecology of the spiritual process involves the fact that the shell, which often has a kind of fascination, does provide something even if it takes (steals) value from the holy and gives back less than it takes.

The mosquito is part of the shell, part of the framework of nature, while the sinner is not necessarily a part; he is only a possibility. He is the result of a choice, made as a direct result of man's free will. In the animal world, even the wild beasts, who may cause injury to man, are part of the manifestation of God's will. (As an aside, it should be mentioned that wild animals rarely, if ever, prey on man. Man is simply not part of their ecological balance.)

The real issue for the spiritual man is martyrdom in the human world. Does a person have the right to choose to be killed rather than commit some transgression? As it is written: "Better to violate one Sabbath, that one may be able to observe many Sabbaths" (*Shabbat* 151b, *Yoma* 85b). For every action then, good or bad, there are counterbalances, another set of considerations, including the intention involved. The more free and complete the choice, the more the responsibility and the reward. Concerning the performance of mitzvot, the person who observes a mitzvah only by force of habit is still under the sway of a free choice made at some point in his life. Therefore, great importance is attached to intention. There is the story of the Tzadik who wanted a special person to blow the shofar on the New Year festival. There were a number of outstanding candidates, and he asked each one what his intention was— why did he wish to blow the shofar? One after another, they gave very fine answers about their motives and thoughts; one mentioned the *kavanot* of the Ari, another, the intentions of another sage. Finally, they came to one who said he needed money to feed his children. Upon hearing this, the Tzadik said that this man was the right man—one could never be sure about the sincerity of the others, but this man's intentions came from the very core of his being.

What then is *kavanah* (intention)? It would appear that intensity of will, of truth, is of more value than intellectual content. Often the actual level of a sincere action is far above that which a person assigns to it in his thoughts; he does more than he realizes. Similarly, actions of a low intensity of purpose cannot be made higher, even with the aid of the loftiest thoughts.

Consequently, too, it is very difficult, if not impossible, to be certain about the lightness or severity of punishment for a particular transgression. At the moment of choice, whether to perform the deed or not, there can be no such distinction. For the essential question is: Am I for God or against Him? If one is against Him, then one is a rebel, and it doesn't make any difference whether it be a light charge or a severe charge. And extenuating circumstances do not count. In war, men are killed for a trifle. And in life, too, failure to perform a certain small duty may have very serious consequences. One simply has to be constantly on the alert and attentive to all the possibilities. At the moment of decision, one cannot determine to what extent a person merits punishment. Only after the performance of the action can one distinguish its true nature, whether it belongs to the outer shell or the holiness.

There is a phrase in the book of Ecclesiastes: "Or ever the silver cord be loosed. . ." (12:6). This cord has been likened to an umbilical cord binding man to God, a cord made up of numerous strands, the six hundred and thirteen commandments of the religious life. Whenever a man transgresses, he cuts one of the strands and, strand by strand, severs himself from God; each severance is called *"karet."* As we know, it does not usually work that way immediately—death does not follow sin. Man is given a certain amount of time to continue to live, a time to try and repair the severed thread, to tie it together by repentance and right action. And it is said that a strand so tied together is stronger than one that has never been torn. Just as a broken bone that forms a hard knob when it knits together, making it stronger than before. This ultimately is the proof of the repentant sinner: He is more steady and powerful than before.

At the time of transgression, or rather, in the moment following, when a person is suddenly cut off, he is cast to the other side. And here we must think in terms of a four- (or more) dimensional world, with existence focused in terms of time and soul. Every moment has a corresponding soul state; after sinning, a person becomes *tamei* (unclean) and forms part of the Sitra Achra. His actions become a blemish on the Being of the world and work against the very order of the universe.

On the other hand, there is a certain point in every human being beyond which he cannot transgress. That is the inviolable point where God resides in him, the Divine Soul in him. This makes it possible for anyone who, in a moment of weakness, has been cast to the "other side" to come back to himself. For there is always a way back if a person has not done something unforgivable (like desecrating the Divine Name). The unforgivable transgression need not be anything specific that is listed in the Scriptures; it can simply be a matter of not living up to a situation in which one represents the Divine: a Jew among gentiles, a wise man among children or fools, a decent person among perverts, for example. Even if the particular infraction may not, under other circumstances, be considered serious, under these circumstances, in which a person represents the Divine in a human situation, transgression may be unpardonable.

There is the story about the Rabbi of Rizin relating the Talmudic allegory of the donkey crouching under a heavy pack, unwilling to budge. The Talmud says that one should consider: If the donkey is indeed overburdened, one should ease the load before compelling the animal to rise; if, however, the donkey is habitually given to crouching, under the slightest provocation, then one may force it to get up. "Whereas," says the Rabbi of Rizin, "when it comes to man, it is said, 'God, Thou art all too ready to forgive Israel.' We sin and He forgives us. We keep on sinning and He forgives us. We provoke Him endlessly and still He forgives us."

25

The Power to Do Good

Irrespective of the kind of mitzvah it is, a mitzah is not a private action or an action that can be considered good or bad. The important thing is that by performing a mitzvah a person unites with God in some way. And when a person transgresses, he betrays the Divine holiness in himself and rebels against God. In other words, it is not a matter of violating the law or breaking a particular rule; it is a matter of making a fundamental choice of being for or against God. As it has been said: We know from age-long experience that when a Jew is confronted with a choice of being connected with God or of being cut off from Him, he will generally not even pause to consider, but will choose the Divine. When, however, tempted by some trifle, he may not realize that he is being confronted with the same choice. For it is the same thing, the same sort of choice between being connected with God or being cut off.

It is written: "For the thing is very nigh unto thee, in thy mouth and in thy heart to do it. . . ." And included in this love, so near to one, is also fear, the dread of separation from God. Nevertheless, at the moment of choosing evil, one descends to the lowest degradation, the betrayal of God and the betrayal of the Divine spark innate in oneself.

One can always repent, of course, for all sins; even the sin of idolatry can be overcome by repentance. At the same time, one cannot say: "I will sin now and repent afterwards." It is not as easy as all that. The circumstances of life will simply not allow it. A person who transgresses in ignorance or error will be afforded many opportunities for repentance. Whereas one who sins with the deliberate intention of circumventing just deserts by repenting in time, will not have many such opportunities.

There are many explanations for this moral equilibrium. One of them is the observation that a person who says, "I'll sin now and repent afterwards," is convinced that he has lots of time. In this case, he is always returning to the same refrain: "One more little transgression, and then I'll stop . . ." until it's too late. The absence of pressure, the feeling of leisure, make it almost impossible to arrive at any real release from the oppressiveness of sin. The Baal Shem Tov once said that the act of repentance depends on the sinner achieving a higher level of understanding and knowledge than he had at the moment of sin. This is what makes all the difference and affects a restoration. A person who sins in sleep or in ignorance, or under some sort of compulsion, can easily enter into another frame of mind when he is in a moral state and thus can repent. But the one who sins deliberately finds it very hard to attain a higher state of consciousness, and repentance is far more complex.

It sometimes happens that a certain inauspicious situation turns crucial. There is an interruption of the routine flow of life, and one is suddenly faced with something new. To be sure, this is not uncommon in the biological world—a sudden veering from established patterns at an unanticipated signal, whether ecological or genetic. So too, man continues to live his ordinary life according to the comfortable principle of free will—which can bring him to the very gates of Hell—and then, at a critical moment, his whole system cracks and changes, and a new set of motivations and principles enter into operation. This phenomenon of martyrdom is not something that takes place in time, or by the process of thought, or by any calculation of reward or punishment, or by any other consideration of one's own good. It is something beyond the reasonable or definable, and it is relatively sudden and overwhelming.

All of this shows that the essential core of truth and power lies within a person. Whatever it is that one must do, one has the capacity to do. The problem is to harness this power and to make it useful in our daily lives, as well as in moments of crisis.

Thus too, the rather general behest to "do good" is not merely an instruction to perform that which is required or that which is satisfactory in spiritual terms. It means, rather, to make the effort to identify with holiness in everything, especially when one is engaged in the intellectual study of Torah or in the emotional effort of prayer. What is necessary is a focusing of will, a concentration of one's entire being. There are, of course, occasions when one concentrates quite naturally on whatever engages one's attention in the course of life. But this other conscious concentration of the spiritual habit is a matter of looking at oneself in a certain way. To stop and think, for example, and examine what one is saying or doing— whether it be in worldly business or study or whatever. How much of one's sincerity is involved in actions such as giving charity or giving of oneself in study? How much concentrated truth is one putting into it? Charity, for example, is measured not only by one's recognition of the objective requirements, but also by the penance one has to pay for one's various defections—neglect of prayer, anger, lust, among others. And our capacity to absorb more, to receive ever more instruction from Torah, is a function of our zeal and desire, for Torah study is not mental learning, but "Devekut," clinging to God. Just as prayer is the union with God.

The mitzvah makes an incision into the veil of the hiddenness of God. If, as has been indicated, the world is made up of many graduated levels of reality, all hidden behind the Divine "withdrawal" which made Creation possible (which we call a veil, like that which separated the Holy of Holies), then the mitzvah is that which causes a tear or a slit in this veil. For "Devekut," clinging to God, accompanying the mitzvah, is an unquestioning and total attachment, and it is, therefore, capable of penetrating the concealment of His countenance, the inability to know the Divine.

To elaborate on this, let us recall that all of reality can be viewed as shell upon shell of covering; and in every such layer of covering, there is something of the Divine essence. That is its only positive and genuine aspect. However, since the reality is a result of God's Contraction, Hiddenness, "Vaulting Over," and Transformation, we cannot possibly grasp it; nothing in substantial reality seems to relate directly to the Creator. On the contrary, as one looks closer, it becomes more and more confounding. Therefore, one can dissect and deal with the world without ever approaching the Creator of the World. Because the structure of the world is such that it does not lead one out and above, but rather inward, always into deeper mysteries of itself. This basic distortion, or evasion, has been partly explained by the Contraction or Withdrawal of God to enable something besides Himself to exist. From this, we have also been able to explain evil as all that which does not naturally and promptly praise God. This, in turn, makes the praise of God optional, of course. Rabbi Nachman of Bratslav once said that there is a certain distortion in the world, and before one can relate to any reality beyond it, one has to straighten the distortion out; that is, one has to effect a certain series of transformations in order to get to some semblance of the Truth. And once one has reached such a valid picture of the Truth, one can function in the world in an effective manner. And this is what is known as the Secret of the Fathers, which is the Chariot, the secret of those who possess the Truth. It may be of interest to mention that the Maharal of Prague said that miracle, as such, does not exist; it is only the effective action on the part of someone who sees the true relations between things in the world. For as soon as one is able to observe the true relation, one can also effect changes. Knowledge of the way a system functions gives one power over it. Just as various types of locks operate on different systems. For those without the proper key, the world remains locked, because each system has its own "distortions" which keep it apart from the Divine flow. This is true of the world only; it is not true of the mitzvah. One of the characteristics of the mitzvah is that a direct connection is maintained between the focal point of the mitzvah and that which acts upon it. There is no distortion. True, the direct connection is not necessarily kept on the same level; it remains, however, within the same dimension of truth. Thus, when one performs a mitzvah, there is a direct relationship. The circle is closed.

On the other hand, the mitzvah is made up of three parts: the will of the One who commands it, the system or technique of the action, and the person who performs the mitzvah. None of these by itself is enough. Only by someone performing it is a mitzvah genuine and holy. Phylacteries lying on a shelf are no more than little boxes and straps, the *tzitzit* are no more than a few threads. A Torah Scroll is holy only when the right person reads from it in the right way. In short, only when the circle of Divine Will is closed and the circuit of holiness is complete is there a mitzvah.

Thus, the person who performs a mitzvah is in two dimensions of reality, that of normal existence, in which the mitzvah is a fixed act at a very specific point in space and time, and that in eternity, where time altogether ceases to have any meaning. There is the story of the rabbi who was jokingly asked by a well-to-do member of the congregation: "Tell me, Rabbi, is it not true that in the prayer of the Shema it is written that for someone who transgresses, the rain will not fall and his work will not prosper? Well, look at me; all my life I did not pay attention to the laws of the Torah; I don't keep the mitzvot now, and yet, I have wealth and honor. How do you explain it?" And the Rabbi answered: "From what you have said, I gather that you were once accustomed to reciting the Shema prayer. And you should know that there is nothing great enough to reward you for this single mitzvah of reciting the Shema. As for your transgressions, that is something else." Thus, every mitzvah is a genuine moment of contact with the Eternal, and there can be nothing in life to balance it.

This brings us back to the matter of martyrdom—the act of utmost devotion—offering one's very soul to God. Why should a person who is able to be a martyr be unable to resist temptation in little things? Because the tempter can be evaded.

If only the whole of life could be divided into equal moments of decision, if only we could give equal weight to all the alternatives. Just as the sinner says to the mitzvah, "Wait a moment," and the saint puts aside the evil impulse, at least, "for awhile." No matter what the situation, it is always a matter of being for or against the Divine. At one moment a person may decide for God, but what about the next moment? One need not consider the whole year; it is enough to grapple with each moment as it comes. In that way, one can manage to stand up to the basic struggle of life. For, often enough, one can barely do more than cope with one moment at a time. Thus too, all worry, sadness, and the like, are a total loss, a waste of time—one could be spending it in achieving something genuine—if one takes life bit by bit, moment by moment.

26

The Meaning of Sadness

Sadness is a great obstacle to the worship of God, and man must struggle against it as much as he can. Even though there is a passage in the Bible that states: "In all sadness, there would be profit. . . ." (Proverbs 14:23), which may appear to be a contradiction. Of course, the meaning is not that sadness in itself can ever be profitable, but that there is a joy that often follows on sadness, which, thus, may be good. For there is also the matter of catharsis or purification, as well as the fact that there is a time for everything.

Sadness can, therefore, be a vehicle for attaining something else, a bitter remedy for a worse ailment. On the other hand, life furnishes enough genuine reasons for being downcast. Thus in order to prevent sadness from being a dominant factor in life, we appoint special times for it—such as fast days or days of penitential prayer—and banish it from the rest of our lives.

Nevertheless, there is sometimes a real need for a contrite heart. Because the greatest hindrance to spiritual awakening is a certain smugness, a dullness of the heart and mind. In this case, all the books and all the messages of spiritual love will not avail. Indeed, self-complacency is a more serious obstacle than depression or stupidity. To overcome it, to smash through the barrier of "fatness" of soul, it is often necessary to pass through some sort of crisis or tragic experience. And this is often brought about by heavenly intervention, against one's own wishes and designs.

Indeed, it is a disquieting fact that it is more difficult to gain knowledge of the Divine through ordinary, positive living, than through negative or tragic experience. The negative seems to have much more power to break down one's resistance; the positive tends to reinforce one's smugness. Of course, sadness can also drag a person into depths beyond sensitivity, but, here too, the direction is important. And when one is aware of one's degradation, the sense of shame or of self-pity can function to restore the balance. Because it is sometimes necessary for a person to come to the conclusion that his life is not worth anything. Only when a person is burned so badly that his skin begins to peel, will he begin to feel himself.

A Kabbalistic insight claims: "It is Jacob who redeems Abraham." Abraham is Chesed, or love, and Jacob is Tiferet (mercy and beauty). One may discover in life that grace is absent and that one cannot awaken love in one's heart. Upon such discovery, one falls back on pity, and this stimulates the love and the grace which had been absent. This stirring of compassion in the heart awakens great love, even the love of God. Here too, the essential confrontation is with Truth, the truth of oneself, and the need to break down the partition or veil that separates one from the Divine.

The Psalmist expressed it: "A broken and contrite heart, O God, thou wilt not despise" (Psalms 51:19). Just as a ladder cannot be useful unless it has something to lean against, so too, is there nothing more whole than a broken heart. Even though, to be sure, God prefers vessels that are without blemishes or cracks, and it is written in the Zohar that the Shechinah does not lodge itself anywhere except in a whole vessel. Nevertheless, this does not include a broken heart. As Rabbi Schneur Zalman of Liadi mentions elsewhere: If one does not have a broken and contrite heart, one cannot be said to have a heart at all.

The central factor here is the demolition of sadness, the

explosion which releases the joy. And many men do not really know true happiness, because they have never experienced the release from sadness. It is not a matter of contrasts, of course; it is a matter of getting to the truth of experience, of breaking out of the self-delusion, entertained by many, that they are alive. Something that only a genuine shock can bring about. For a great number of civilized human beings live comfortably with the notion that they would like to know God; and this is as much of a search for meaning they can indulge in. They do not get beyond the daily obligations of ethics and religion. Their search is, at best, the search for an earthly fortune, a matter of putting effort into something and getting a more or less just compensation. However, using the same logic, the story of the rich man who asked the rabbi: "What will I get out of the next life?" The rabbi answered: "At least as much as you invest in it." If you put a lot of money and effort into an earthly endeavor, you are likely to earn even more; if you put a lot of thought and energy into your spiritual endeavors, you're liable to gain more in the heavenly hereafter. The trouble is that men are much more troubled about the loss of a ten-pound note on earth than about losing a spiritual opportunity to perform a kindness.

For the heart is dull and heavy, and it is difficult to reach true joy. Thus, we have had to set fixed times for sadness and times for joy. The Ari used to teach his group in Safad to practice Tikun Chatzot, the nightly midnight sessions. These were mainly devoted to the recitation of Lamentations and the confession of sin, followed by hymns of praise and hours of joyful study of Torah and Kabbalah. The rationale is that when one thinks of the Exile of the Shechinah, we invoke a feeling of loss and abandonment. When this does not have the desired effect because it is too abstract, then one must think about the exile of the Shechinah in oneself. Then a person can experience the sorrow and the heartbreak of his life. And afterwards, he can more easily come around to the joy of prayer and study. So that sadness at fixed times can be a way of release from routine dullness and an opening for light and inner happiness.

The light that comes from the darkness has a certain excellence, like the wisdom that results from folly. To feel true happiness, it is perhaps necessary to go through the darkness of pain and the pit of anguish; in order to truly know happiness, one must make a place for it in oneself, and this can best be done by great pain which thrusts all else aside. For example, the greatest happiness of all, the pleasure of being alive, is hardly ever experienced in ordinary circumstances; and only when life is threatened, in passing through the danger of death, does one know it fully. In other words, only when a person realizes the full pain and terror of his life, can he make a place for God in himself. But of course, this applies to the times in history or in personal life when a person can allow himself the luxury of experiencing sadness at fixed times, when one is not the victim or the object of suffering. Sadness is well and good if it can be taken out and put away at will. As the instructions in certain old prayer books directed: "Here one is to weep. . . ." The fact is that life was perhaps harder in the old days, and in order to overcome the immense sadness of it, Jews had to put aside certain times for grief and weeping. It used to be a wry joke among Jews to say to someone full of complaints against fate, "Save it for the proper occasion in the course of prayer."

This preponderance of suffering in the world naturally caused wonderment in previous generations. Largely, it was attributed to the Exile of the Shechinah, the general scheme of incompleteness in the world. All of an individual's personal pain was part of this universal impairment of the world, like the defective moon prayed over by Israel until it becomes full. The incomplete moon was a sign of the crippled world, an omen of what was missing. And the praying Jew had only to recollect that his own and the world's suffering betokened the incompleteness and pain of the Shechinah, and that he could help bring about the restoration of the wholeness by prayer. One's own anguish was a part of the greater anguish of the Shechinah in exile.

Sadness is, thus, only a stage on the way, a passage to joy. Essentially, a person must worship God with a "glad and joyful heart." It is even said that much of the suffering of Israel has come because Jews did not worship with gladness. Because when a person worships with gladness, it shows a certain connection, a oneness with God. And what is sin, if not separation from God? Can any man be judged whether he keeps the mitzvot properly or acts in righteousness for its own sake? This brings to mind a story about a king who had to decide whether the commander of his army, who had just lost an important battle, was a traitor or whether he was inept, a victim of his own error. To help make the decision, he sent another general to do battle with the same foe, and when he returned victorious, the king observed the reactions of the commander who had failed. If he was happy at the victory of his rival, it proved his loyalty to the king; if he showed any sign of unhappiness, he was a traitor at heart and deserved to be dealt with accordingly.

Indeed, if one worships God with "gladness and a joyful heart" then, in spite of sin and misfortune, one remains strong in the attachment to the Divine, and it is simple to return to Him. But if one does not worship God in this heartfelt, joyful manner, if it is a matter of some agreement or pact with God, then to transgress invites endless trouble and tragedy for the soul. It is all the difference between being a son of the house or working for the house as a day laborer.

Sadness then is something to be used with restraint and caution, like those little bottles of medicine labeled "poison." It may become necessary to imbibe a little for the sake of overcoming sickness, but great care has to be exercised in doing so. Only at certain times, and only to restore life, can sadness be useful. There is a sadness, however, that comes when a person feels his inferiority and impotence, which happens often enough with those who are of the category of the Benoni, the intermediate personality between the saint and the sinner. Even then, melancholy has to be controlled, allowed to surface only at specified times, and at other times kept submerged. As the Rabbi of Kotzk is purported to have said: "Everything has its own time. For eating, when one is young. For sleeping, only when a person is in the grave. For sadness—never!"

Thus, it is impossible to conquer one's nature with a sluggish heart. Alacrity, which is derived from joy, is needed. But what about the incessant problems of existence—besides the daily cares of eating and sleeping and money—the worry about life and love and death and children?

There has never been an easy answer, and it is known to be far more difficult in the doing than in the saying. Consider the story of Rabbi Meizlish of Cracow and Warsaw, who was a well-to-do merchant before he became a rabbi. Even then, when he was sending timber along the river to Germany to be sold there at a profit, he was famous for his erudition, and he used to teach brilliant pupils at the yeshivah. Once the news came that the timber rafts were wrecked in a storm, and the whole of the rabbi's fortune was lost in one day. They did not know how to tell the rabbi and chose one of his favorite pupils to do so. The young man selected a passage in the Talmud and came to the Rabbi with his question: "It says here that one has to thank God with blessings for the evil that befalls one as well as for the good. How can this be done?" The rabbi explained the matter in terms of its hidden meaning as well as in straightforward theology. To this the pupil replied, "I am not sure I understand. And if my rabbi were to learn that all his timber rafts were wrecked on the river, would he dance for joy?" The rabbi said, "Yes, of course." "Well then," said the pupil, "you can dance—all the rafts are lost!" Upon hearing this, the rabbi fainted. When he came to, he said, "Now I must confess I no longer understand this Talmud passage."

In other words, there is a difference between theoretically knowing that God is always present and knowing it when one is crushed. To be sure, there are many saints, and even ordinary men, who are able to bless the evil as well as the good, not only to receive it without complaint, but also to accept it with joy. The capacity to do so is a function of deeper comprehension as well as of faith or certainty in the wisdom of the hidden workings of God. Hence we understand the meaning of the verse: "Happy is the man whom Thou, O God, chasteneth . . ." (Psalms 94:12).

To be sure, everything is good, in the sense that it comes from God. On the other hand, there can be no denying that suffering exists and that the cause of suffering is something that may be called evil. In this case, the good is hidden, and several levels have to be excavated in order to get to it. On the simplest level, one can sometimes see it quite directly—my cow broke a leg, and I found a treasure at that spot. Or there is the story of Rabbi Akiva who, traveling, could not get lodging at the inn. He had, however, a candle to read by, a donkey to take him to the forest where he could sleep, and a cock to wake him in the morning. So, he was pleased and said, "This too is for the best." Then a lion came and killed his donkey; a cat devoured his cock, and the wind snuffed out his candle. "This too is for the best," he said, and he curled up in a tree and slept soundly. In the morning, he learned that a band of wild robbers had come to the inn, looted and taken captive all who were there. Had his donkey neighed or his cock crowed, or had the robbers seen his candle, he too would have been plundered. So that he was able to say again with conviction, "This too is for the best."

Of course, in most instances the matter is far more complex. There may be a considerable time gap, as in the case of Joseph and his brothers. Or the true nature of evil may never be made evident to the outer eye. Even a very cursory reflection upon the events of one's life can often lead one to contemplate the relative nature of what were once considered calamities. This notwithstanding, we are still confronted with the existence of evil.

Whatever it is, evil is not the same as what many would classify as unmitigated wickedness. As in most things, a certain education of the moral sense allows one to see things differently. In matters of taste—the bitterness of certain beverages, like beer, has to be cultivated in order to be enjoyed, in contrast to the obvious sweetness of sugary things, which is almost always enjoyed. Or consider the whole gamut of sophisticated taste in art, as well as in culinary matters. The development of "good taste" requires time.

So too, it is easy to bless that which is universally good. It is difficult to comprehend the true nature of suffering, and even more so, to "enjoy it." For the truth of things is hidden, and the true good is on a higher level of reality, making it less available to our understanding. That is to say, suffering comes from the revealed aspects of the Divine (the letters *yud, hey*). A more profound happiness comes from the hidden aspects of Divine reality (the letters *vav, hey*).

To be sure, most men are willing to renounce this Divine chastening, preferring to receive the good portion of the simple man. Thus, in praying we say: "May it be Thy will to forgive and wipe away our sins, but not by suffering and affliction." Also, it is written in the Talmud: "Lord of the Universe, truly Thy gifts are good and sufferings are among the greatest gifts, for nothing truly valuable comes without suffering, and no man attains to the Promised Land or to Torah or to the life in the next world, except through suffering, from the earliest breath. . . ." Nevertheless, we do pray, in all humility, in all simplicity, for release from suffering.

The relation, however, between the evil person and suffering is rather puzzling. Obviously, the wicked should receive the just deserts of their actions and suffer the consequences. But life is more likely to be the paradox of the sick person getting all sorts of delicacies to eat while the healthy person has to suffice with whatever is available. Or the disobedient child getting much more attention than the obedient one. If suffering can be seen as a gift from God, how can we accept punishment as the evil effects of sin? Do the wicked have it good from all sides?

The answer is that suffering is, of course, not always the same thing. To the wicked, suffering often comes as a means of release from a certain constriction. And the real punishment lies not in the virulent reaction of life and society against the sinner, but in the exemption from suffering—when the one who has sinned is discharged before he has made right his evil deed. Like in the explanation given concerning God's punishment of the snake for tempting Eve in the Garden of Eden, the snake is made to crawl in the dust of the earth to "eat of the dust all the days of thy life." This means that, in contrast to man's punishment—"Cursed is the ground for thy sake; in sorrow shalt thou eat of it all the days of thy life"—the snake always has enough to eat, and he can survive without effort no matter where he is. "Not much of an affliction," one may say. The real punishment is that God is ridding Himself of all responsibility; the snake can go and do what it likes; it doesn't even have to pray to God for anything. And this disconnection from the Divine is the worst that can happen to any creature; it is the nature of Hell.

Suffering is then a means of restoring a person to God. As we have said, there are many who will never awaken to holiness without some life crisis. Just as it is interesting to observe the effects of what is considered "success." Not only does success often bring a certain crassness and insensitivity, but it also brings a forgetting of how to be grateful.

It is written in the Talmud that were it not for the sins of Israel, only the five books of the Torah and the book of Joshua would have been given and no more. If so, we have to thank the sins of our fathers for much of the wisdom, poetry, and prophecy in the Bible; their recurrent wrongdoing apparently demanded that much more Divine care and intervention.

Another way of looking at it is that man oscillates between periods of spiritual soaring and periods of rest from the spirit, when he is content with the simple things of life. Also, there seems to be some danger in all extremes. Riches lead to one sort of temptation, poverty to another.

Thus, while the wicked get God's attention, causing Him to occupy Himself with them, the saintly are privileged to suffer as their portion, and the mediocre are usually happy to avoid either extreme and are satisfied to live out their lives in tranquil dullness and insensitivity. However, since nothing shakes them, there is no thrust forward or awakening to another world. And indeed, suffering is often "wasted" on the complacently mediocre. This is a very different sort of thing from the "wasting" of suffering on the saintly who simply do not see it as something evil. For the conscious person, the gift of suffering comes as a test, an opportunity to learn something and to progress into an acceptance of suffering as a hidden blessing.

The point is that man needs to see suffering as something given to him for his own benefit, whether as instruction or as a bitter medicine. If it is so hidden that one fails to see it, something very serious and complicated happens to one's relationship with God—a kind of destructive bitterness. On the other hand, the person who is ready to receive the Divine chastisement is the one who is closest to God, even though He is hidden. In chastisement, God is closer than in correct or formal relations. As is true in ordinary human associations, rebuke is a part of genuine cherishing.

Moreover, the person who is prepared to accept chastisement is not simply passive and obedient. The problem is far deeper than that. If a person is sick, he should not merely take medicine and lie in bed in order to be able to enjoy the chastisement of suffering, nor does the poor man have to resign himself to poverty. The problem is: What is one to do with the suffering that is inflicted? Is it in the nature of a calamity or a revelation? The only answer lies in the certainty that no matter what the nature of the situation, one is always interrelating with God. If there is suffering, He is contending with me, bringing me to some new appraisal of things. He may be right or He may be wrong, in my opinion; but at least I can argue the matter with Him. That is what God wants—a living relationship.

Ordinarily, men see the world through a thick veil—and the image of the sun coming out of its covering represents a real event of revelation. In the resultant brightness, the Tzadik will be healed, and the wicked will be burned. The Tzadik, or saintly person, who was ready to accept God in His hiddenness, in the darkness of suffering, will be able to receive the greater light and be healed, while the one who wished only to avoid God or any kind of Divine interference in his life, is consumed by the revelation.

To say, "This too is for the best," is hardly the same thing as superficial optimism. It is a recognition of the reality of pain and evil and an attempt to get to the root of suffering, to get beyond the fact that everything bad has something good in it, and that salvation often emerges from tribulation. There is no longer any consideration of the ultimate profit or hidden goodness in the reality of suffering. Besides, what kind of release or consolation resides in the thought that the pain will pass? One who is in agony of body or spirit can hardly be made to feel better by philosophic or religious ideas.

The Jew who sincerely faces suffering does not seek an accounting with God—he does not reproach Divine justice or defend his own innocence. Nor does he seek ways of reaping some advantage. He relates entirely to the present, to that which is now, not to what was in the past, or what is liable to be in the future. No solace is sought or vain imaginings. If God wills it, the situation will improve; otherwise, it's none of my business. The argument is that since suffering is something that comes from God, it is in the nature of a gift, or at least something that is given. Because, to be sure, not everything that is given can, at first sight, be recognized as something positive. And this takes a lot of time, a great deal of tumultuous repudiation before one reaches a relatively peaceful state of equilibrium. In other words, the Chasidic teacher tells us that his wisdom cannot really remove the pain or resolve the sadness. It can only eliminate the anxiety, the tension, the fear, and the uncertainty.

The problem becomes focused on the nature of passivity in the spiritual life. First, there is the simple situation of a certain distress, whether of a greater or a lesser degree—a lack of money or illness or a calamity of tragic proportions or despondency. The distress is genuine enough, and there is no point in claiming that one should be glad about it, or that one should not do everything possible to eliminate it. The usual way of relating to distress is to experience a certain drop of spirit, a sadness, or bitterness, which can be interpreted as stemming from an attitude that one does not deserve the pain and sorrow, that one has somehow been unfairly or wrongly treated. And it is this that can be remedied by seeing the suffering, not as punishment for some wrongdoing, that one may or may not have done, but as a sort of reward—which is not immediately apparent as such. It takes a while to distinguish it.

The second part of the problem lies in the nature of whatever causes distress. What if it gets worse? What if no good comes of it? The hiddenness of the Divine necessarily brings on its wretchedness and suffering. God does not appear to the one who is in misery in the same way as to the same person in ordinary life, when the evil and the pain come from outside oneself, from the structure of the created world.

In other words, the problem focuses on the fact of suffering as a trial. For suffering can lead to many things. Some rise; others fall. Suffering is the test. Can a person receive it without sliding into hatred? Can he grow from experiencing it? And if he can, is he able to persist and reach a world illuminated like the "sun emerging"?

In other words, the sun comes out of its sheath or covering gradually; it is a process that one has to pass through. Otherwise it would consume one instead of heal. The revelation would be too much for anyone who is unprepared. It is necessary to become accustomed to, or rather, made able to absorb the light. Like any learning process, there is the need to make mistakes, the need to repeat and exercise the correct action or word or concept. Nothing in life, or comparatively little, comes of itself. And the light of God is made available through a growing process, a learning through hardship, an exercising of one's ability to accept suffering, to receive it as a gift from God. This gift does not carry any obligations beyond the requirements, perhaps, to relinquish self-pity, the sweet solace of feeling sorry for oneself. And not to worry about repairing God's world for Him, leaving Him to care for it.

This does not mean that there is nothing for a man to do. On the contrary, a person has to try to do the maximum possible in the way of fixing himself and the world, which is all in the realm of the World of Action. After that, he is released from all anxiety and sadness. Because anxiety and sadness come from a certain lack of proportion, from the fact that a person thinks God is able to do wrong, or that it is up to me to set Him right. Suffering by itself is not a matter of being mistreated by life; it is something given that has to be received, sometimes as a gift. I have to relate realistically and not become sad or downhearted. Pain and sadness are two very different qualities. Sadness is a state of mind in which a person perceives himself as rather justified and decent, and God as rather unfair. Thus, one should avoid falling into anxiety and sadness.

27

The Need for Struggle

The problem of the Benoni, the intermediate man who is neither saint nor sinner, is the persistence of temptation. The saint is beyond it, and the sinner yields to it; the Benoni has to live with it and struggle with it. This makes his life neither simple nor easy, and he will often feel that he is on the verge of losing his hold—either by succumbing to temptation or by resigning himself to the sadness of frustration. Thus, underlying the virtue and courage of the Benoni is the hopelessness of ever being able to solve the problem of attaining some sort of genuine freedom. This in itself can well be grounds for a certain melancholy.

As Job said: "You have created the wicked and you have created the saintly. . . ." Which suggests that free choice may be questioned—how can one act except in accordance with what one is created to be? Why should one endeavor to be anything else? But the meaning is not that those so created must actually be wicked in their thoughts and feelings. There is no predetermined life. There is always the freedom to choose, to be sinful or otherwise. There is the Talmudic allegory of the letter *"kuf"* (as in *kadosh*, holy), which has two openings, one above and one below. Every man may decide for himself which he prefers to go through—below, through transgression, or above, through righteous living.

Those created as wicked, or as Benoni, have that much more of a task cut out for them—to subdue the Sitra Achra, the forces of the unholy. The saintly have no such struggle; they do not know the forces of evil by experience, and they can only learn about them secondhand, as one learns of the life of the birds and the beasts. The deeds of the saintly are therefore relegated to a different sphere of influence, and the battlefield is left to the Benoni. It is he who must fight to subdue the Sitra Achra; and at each victory in the contest, no matter how small, he manages to light up the world for a moment.

Each then is necessary to God, the saintly, the Benoni, and the wicked. All have their task, and there can be no comparison or value judgment about which is better. Each has only to fulfill his task within the given reality to the utmost of his ability; and this is what is most satisfying to God.

The Tzadik, or saint, transforms the evil to good within himself, as well as within the context of the world. It has been mentioned that the Tzadik does not feel suffering in the same way as other men; he does not recognize it as something special to be feared and avoided. It is, for him, like all else in life, a fact of existence; one eats, one sleeps, one acts, one suffers. Everything is translated into good by the very essence of his being.

There is the story of Rabbi Zusia of Anipoli, who was known to be very poor and living in quite miserable conditions. Once, two scholars came and asked Rabbi Zusia's teacher, the Maggid of Mezritch, the meaning of the precept that one has to bless the bad as well as the good. The Maggid said: "Go and ask my pupil, Rabbi Zusia." They went to Zusia's house, saw how he lived, explained themselves, and put their question to him. He answered: "I really don't know why my teacher sent you to me, one who has never known the bad in life at all." In other words, he who reaches the stage of the Tzadik does not come to grips with the problems of evil; it does not even touch him. By his very existence, he simply transforms all darkness to light.

It is the Benoni, then, who is occupied with the task of

subduing the Sitra Achra, thereby making it possible for the glory of God to rise. The Tzadik is not concerned with evil at all; it simply vanishes before him, just as the darkness is nullified by the light. There is no need for a struggle, whereas, for the Benoni, there is a very real struggle. For him, the Sitra Achra is not a shadow that is nullified by his approach; it is a strong and genuine reality.

The Tzadik, for example, simply cannot understand what temptation is; he is repelled where others are attracted; he finds the evil fascinations of men to be rather silly. Consider the contrast of widely different cultures, such as the Australian aborigine with the European; what is pleasing or absolutely vital to one may be disgusting to the other. So the Tzadik views the vanities of his own generation to be as pathetic and stupid as the aborigine's removal of the front teeth or the tattooing of the face in order to look beautiful.

The Tzadik is thus a higher type of human being—more like a Jewish "superman"—one whom evil cannot touch. In terms of the great yearning or hope that "the spirit of corruption shall pass from the earth," the Tzadik may be seen as a sort of harbinger of the end of days. In the world as it is, however, there are two categories of men: those few who are immune to evil and the vast majority for whom evil is very real. For the latter, the ordinary man, life is a terrible struggle against evil, while God, the Creator, looks on admiringly at the feat of one, merely human, who is able to overcome something He himself formed.

The Tzadik is not born a finished product, a saintly person from the start. He grows by continual self-correction until he reaches the point where the Sitra Achra is no longer within him, when the evil impulse comes from without, from the world. For this reason, it has been said that the Tzadik is higher than the angel. For the angel is one-dimensional, without conflict, while the Tzadik is vulnerable to both the material and the spiritual. The angel does not even understand what the physical consists of; he is beyond it to begin with. The Tzadik is thus on a higher level, precisely because he is physical and is able to maintain a double perspective, a capacity for seeing the two aspects of existence at once. At some sages once said: "The

Tzadikim will someday recite the 'Holy, Holy, Holy' before the angels in hierarchical order."

In the same way, the Benoni also stands between two orders of being; but he remains within the struggle against evil, and he can never get beyond it. The Tzadik, on the other hand, is able to transform the evil to good, the bitter to sweet, the darkness to light.

It is written that Isaac instructed Jacob to "make me some savory meat, such as I love . . ." (Genesis 27:4). This is what God wishes man to do with his life—to make something satisfying to the Divine. The Benoni can repair or correct some of the wrongness of life; he cannot sweeten it or give it to the savory quality of perfection that God loves. He can only flavor it to a certain extent; he cannot transform it in the same way that the Tzadik can. God, however, needs both of them: He wants the Benoni to be what he is just as He enjoys the Tzadik's existence. They complement one another.

In the same way, the wicked can effect certain changes in solving the problem of evil, changes that are out of the range of the Benoni because he is susceptible to evil. Being on the same "wavelength," the wicked can alter and correct and sweeten much of the evil in the world. But it is the Benoni who, although he does not necessarily commit a sin himself, is the one who really struggles with sin. Evil for him is very real, and he is always suffering, even without cursing or complaining. He is unable, like the Tzadik, to see only the good and the beautiful of existence—as in the story of the impoverished Rabbi Zusia, who once stood on a street corner feeling very hungry, and all he could think of was: "Lord of the Universe, thank you for giving me an appetite."

The Benoni is thus a warrior, a person of great courage and an unusual capacity to keep on fighting without ever giving in to despair. Even though he is well aware of the fact that there is no end to his struggle, that is his destiny, he does not let this thought afflict him. His life pursues its course with a certain steadiness; the fact that he experiences temptation again and again is not an indication of his unworthiness; it is a sign of unmitigated struggle and serves as an opportunity to manifest strength and to rise to a higher level. Because every rise is the result of a successful confrontation with new problems—in contrast to the *modus vivendi* of most men, who continually sanction their provocations and desires.

Consequently, the struggle of the Benoni is not necessarily against evil or temptation—it is a contest against himself, within himself, as is ultimately true of all the great heroes. And it takes place within the narrow confines of a natural urge, like the eating of food at a certain fixed hour or the impulse to dispute something within the course of a conversation. At which, the restraint, deliberately exercised, even one so slight as the pause in the moment of blessing, can be a part of the great task of subduing the Sitra Achra. As it is stated in the Talmud: "If a man consecrates himself in a small measure here below, he is sanctified much more from above . . ." (*Yoma* 39a). That is to say, the moment of overcoming the smallest wrong impulse is a thrust into the circle of sanctity. And sometimes, that is all that is needed, a small thrust into the circle of the holy in order to extricate oneself from the powerful current of some evil, sin trailing sin, in which one's life may be caught.

The Torah says: "Sanctify yourselves and be ye holy" (Leviticus 20:7). This means that in those actions that are not specifically prescribed by the Halachah, there is great opportunity for sanctification. Similarly, within the prescribed limits of Halachah, a person may be as unholy as the most wicked, and thus be separated from God. Even the greatest of men are structured this way—those potentially capable of the highest sanctity are also more vulnerable to the force of the evil impulse. That is, the one who instincts are stronger is just as capable of being a saint as a sinner. The point is to utilize the opportunity presented by one's potential.

The Benoni is, thus, the one who is presented with a possible greatness of soul, an opportunity for holiness. What, for another, would seem like assuming a terrible burden, one that is almost inhumanly difficult, is, for the Benoni, his chance to prove himself. And he can succeed only because he does get help. He cannot solve all his problems by himself; he can only alter them, set them up in a different manner. While the Tzadik can attain a total victory, a state where there are no more enemies about, the Benoni is always beset by antagonists, by problems; he overcomes one, and two spring up in its place. He can never terminate the struggle. Nevertheless, the more he perseveres, a certain advantage accrues to him: He becomes more capable of accomplishing what he wants to do. Not that he can ever say with certainty that anything is completely solved; a forgotten problem can always slip back into his life. No impulse is overcome forever. The important thing is that even this is no reason for sadness; it is only another aspect of the process of life, of progress, of striving, which is the very essence of the Benoni.

28
Extraneous Thoughts

Thoughts come to a person from the outside like forces of nature bombarding one with a limitless variety of meaning and value. What happens, however, when a stream of such extraneous thoughts comes upon a person engaged in prayer or study of Torah? And so it happens that the "evil impulse," for all its being only one thing in essence, shows itself to every person as something unique and special to him alone. In any case, no matter what the nature of this extraneous thought, it may easily throw a person into a state of despondency, especially if one is in the midst of earnest endeavor or prayer.

The answer, of course, is not to relate to it as anything more than a troublesome distraction. To struggle with it is to invite real difficulties. It is hard to avoid getting dirty when one is wrestling with filth; invariably some sort of communication is established with the source of trouble, and it clings to one. So that by far the best thing to do is to cut oneself off from the thought, no matter how and when it comes.

To be sure, certain Chasidic texts speak of this as an opportunity to perform an act of Tikun, or correction of evil; that is to say, to raise the uninvited and chaotic impulse to some higher level. This idea is based on the view that there is the force of desire, and there is the object of desire. And theoretically, at least, a person can separate between the two, and in doing so, redirect the force of his desire to something that is beneficial or good. Techniques have been devised to help one do this, guiding one in the unmasking of instincts. One can say, for instance, that the source of all beauty is God, and therefore, instead of pursuing some transient reflection of beauty, would it not be better to cling to the Eternal source of splendor itself? Thus, an impulse or temptation on a lower level can be raised to a force of creative action on a higher level. To be sure, certain Chasidim carried this to absurd lengths, and there are many amusing anecdotes to this effect.

This may well be why the Baal HaTanya maintains that this sort of spiritual effort is theoretical only: One can perhaps elevate an extraneous thought or an evil impulse, but not if it is one's own. When it comes from within oneself, when there is no distance and no objectivity, it is impossible to act on it. Whoever is given over to a thought, an impulse, a strong emotion or desire, cannot detach himself from it by himself. Just as it is impossible to extricate oneself from a swamp without fastening on to something outside.

Indeed, any proper relationship requires a certain distance. One cannot relate to beauty, for instance, unless one detaches oneself from it and looks upon it as art. For the world presents itself to us in a myriad of images and perceptions, and, in order to come to grips with anything, one has to be able to relate to its inner content. Only a thought with which one is not identified can be raised to a higher level; one can help other people with their problems—only if these are not one's own. Moreover, as Jeremiah said: "The heart is deceitful above all things." Often a person will feel himself to be immune to some enticement or provocation, only to discover, to his dismay, that he was mistaken. Even the greatest sages have admitted as much.

Nevertheless, in spite of the difficulty, or rather the impossibility, of elevating the evil thought or impulse, a person has to be in a state of gladness. That is the first condition in the Divine service to which every human being is called. Instead of feeling despair because one is helpless and weak in the face of an extraneous thought, one has to divert the things of the outer shell, resorting to a certain wrestler's skill, using the weight of the opponent to topple him and then slipping from under his grip by an ingenious clarity of purpose and will. For, as the Baal HaTanya says, there are two souls waging war against each other in a person's mind. And the prize for which they are fighting is the individual's progress toward God. How often it happens that one succumbs for a moment to the extraneous thought while praying, and, consequently, one ceases to pray; the battle has been won by the tempter, and yet, at the same time, the extraneous thought that started it all collapses. In other words, the victory or defeat of the extraneous thought wasn't what the struggle was really about in the first place. And the retreat continues; a person loses heart and becomes depressed; and then, even if he doesn't commit a transgression, he is, nevertheless, caught in the vicious circle—and one thing leads to another.

The Benoni, or intermediate person, is, thus, himself the battleground of an unending struggle, a battle for human consciousness. Because there are layers of consciousness above and below outer awareness, over which he has relatively little control, he can never resolve the struggle; he can, at best, gain such control of his consciousness that a sizable portion of life is secured. The same sort of thing, from the opposite side, can be said of the common sinner. Since he is always feeling sorry for what he has done, it may be surmised that the holiness in him is not that far below the surface. And in him, the extraneous thoughts would tend to be those of his conscience, disturbing him with unwanted diversions, making his transgressions lack sincerity and wholeness. In other words, there is always that other part of us—below and beyond our control—that prevents wholeheartedness of activity, whether for good or for ill.

To be sure, there are people who can present a hard surface, seemingly impenetrable to the invasion of outside thoughts. These are individuals who have such powers of concentration that they may feel themselves to be superior human beings or Tzadikim, so little are they disturbed by the evil impulse. But very often, such a peace is only a temporary truce hiding a change of form; the evil instinct is only taking time out to transform itself and to burst forth—in a week, a month, a year—as something else, different from what it used to be, and yet the same. And then, if a person is not acutely conscious of the unending struggle within him, he may really stumble and fall.

The straightforward advice given by the Chasidic master, then, is simply not to pay attention to these other thoughts, "to pretend to be deaf" and to further stengthen the power of one's concentration. The assumption is that one is capable of directing the subject of one's thoughts, just as one can change the subject of a conversation at will, even if the more profound impulses behind the conscious expression are out of one's control.

Let us take as an illustration the frequent instance of a worrisome thought, not necessarily anything sinful or objectionable. It turns up at the very moment one stands up to pray. And, indeed, there are all too many reasons why it should happen in this precise, frustrating manner. One brushes the worry aside; it returns with increased force. One makes a more sincere effort, and one may even succeed in concentrating for a moment on the words of the prayer, only to have the worry rush in like a flood, overwhelming one completely.

The problem obviously is not the thought itself, but the energy behind it. And the advice is to discharge it, somehow or other to nullify its fury. A joke is sometimes appropriate—humor can bring peace of mind when seriousness fails. And there have been great rabbis who always began their studies or lectures with a joke, in order to put themselves and their listeners into the proper frame of mind for awesome truths. And it has been found by many that, by far, the best cure for heartache is the sudden impact of the grotesque. There is the story—one of the innumerable stories of the prophet Elijah's sojourns among men—of the prophet finding himself in a marketplace full of people. One of the local elders approached him and asked: "Who, of all those here, belongs to Heaven?" Elijah looked around and said, "No one, as far as I can see." Just then two more people, strangers, entered the marketplace. Elijah pointed to them and said, "These two are among those that belong to Heaven." The elder then inquired who they were; and it turned out they were clowns, jesters who earned their living by making people laugh.

If a person, despite all efforts, does not succeed in concentrating on his prayer, he can resort to supplication, asking God to have compassion on him, like a father who takes pity on his children. For we are a part of God, as children can be said to be a part of their parents. It is, in a sense, the last argument: "O Lord, even if we are not worthy of Your glory or grace, at least for Your own sake, since we are a part of You, a spark of Your holiness, come to our aid."

There is a hint here of something more profound than a self-centered call for salvation. When people are in trouble—in the narrow confines of sorrow or pain—they tend to become more selfish, if anything. Everything revolves around them. To overcome this apartness from God, it is necessary to reemphasize the essential oneness with Him. Each of us is a part of Israel—and not only of Israel, but of the Shechinah, for it is written, "His people is a part of the Lord . . ." (Deuteronomy 32:9).

When in difficulty, then, the best thing is to try to avoid seeing only oneself. Jewish prayer seeks to extricate one from the individual problem or pain and to reestablish the pattern of the wholeness of things. The suffering one is not "I," but the Shechinah. "Therefore, for Thy sake, Oh Lord, come to my aid. . . ." Thus, in the midst of prayer, when the evil impulse assails one, this is often the only way to save oneself.

The trouble is that, in the very enthusiasm of prayer, a person may very well begin to be aware of himself in questionably self-admiring terms: "Such a fine figure of devotion, such fervor and wisdom!" And this of course, even when most sincere, is just the opening the negative forces of various kinds are waiting for. This is why it is said that a broken and contrite heart evokes the quickest response. It is best to affirm that one is nothing in oneself, that one is something only because one is a spark of God.

This removes the ground from under the extraneous thought or evil impulse. When a person identifies himself with God and asks God to act for His sake, and not for one's own sake, there is safety. Even when one asks for no more than a livelihood or health and happiness, one can do so in several ways. It makes all the difference whether the request is made in a calculating fashion or with complete trust in His judgment.

29
Dullness of the Heart

We have been directing our attention to the problem of dullness of the heart, the inability to feel and be responsive to things. It is not connected to any lack of intellectual understanding. A person can comprehend, clearly and in depth, and still be in a state of "dullness of heart," incapable of feeling what is happening; nothing moves, it is impossible to make any progress.

This spiritual numbness comes when the shell, the animal aspect of man, prevails over the human; and there is no other remedy but to shatter it—as one chops up a wooden log in order to get it to catch fire. A heart that cannot respond emotionally to life has to suffer itself, to be broken into pieces. How is this to be done?

It must be remembered that the standards of the Benoni are much above the average; he is what the average individual endeavors to be, free from sin or evil in thought as well as deed. And the fact is that even a Benoni can be in a state of "dullness of heart," requiring a shattering of the ego. Because the ego is an expression of the animal-soul; and the shattering of the ego is like a peeling of the shell, a penetration of the dense hardness that blocks genuine sensitivity.

There is the question in the Psalms (24:3,4): "Who shall ascend the mountain of the Lord? And who shall stand in His holy place?" To this, the answer is given: "He that hath clean hands and a pure heart." For it is possible for many men to ascend the mountain of the Lord; the difficulty is to remain, or to stand, there. After all, remaining in the holy place is not simply a matter of inertia, of staying put; it is a dynamic art, requiring constant effort. And the most significant factor in the formation of the dullness of heart is a certain self-satisfaction. This is the pitfall of almost all decent and pious men. A wholly wicked person will hardly suffer the temptation, and a partially wicked one, full of self-doubt, will also be free of it. It is the sin of the sinless, the snare of those who do no evil in thought or deed. Thus, it becomes most urgent for the righteous man to berate himself, and in anger and indignation call himself "such-and-such, a good for nothing." Anger is important—to be exasperated with the animal-soul and its temptations, despising it and railing at it. A kind of slap in the face to shock oneself into wakefulness.

This numbness or dullness of the soul can be considered a state of separation from the Divine light. But unlike the concealment of God in the act of creating the world, this is a matter of man hiding from himself. He does not want to see, as though he were under the hypnotic spell of his own self-suggested repudiation of the Divine presence. He sees only the things of the world. Indeed, one may say that at most of the levels of his existence, man is a sort of amphibious creature, living in two worlds: that of matter and the senses and that of the spirit. And the concept of spirit, here, is not necessarily that which is highest, but simply that which is not material, that which is the source of the nobler expressions of love and hate, honor and humiliation.

But the animal-soul in us constructs a whole system of reality made up of material things only. And we tend to give this so much significance that we may be said to be blind to all else. In short, the power of the animal-soul is such that a person does not want to see the spiritual truth of himself and feels himself unable to experience that kind of joy. Therefore, says the Baal HaTanya, it is necessary to use drastic measures, such as indignation and verbal violence, on oneself, in order to be reminded that God is present. He is here, as it is written: "I, the Lord, do not change!" (Malachi 3:6).

For the Holy One, blessed be He, existed before Creation and He continues to exist, unchanged, in the hereafter and forever. This brings to mind the explanation offered by the Tzemach Tzedek to the philosophical problem of faith. There is a mitzvah to believe in God, he says, but it may be defined as an injunction to believe that the "Lord is God"—that the transcendental and the immanent are of the same essence. This is the gist of the mitzvah, or the commandment, to believe. The recognition of the reality of a higher power, a creator and omniscient presence, is not a matter of faith; it is more a matter of a point of view. It belongs to the field of one's vision—the Torah does not obligate one to believe in the soul; one feels it instinctively, and there is no need for specific instruction.

Similarly, "I am the Lord, your God" is not a commandment to believe in the reality of a Creator of the world; it is a commandment to believe in the special connection between the ungraspable essence of "I am that I am" (Exodus 3:14), which is beyond all reality, and "your God who brought you out of the land of Egypt" (Exodus 20:2), which is the active and the activating power within the world. The latter is a matter of faith; the first is not. If, however, a person allows a barrier to form in his soul, in reaction to the temptations of the animal-soul, or the evil impulse, then he will be like "a scoundrel, who said in his heart 'There is no God . . .'" (Psalms 53:1) to prepare the way for evildoing. Indeed, the knowledge that God exists can be very disturbing to anyone who is bent on acting as he pleases. Therefore, the animal-soul will clearly do away with God to begin with—faith is turned into a jest and the clever intellectual becomes blind to the basic sense of a higher reality, which is common to all men, even the most primitive.

The fact is that the elemental sense of the Divine is not a matter of mystical realization or any kind of emotional or cerebral experience—it is the simplest, most fundamental perception granted to all human beings, a certainty that there is a Creator, or some sort of greater reality, responsible for the world. It is a recognition of the obvious, not an extraordinary vision of the hidden. This brings to mind the story of Sammy Groneman who, after a lifetime of Zionist activities in Germany, came to the Land of Israel in 1929 to tour the country and, in his farewell speech in Tel Aviv, said, "Gentlemen, I must make the shattering admission that all the lies that I've been telling for thirty years are true."

In other words, there are many God-fearing Jews who, at a certain point in their lives, have to experience the simple confrontation with Truth. Beyond the theoretical knowledge, to see beyond the picture or image of what exists, to understand for the first time, the living reality itself. After all, it is all different. Like the Kabbalistic answer, given by Rabbi Tzvi Hirsch of Ziditzov to the question "What did Chasidim bring into the world?" He said, "Let us imagine someone returning from a long journey to a distant land and telling us that he saw a bird with a human face and the legs of a horse. Afterwards, someone else goes to the land and, upon returning, says that, indeed, he saw the creature; but it didn't have the face of a human, although there was a certain resemblance; and the legs were, in the abstract, like those of a horse, even if not at all identical. Hearing this, there were more people prepared to believe the story. But there still remained many skeptics. Whereupon, a third person made the same journey and brought the very bird back with him. This, of course, was decisive. So, too, there are three levels of insight into the mystery of God. First, there was the level exemplified by Rabbi Shimon bar Yochai, who came and told us about the Divine presence in the Zohar, which is full of such fantastic tales, strange configurations, images, and countenances that one could hardly believe him. Then, after a number of generations, came the level exemplified by the Ari; and his pupils wrote down the evidence he conveyed with all its greater attention to detail. Finally, the Baal Shem Tov came, and he exemplified the third level and brought the reality of the Holy One, blessed be He; and it was no picture or abstraction of Divinity, but an actuality, and all that was required was that one should look at it and see it for what it was."

Why then is it necessary to shout and grow indignant at the extraneous thought in order to drive it away? Why does one have to struggle so hard to maintain the Divine presence? The answer hinges on the very nature of the Sitra Achra, on the questionable character of the power of evil. For the fact is that the Sitra Achra, the other side, is like the darkness—it is an absence of light and without any reality of its own. On the other hand, what is that darkness or the emptiness if not the very condition for creation? In order for the events of Genesis to take place, God had to create space for the world, a vacuum empty of Himself, in which the world could be contained. But it was essentially a negative essence, a darkness and a void.

After the creation of the world, this darkness or absence of God subsisted as a parasitic power of evil. It maintained itself by living off the holiness in the creation. It could not possibly retain a hold on existence by itself; there can never be any such thing as a total lie, or a complete shadow—even a little truth or light is enough to give them substantiality. Otherwise, they revert to nothingness.

Evil is, thus, a distortion of holiness, an abuse and a misuse of the sacredness of the real. It creates an image for itself, a reflection of the world in its own image, in which falsehood and the nothingness take vitality and being from the sanctity of that which is genuine. Like certain viruses or parasitic cells that have no more than a genetic code and can only live off something else. All that these parasitic creatures possess is the capacity to distort things in a certain way; they have no independent existence. Evil is, thus, parasitic by its very nature; unable to survive by itself, it has to be nurtured by something alive and capable of taking form. This nurturing, however, is suicidal because it tends to kill the life source upon which it draws. Hence, evil does not really wage war against good; it is actually interested in the survival of good, for its own sake. Just as light need not flee the darkness, since a little light can easily make a great darkness retreat. Why then do we have to fight the darkness, why the struggle against falsehood and evil? Why cannot the Divine Soul simply take total possession of a person?

The answer given is that the evil in a man is compounded of many factors; it is not at all a simple opposite of the good. The ambience of its vitality stems from the fact that it draws upon

the holiness in life, using it, as we have said, for its own
purposes. Man seems to have been granted an almost infinite
capacity for both good and evil as a result of the free will
inherent in having been created as what he is—a creature able
to awaken to the consciousness of God.

The capacity to rise up against the Divine is, however, as
ephemeral as the darkness which retreats before the light. As
has been said often enough, there is a certain inner logic to the
situation. For instance, there is the commandment to Israel to
"wipe out all trace of Amalek" (symbol of unregenerate evil)
and, on the other hand, the Holy One, Blessed be He,
promises, "I shall wipe out all trace of Amalek." Now both of
these are connected in the sense that you, man, have to do
what you can to battle against Amalek so that I, God, shall be
able to complete the task and demolish the very memory of
Amalek.

In short, the relationship between good and evil and the
struggle within man are dependent, as it were, on the continuous existence of God, Who allows things to happen and
permits the anomaly called evil to flourish. For evil is what God
uses as an instrument to raise man up to Him. As it is written
in the *Sefer Yetzirah*: "Good distinguishes the evil and evil
distinguishes the good." The greatness of man stems from this
struggle between good and evil; this is why God has to build
the anomaly of evil, making it possible for it to exist and
flourish and then, when it has performed its function, making
it null and void. After one has defeated the evil impulse, it
ceases to have any meaning. Thus, the ceaseless war that man
wages can be interpreted as a challenge for him to do all that he
can while God is working against him at the other end. And
then as soon as man proves that he is able to stand the test, it
all collapses and has no more significance, and something else
starts up all over again.

There is a story in the Zohar of the king who wished to test
the virtue of his son and thus sent a whore to tempt him. Her
task is rather ambiguous, if not actually frustrating, for her
success might be, in reality, failure for all concerned; and yet
the test has to be a real trial; it cannot be make-believe.
Therefore, she hires another whore who, not understanding

the meaning of the test, tempts him wholeheartedly. From which, it may be gathered, the actual essence of evil is complex—the lower levels of evil do not even know that their function is only to serve as a temptation; they enter the contest in all enthusiasm, even though their whole function will collapse as soon as man succeeds in standing up to the test. It is as though God says to evil: "Very well, it is all over; the tempter may go home." Man, however, cannot do this; it is God's task. Man's task is to stand up to the trial.

From this, we may conclude that as soon as the light of the Divine is directed toward the Sitra Achra, the evil evaporates, and there is no actual struggle. The struggle takes place only when there is no real confrontation, only when it is all a show. So that when a person shouts in sincere anger at the animal-soul, whenever there is a genuine confrontation, victory is easy.

As an illustration, consider the biblical incident of the spies sent by Moses to search out the Land of Canaan. They return full of defeatist information about giant inhabitants and their prowess, saying, "We are not able to go up against these people, for they are stronger than we" (Numbers 13:31). By implying that the giants are stronger than God, these words are heresy, for they suggest that evil is undefeatable. What does Moses do? Not as on other occasions, when he performs miracles, evokes signs, or activates some sort of convincing omen; he now simply gets angry and tells them that they are not worthy of entering the Promised Land, that they shall remain in the desert for forty years and die in it, and that only their sons, a generation of greater courage and faith, will be able to conquer the land. Whereupon the Children of Israel, instead of crying out in dismay that they want to go back to Egypt, or that they want to change their leader for someone more congenial, call out: "We are here and we shall go up" (Numbers 15:40). This proves that Israel is essentially a people of faith; it is only when the Sitra Achra gets into the picture that poverty of spirit and crudity of taste prevail.

So too, all the blasphemers, manipulators, and unbelievers have to be shouted at and put in their right place: "You are small-minded and low; you have no real desire for the Promised Land—therefore, you shall die here."

From this, we conclude that neither the force nor the arguments of evil can stand up to the action of the light; they have to descend and sink into the crudity of the Sitra Achra, a crudity expressed as doubt. Doubt strips one of the power to act and think meaningfully by making one wonder whether a thing is true or not, by making one believe that one has no inclination for anything or certainty about anything. Indeed, doubt is always present. One may take even the most familiar word or fact, and by repeating it over and over, there enters an element of doubt, an uncertainty about its form and content. And everyone is acquainted with the sudden loss of assurance about a date, a person's name, a place, or anything well known. One becomes vexed about forgetting and wonders whether one ever knew it properly; it seems to be so unlikely that clarity can become obscurity so easily. It is impossible to deal with it rationally, of course. Something has moved from its right place; it is a matter of the Sitra Achra rising up and causing a distortion, a misplacement.

The people of Israel, however, have the capacity for faith and can thrust aside this doubt, and they have no need for discussion or convincing argument. Doubt is a sickness of sorts, an invasion of the nonbeing trying to gain some life-force from the innate certainty in a man.

Just as it happens sometimes that, without any reason, there is a change in one's relations with another person. Depression follows; there is a tendency to withdraw from the other, to dread confirmation of one's fears about his aloofness, and there is less and less chance of bridging the gap. Doubt has a subtle way of injuring the most profound of relations. It is a definite process even if it is beyond examination; what is worse, it is capable of producing wild fantasies that can continue to flourish on their own. There is no need for these wild growths to have any truth or wisdom; the process is known as the dullness of the heart—a wall between man and man, a wall between man and God, that keeps getting higher and eventually cannot be crossed. Thus, as the Baal HaTanya says, it has to be smashed.

30

Critical Insight into Oneself

Asn has often been repeated,
it is good for a person to be humble before all men. Even if one
is an upright Jew who does all that he is obligated to do and
more, he should humble himself before others, even before the
poorer in spirit and even before evildoers. But how can this be
achieved when even humbling oneself before those who are
greater is often as much as one can do? The answer is that it is
not possible objectively to compare men in terms of their
transgressions, because this is not the correct gauge of worth;
one should compare them on the basis of the degree of effort
required to overcome temptation. What for one person is a
terrible temptation, on account of his personality or history, is
for another of no import whatsoever. For a gambler, playing
cards has a different weight than for someone who has never
played. Thus, it is always easier to tell someone else to
overcome a wrong impulse. The question is whether I myself
can do as much even if I am a very righteous person. And it is
not necessarily a matter of correcting conspicuously appalling
sin, but rather of the ordinary virtuous man's capacity to flee
from the passionate urges of his own heart, to avoid the evils of

slander and other such seemingly trivial modes of behavior like thoughtless speech or careless dealing in money transactions.

All of this concerns the need to avoid transgression. But there is also the matter of sanctifying oneself. To conduct oneself properly in matters that are permitted is still fairly straightforward. To do so with a degree of holiness is another matter. One can be a scoundrel even within the bounds of the legally permitted in Torah, as the medieval sage, the Ramban, said. It is a matter of how one eats and drinks, how one goes about one's affairs, even in the most intimate of life's details — where, in fact, the temptations are the greatest and the failures most common. The struggles here, as the sages have frequently noted, are real battles of life, and the need to be careful and circumspect cannot be overstated. There are transgressions that are so instrinsically habitual that they are no longer considered sinful. The repetition makes them commonplace and acceptable. What is shockingly bad the first time is no longer even perceived the tenth or twentieth time.

This is as true for the scholarly Talmid Chacham as for anyone else. His very superiority, his knowledge of Torah makes it all the more urgent for him to be more aware of the Divine presence at all times. His life, as a whole, is an attempt to approach God; hence even the smallest trangression may be more than he can bear, and his guilt is all the greater.

How vastly different is this case from the person who is free to roam the streets of the world unencumbered by Torah, where everything is allowed and even given to him as a gift. When one demands that such a person must exercise control over his thoughts and actions, to fear God and respect the Divine glory, one is asking far more of him than of the righteous. He has to struggle much harder against himself and against all the habitual ways of his being. Therefore, too, the degree of guilt varies from one person to another, and the atonement required of each, even for the same sin, is proportional to one's level of knowledge and awareness. The guilt of one who knows Torah and who has ascended to spiritual heights is far greater than that of the one who is ignorant.

Therefore, he who is satisfied with himself, smug in his

proper performance of mitzvot and the correctness of his life, may be somewhat perturbed by the injunction to be humble before all men, irrespective of who they are. He has to compare himself in subjective terms: Does he, indeed, struggle with himself to the same degree he requires of the most casual delinquent? Can he put himself in the other's place and overcome the same temptations?

There is the story of the Tzadik who, after passing through a forest, said that he was amazed at the awe and fear of God he had seen displayed by some nameless person there. An uncouth and unlearned youth had been standing among the trees, shouting at his father: "Were I not afraid of God I would smash your head with my ax!" This indicated, said the Tzadik, that the youth had overcome a powerful urge to kill his father and had done so because of a genuine fear of God. "Such a victory," said the Tzadik, "is more than I can claim for myself, never having struggled with such a terrible passion; and I am humbled by it—not at all sure whether, I, or those around me, would be able to make the same sacrifice."

Mention has already been made of the ways of breaking the outer ego of the self, a need that is quite fundamental in the process of Tikun, or correction. For the self is like a big log that cannot readily catch fire; it has to be chopped up and broken into inflammable pieces. The ego cannot be consumed by the fire of God's mercy unless it is first shattered and subdued. It is in this way that a person can be humble before all men— when he compares his own struggle against temptation with others' and defines his soul—reckoning in terms of what he should have done. Then, instead of blaming others, he can begin to envy their capacity to overcome the evil impulse, and the question becomes: "Where do I myself stand in the great struggle against the trivial?"

In this manner, those very thoughts that cause dejection and heartbreak may also be the instrument for a revival and renewal of the person; although they are essentially sad thoughts and, therefore, reprehensible, they have a place in the Klipat Nogah and can serve the purposes of the holy in its struggle against darkness and the evil impulse. Indeed, in every sadness, there is also something of the permitted. The contrite heart, with its apartness from the Divine and the vestiges of its involvement with the Sitra Achra, invites a sadness that has more than one aspect to it.

Obviously, it does not lead directly to joy and openness to God, but it may be a stage that provides the force and energy for change. The kind of sadness, which is melancholy, makes a person withdraw from activity and has its own kind of satisfaction and pleasure. But bitterness of heart is another sort of sadness; it is accompanied by a certain passion, by a repressed anger against oneself and by an inability to linger in this state. It exerts an urgent pressure for change and may cause an awakening of the soul. When it is so oriented, bitterness can be considered a vehicle of Gevurah, the holy Sefirah of severity and judgment. It is then a vital and energizing state of being, for all its inherent disagreeableness. To be sure, for the person suffering from bitterness of heart, it is not at all easy. Nevertheless, it belongs, together with the grace of Chesed, to the essence of the soul. In life it may sometimes be necessary to awaken one or another of the Sefirot in order to accomplish an urgent spiritual task.

True, there isn't much choice; but naturally, one may be rather reluctant to get involved with the severe side of Gevurah, tending as it does to set firm limits on one's spontaneous conduct and to open the door to matters we prefer to ignore. Nevertheless, we may have to call on Gevurah, the power of severity in one's own soul, in order to lighten the severe judgment of Divine providence. That is to say, we need our own bitterness of heart to sweeten the bitter dispensation due to us from our animal-soul and the evil impulse. Tikun, or spiritual correction, is a matter of lightening or sweetening the judgment, rather than uprooting or displacing it. The latter— the uprooting of the animal-soul—can only be accomplished by other forces, while sweetening is the action of something higher and better exerted on the soul, thereby affecting a certain change of quality, a kind of cooking process, converting the impalatable into something edible. On the other hand, there is no other way of tearing out the evil except by relating to the fundamental substance of change, the root of the condemning sentence, which is Judgment, or Divine Truth in action. Therefore, since only the Sefirah of Gevurah has the power to deal with Divine Judgment, or Divine Truth in action, the Sages have said that a person should always let his good impulse be angry at his bad impulse.

This may sound strange; but the meaning is that, even though bitterness and anger are not to be sought after or even to be considered a desirable way of progress, nevertheless, whenever a person feels smugness stealing up his soul, and whenever his heart grows dull with self-satisfaction, he should let his good impulse be angry with him and invite bitterness and self-denunciation.

The time to do this varies, of course, but it is best to do it when one is in a sad frame of feeling anyway, for whatever reason, or even for no reason at all, as in the natural rhythm of things. It may be a good opportunity then to transform the feeling into bitterness. Not necessarily to get oneself entangled with negativism and denial, which only serve to pull a person down, but, on the contrary, to convert the sadness into a rebelliousness which compels one to give an account of oneself, a straightforward and honest account before a higher tribunal. One forces the smugness to admit its parasitic existence, and one's life is contrasted with what it should be. At this point, of course, the melancholy sadness itself is banished, because melancholy is usually the expression of some sort of subjective conviction that one has been abandoned or insulted or injured by others. If one is fully aware of what one is dejected about, capable of analyzing one's sadness, one can more easily slide into genuine bitterness of heart, with its painful insights into one's own faults, weaknesses, and omissions.

The ache of self-revelation may well turn into real happiness, however. It is a process that stems from the fact that one is making a reckoning with God. He, Divine Reality, may still be far from one, and one does not have to probe deeply to detect this; but there is no need to justify one's faults any more, and being alone with one's whole existence, with both the inner self and the outer self, provides a recognition of naked truth about the body and about the fact that there is something in one which is a spark of the soul of God. The soul, or at least the unmistakable indications of its existence in oneself, is then seen as having been expelled from consciousness. A life spent in idleness and gloom is really a state of exile from God. The soul has been dragged along after the body into exile, and one's whole desire then becomes to raise it up and restore it to the Father, to redeem the Divine element and free it. The soul is seen as the true daughter of God, the one who has been taken captive; and in order to restore the soul's freedom, one has to concentrate on precise action as defined by the mitzvot. The totality of one's thought and action has to strive toward this one purpose. It may even be necessary to pray and cry out to God in one's agony of exile and confinement in the body. The idea is to seek joyful repentance and good deeds, modes of restoration of the soul, rather than the grievous confession of specific sin or transgression.

How much more so is this applicable to the Benoni, the conscious man who does not have to struggle with the things that trouble ordinary men, whose chief aspiration is the restoration of the Divine Soul imprisoned in the body. This is repentance in a higher sense, accomplished by a life of Torah and good deeds; and it is done with great joy, the joy of the soul gradually being liberated and restored to Divine holiness. To devote all of one's life to this kind of repentance is, thus, not necessarily a way only for the sinful, and it does not have to be connected with any specific transgression. The Jew who is called upon to do it is simply returning to God and striving to approach ever closer to Him, which is the highest happiness.

31

Liberation of the Self

The method by which bitterness of soul can serve to break the resistance of a person and bring about a renewal is by penetrating the dense covering and dissolving the fat around the heart. When the person is thus subjected to humiliating self-criticism he may then awaken to the feeling that there is something important to be done. He will realize that, in his body, he is beyond correction, but that he is somehow responsible for the Divine Soul; and if he can learn to pray and give himself to holiness—in thought and intention at least—the Divine Soul could be liberated and begin to approach the Divine light. The body may well remain unaltered by this; and the part of the soul that is bound to the physical also may not change, being what it is, namely, an animal-soul, which cannot become holy. Even the conscious criticism of the Benoni cannot have a profound effect on it. In fact, the efforts of the Benoni are not intended to criticize the animal-soul for being what it is, but to reproach it for continuing to sin, for being unaware of itself even after all the attempts to influence it.

Nevertheless, this should not be a cause for despair. In spite of the downward pull of the body, the soul has to find ways of being happy, to feel a permanent joy beyond the capacities of the physical. Why does one have to identify oneself with the animal-soul? Why suffer its sorrows and be dependent on its simple pleasures when one can rise with the Divine Soul to heights of holiness and blissful oneness with God?

Spiritual joy is of the nature of the Exodus from Egypt—it has been said that the Exodus represents the emergence of the self from the narrow place of restriction, the breaking out from the gloomy darkness into joy. It is not a matter of ignoring the existence of evil that surrounds and is within one, but rather of using the evil and transforming it in the process of living.

Think not that this is the essential purpose of life; in the endeavor to build up one's own soul, there may not be ample opportunity to stop and repair all the evil one meets on the way. The important thing is to provide the Divine Soul both with powers of adaptation to deal with these forces and with the light needed to make its way. In this respect, too, the process is in the nature of an "exodus"—full of questions and doubts. Why did the Children of Israel have to wait for Pharaoh's permission, even if he was forced to grant it? Why could they not have just gone forth with head held high, under the glory and power of God, instead of relying on all sorts of stratagems—such as requesting to go for a period of ceremonial worship? The point is that the evil in the soul of the Children of Israel was still active in the left chamber of the heart, and its force continued to be felt until the giving of the Torah. Only then, when they were standing before God at Sinai, did the evil in the soul of Israel cease to have any effect.

For the state of slavery in Egypt is not only a banishment from the Holy Land; it is also a matter of participating in the "defilement of Egypt," which is said to be equivalent to the abomination of the earth. To get out of this state of defilement and to cleave to the holiness of God was, therefore, in the nature of a flight, of running away, not only from Pharaoh, but also from one's own uncleanness. There was no thought of solving the problem in its entirety. Thus, too, when the soul is struggling against the body, it usually has no time to answer all the questions of the self; all it wants to do is escape, as well it may, to the saving hands of God. Hence too, in the future, when the spirit of God will begin to sweep away all the defilement of the earth, there won't be opportunity to do much else but make one's escape. The difference is that in that future, there will no longer be any need to hasten; one will be able to walk. Because the Exodus from Egypt was also an exodus from some inner servitude—which cannot be done at leisure (the Torah relates many occasions when the people complained that the journey was too much for them and they wanted to go back). Whereas in the future redemption, it will be possible to walk to Divine holiness with the feeling of wholeness and with the happiness that follows the sadness of despair.

True, the person who reaches this spiritual joy following dejection knows that he has not achieved a high level of holiness and that he is hardly able to be a messenger of God. Nevertheless, he does feel that he has a great task in the world, that it is a matter of expressing joy and overcoming the sadness of the body, of being a penitent in the deep sense of one who "returns." This means an ever increasing amplification of the great joy by embracing the elements of knowledge and understanding. The purpose is to sharpen intellectual comprehension, after having made a thorough reckoning of one's life, in order to be able to see the shallowness or disinterestedness of one's previous efforts.

For one remains connected to the body; one can even be in a situation wherein a slice of bread is more real that Divine holiness, where only by very substantial effort can something in oneself be changed. Questions may well be asked: Why did God make a person like this? Why did He create the world this way—clothing the light of one's Divine Soul in the "skin of the serpent" and in a "fetid drop" like the body. For the human body is flesh, like all animal flesh, and, in addition, it has the animal-soul, which is like having the human body in the serpent's skin.

The answer is that God introduced the Divine Soul into the physical body in order to lift it up. It was not a descent of punishment; it was a descending for the sake of ascending and raising up, in order to make the elevation an achievement. Every human soul has its source in the Klipat Nogah, the Shell of Light; and its garments, thought, speech, and action, are expressly given to it in order to enable it to ascend through a life of dedication to Torah. In this manner, not only does the Divine Soul achieve its purpose in this world, but also the animal-soul manages to make the proper connection and relate to the Divine light directly. Just as the miner is lowered into the depth of the earth to bring up the valuable ore, so too is the Divine Soul lowered into the body and its darkness to seek out the precious stones and minerals in the animal being; it is not sent to undergo suffering or to bear up under some terrible burden. Also, the Divine Soul does not have to think of the final worth of its efforts; it has only to release the lights from the animal-soul and to bring them up. This may well be the purpose of the Creation altogether.

Therefore, the result of one's performance of a mitzvah is of no consequence; it is the moment of the mitzvah itself which is the victory. It is the moment in which the King is presented with sparks of holiness from below, and it contains the whole of one's own significance on earth.

A person should see himself as part of a caravan that is climbing a high mountain; his body and soul are on call, ready to do whatever is needed. When one is busy with one's hands, one is doing God's actions; when thinking or feeling, one is occupied with God's thoughts; when speaking one is uttering His words. Such a life is called "soul restoring" in that Torah brings the soul back to its source. As it is said: "The precepts of the Lord are right, rejoicing the heart . . ." (Psalms 19:9). Their capacity to make the heart rejoice come from the fact that, no matter who the person is, whatever his level, when he does the will of God, he knows that he is redeeming the world and redeeming his soul. The sanctified deed extends in unknowable ways far beyond the confines of the action. In such a life, a person forgets the personal accounts of his own self and becomes absorbed in the task of Divine work.

Accordingly, the next stage, following sadness and bitterness of heart, has three distinct phases. The first phase is that in which a person realizes that he is not moving anymore, that he is no longer able to get excited about anything or even to relate to holiness. At this point, in the second phase, he has no choice but to break himself into pieces, to shatter the egocentrism of his feelings and of his secret self-satisfaction. After this, in the third phase, it is possible to give an accounting of his life by probing into himself and comparing himself with others—not only in terms of outer achievement, but also in terms of the inner effort made to do what he is capable of doing. Then, one is able to experience the joy of release from self and the happiness of raising up holy sparks.

32

Love and Hate of One's Fellow

It has been explained that, for Jews, the love of one's people (Ahavat Yisrael) is not only a commandment concerning the social group, but it is an indication of the way a person stands in relation to God. As long as a person identifies himself with his body and concentrates all his attention on a particular "I" in time and space, he can never really love another person; he can only love himself because the "I" is the focus of his whole being. By way of contrast, when the soul is seen as the mainspring of one's being and as the meaning of life, there is no limit to the possibility of love. Because no two bodies can ever become one; at best, they can make good use of each other. Two souls, however, which strive together toward the primal root of things, come closer and closer; and if they continue on an ever higher plane, they can grow into a genuine unity.

Therefore, the concept of Ahavat Yisrael, the love of one's fellow Jew, points to the love of God. One does not attain it by remaining in the material body and feeling all sorts of sentiments about one's brethren; it is attained by striving for, and ultimately reaching, that level of being in which one sees oneself as a soul. Consistent with this point of view, a rather

211

extreme notion of Israel as a physical-spiritual collective body has developed over the centuries. It is something so sensitively organic in its unity that any separation of one of its smallest limbs or parts was seen to inflict a serious injury on the whole, which was the Shechinah, the Divine indwelling. A common expression of this is reflected in the words of the blessing: "Bless us all, our Father, as one, with the light of Thy countenance." When we are all one, then we can receive the light of "Thy countenance." When we are not one, the Shechinah is not in its right place, and Israel is in a state of deprivation and suffering.

Consider the Talmudic statement that one who sees his friend sinning should hate him; one may add that there are also injunctions against hate in the Scriptures: "Thou shalt not hate thy brother in thy heart." Nevertheless, it is true that, in certain circumstances, it is a mitzvah to hate an evildoer, even to the point of informing on him to his teacher. Again, the dilemma arises: According to the Halachah (legal code), any such testimony concerning a person and his sinful actions would be libel or speaking evil. The popular story goes: "Tuvia sinned and Zigud was beaten." Zigud, the moralist, caught Tuvia committing some transgression, and he promptly brought him before the court. There he was told that one witness was not enough to incriminate a fellow Jew; and all he had done, therefore, was to slander the good Tuvia, for which Zigud deserved to be beaten. And he was. Only in exceptional cases is it permissible to publicly assert that someone has trespassed—and that does not mean in a court room—but before the teacher of the one concerned. Indeed, the whole problem of giving testimony against someone is a very delicate matter, and the sages have always had many reservations about it. This does not alter the point being made here, namely, that in exceptional circumstances it is right to hate an evildoer.

Can one hate someone whose way of life is very similar to one's own, someone living according to the same basic principles of Torah and mitzvot? In fact, one should despise such a transgressor even more. The more learned the sinner, the more deserving of our reproach. Whereas, if the sinner is ignorant and unlearned, if he does not know the meaning of his wrong action, and if it is all the same to him, we may be equally repelled by his actions; but it is forbidden to hate him. Like other matters of this nature, the question has been discussed at length by the sages: To what extent should permissiveness be extended towards those who do not know they are transgressing the law? How lenient can one be with someone who uses his ignorance as a general license to do as he likes? And what about those who feel that they have a general authorization to transgress because "they are not religious"? Is it not the same sort of excuse a thief will fall back on: "It's my occupation—I'm a thief—am I not?" The fact that this occupation involves stealing is of secondary importance; the important thing is not to get caught. In such instances, the Halachic point of view is quite straightforward and strict. But in human terms, we have a different attitude toward someone who understands the meaning of his actions and still rebels against the Divine as compared to someone who does not know what he is doing.

Someone who is not learned in Torah and mitzvot and does not consider himself a part of the religious framework transgresses in a different way, with another attitude toward the whole concept of sin; thus, it is forbidden to hate him. However, if he is your friend, and especially if he is learned in Torah, you should at least rebuke him. Furthermore, you should not sin against him (by hating him), except if he continues to sin in spite of being rebuked. One's brother—who is anyone of the House of Israel—is not to be hated even in the heart; but one's friend, with whom there is a greater intimacy, is to be severely rebuked and even hated if he persists in sinfulness. The words of the commandment do not specify to love mankind or even Israel, but to love people. This is a very general term, but it is not meant as a subterfuge to avoid relating to specific persons. On the contrary, "people" includes all sorts of individuals, even those whom one would not choose to love of one's own free will. As it is said in the Talmud: "Love peace and pursue peace, love people and bring them close to the Torah." The order of performance is not to bring people close to Torah and then to love them, but the other way around; loving peace and loving people—if you succeed—will help you bring people close to Torah. And if you don't succeed, at least you have kept the percept of love; and that is enough—because this love should not be dependent upon anything else—even coming close to Torah. To love people is a clear, unequivocal commandment with no reservations. This brings us once again to the opposite injunction, that is, to hate those whose actions are not of a certain spiritual level, whose transgressions have continued beyond our love and our rebuke. To be sure, this does not mean there is an end to our duty to love them. The question is: How is it possible to hate and to love at the same time? The answer is: The mitzvah to hate can never be a matter of personal malevolence. Like all mitzvot, it has to be performed out of a sense of awe, a fear of Heaven.

The essential problem, however, is one of relationship. On the one hand, it is forbidden for me to judge my fellowman. It is not for me to decide whether he is innocent or guilty. That may sometimes be the task of a court, within the limits of a specific charge and along the lines drawn by Torah or the law. But as it is written in the Halachah, once a person has received his punishment, he is again a Tzadik, a pure soul, as far as I or any other man of Israel is concerned. Indeed, all these calculations—who is a saint and who is a sinner—all belong to God. Only He can make them. As the Rambam said: A person who is bad is inscribed for death; and if we observe that all sorts of people go merrily on their way, it is because we don't know how to make the reckoning. We may calculate according to our reason, but God makes His reckoning according to the truth of the Divine attributes. In other words, we cannot possibly ever make any final judgments about anyone. And if, in keeping with the mitzvah to hate the evildoer who has been rebuked and yet persists in his sinfulness, one does repudiate some action; it is not a judgment passed against him, damning him to Hell and purgatory. It is sometimes part of the need to hate and to love at the same time.

The fact is, every person is something of a duality. Every person has two souls, the animal-soul and the Divine Soul; and one cannot hate the Divine Soul of any man, since it is a part of God. Because of the complex nature of the relationships within a family, our feelings are often ambivalent. We harbor all kinds of resentments and display warm affections for the same

person. One can entertain a thorough dislike of certain personality traits and, at the same time, be in love with that person's
essence. It is not only a simple matter of distinguishing things
that are likable or repellent. Nor is it a matter of having to love,
in spite of everything else, as in the relationship between
parents and children. The truth is that love and hate do not
necessarily cancel each other out. They can continue to exist
side by side on the same plane. In certain Chabad texts, it is
asked: How is it possible to carry out the mitzvah "Thou shalt
love they neighbor as thyself" if the other person is an evildoer
and a sinner? How can one bring oneself to love anyone with
whom there is no natural affinity? The answer given is connected with the words "as thyself." Just as one knows one's
own faults and sins better than one knows those of others, one
does not hate oneself; so it is necessary to relate to another.
Even when a person hates himself, he continues to love himself
also. As it is written: "Love will cover all your transgressions."
Of course, love does not really do more to the transgressions
than put some sort of veil over them to keep them from being
seen. They cannot usually be made to disappear. Nevertheless,
one's evaluation of the same facts can be altered. Just as one
tends to gloss over one's own transgressions, so one should try
to confute the negative reaction to someone else's transgressions, thereby seeing the other as one sees oneself. The
double-mindedness here is not a matter of hypocritically
closing one's eyes to sin, but rather, seeing it from a different
angle—as though it were I who did it and not someone else.

There are many Chasidic stories that are variations on this
theme. An interesting one is about Rabbi Levi Yitzchak of
Berdichev, who was a great champion of the common people,
a lover of Israel. One morning, looking out of his window, he
saw a poor Jew, a teamster, driving his horses and wagon
through the muddy part of the road. The driver was pulling
hard on the reins and, at the same time, with phylacteries on
arm and forehead, he was reciting his morning prayers. "Lord
of the Universe," exclaimed Rabbi Levi Yitzchak, "see how
devout your people are; even while driving their wagons
through the mud of the world, they find it possible to pray to
you!" To another onlooker, this irreverent mode of prayer

would probably have met with strong disapprobation; and
Rabbi Levi Yitzchak himself would scarcely have considered
reciting his prayers while doing something else, much less
driving horses. He was, nevertheless, able to put himself in the
other man's place, to transfer his point of view entirely to that
of another person, another way of life.

This may, therefore, be considered a supplement to the
commandment: "Thou shalt not hate thy brother in thy heart."
Besides personal resentment, there is another more subtle
hatred of the heart, and that is the intolerance of another set of
standards. One frequently cannot stand the actions of someone
who behaves according to a set of values different from one's
own. This, too, is forbidden, for a person is to be measured by
his own heart and not by another's. All of this comes back to
the play of love and hate within the same person. In terms of
the Sefirot of the Kabbalah, love is Chesed, hate (and justice) is
Gevurah, and the resolution of the two is Tiferet (Harmony and
Beauty). Tiferet is also known as Rachamim (Compassion and
Mercy). Thus, when one loves someone because of some
essential affinity, one can also hate him because of his evil
actions and still can have compassion on him because of the
desperate straits he is in. The compassion thus destroys hatred
and awakens love. It is known that any real feeling of compassion or pity will stir up positive emotions. This becomes the
shade of difference between Gevurah and Tiferet, Justice and
Mercy. Compassion, or Mercy, accepts the facts of another
person's actions without passing judgment. Similarly, what is
the difference between Love and Compassion (Chesed and
Tiferet)? In love, the shortcomings of the beloved are usually
overlooked. What is more, the inner impulse of love, or grace,
as it is more precisely called, is a total giving of oneself and of
all one has without considering what the loved one needs. It
gives out of the very fullness of itself, without stint or measure.
The relationship between Compassion and Beauty (Rachamim
and Tiferet) is far more complex and necessarily includes right
judgment and right measure.

When one has compassion or pity for someone, one is
usually aware of his shortcomings as well. It is even maintained
that the more one is aware of the faults of the person for whom

one has compassion, the more intense the emotion. Thus, instead of causing repulsion, this compassion can augment the attraction and cancel out the hate. In other words, if one has pity, it is almost impossible to hate; and it is very likely that love will be aroused. In this case, one no longer sees the shortcomings that started the whole process, and love can take root and grow.

It is in this sense that it is said that Jacob redeems Abraham. Jacob corresponds to the Sefirah of Tiferet (Mercy) and Abraham is Chesed (Love). When Abraham is held captive, bound by a situation where love cannot be expressed, the attribute of Tiferet can usually stir the emotions. Whence, with the aid of this merciful compassion, the door is opened for love to enter. As for those rare individuals whom one cannot love under any circumstances, those whose wickedness is unmitigated, uncompromising, and final, one has to find the point of contact. In almost all human beings there is always, at least, one such point of possible contact, of coexistence with other human beings. If it does not exist, or if it is severed, there is little hope of redemption. To be sure, in an absolute sense, no person can be entirely cut off from such hope so long as he has life in him. Afterwards, after death, it is another matter. Nevertheless, when a person deliberately cuts himself off, he puts himself outside the pale. Moreover, there is a definite relationship between the love of righteousness and the hatred of evil.

Even if, at times, it may appear unjust, the more love a person has for the good, the more clear will be his power to distinguish the good, and he will tend more to be repelled by wickedness; and all that is not good will be regarded with dislike, or more intensely, repugnance amounting to hatred. And of course, the opposite is also true; when one does not hate evil—and not necessarily the evil connected with people, but even the evil that seems to be intrinsic to certain things and situations—when one does not hate this very essence of evil, it is a sign that one is not able to love the good either. There seems to be some common denominator that goes beyond our analytic powers.

The question then is not simply the overtly moral one of

being a good person or a bad person, either in action or in thought. Society needs to maintain a network of reliable, impersonal relationships between people, something that is essentially functional. It is like the neutral relation to things for which one does not really care one way or the other. In many aspects of normal social life, it should not make any difference who the other person is; a basic decency is all that is required. Indeed, love becomes an obstacle in formal relations.

The problem becomes acutely apparent when the situation is carried to its extreme, and one's attitude toward people becomes purely and simply functional, an unemotional and even polite correctness. In certain areas of modern life, this has resulted in unspeakable horror—precisely because people have ceased to relate to people as persons and think of them as things. The worst acts of brutality were done, not out of cruelty or hatred, but out of a mechanical neutrality. Often, it was more a result of not caring than a profound antipathy.

Hence, when confronted by a living person, it does not matter whether one loves or hates him—the important thing is that it be a living relationship. Total hate is possible only toward someone whose actions are immensely disturbing and distressing, threatening the very essence of one's own life structure. In such a case, one really cannot help oneself. But the inner meaning of it is that when one loves something intensely, one distinguishes the good with a vividness that leaves no room for doubt.

33

Gladness in the Presence of God

The soul of man has a profound need for an intrinsic joy. To be sure, this hunger for gladness is felt more acutely when a person has fallen into a dark and bitter frame of mind and is feeling a certain alienation from everything. But there are also times—frequent enough—when one simply gets bogged down, when thoughts and actions seem to be clouded over and obscured. Then, too, one feels the need to "purify and illuminate the soul."

The gladness of heart we are here considering is not merely a matter of being in good spirits or healthy contentment. It is, in fact, a state of being that is open to many kinds of illumination. As the Talmud says, a man should not undertake an act of prayer or other mitzvah except with the joy of fulfilling a Divine commandment. Since prayer is largely an expression of feeling, the desirability of getting into an appropriate emotional attitude is understandable. But this is also true for study of Torah, which is primarily an intellectual occupation. For we know from experience that when a person is in a joyous frame of mind, his spiritual capacities are that much more alive and potent. Just as when a person is in a depressed state, or even when he just feels a little gloomy, everything he does tends to be dark, without light.

To an appreciable degree, the light, or the capacity for illumination, can be induced by correct orientation. One of the ways to achieve this "rising to gladness" is to depict to oneself the unity of God. Of course, it is not a relatively easy matter of simply allowing the thought to take form. It requires a certain deliberate amount of thinking about the subject. Theoretically, one can think of anything one chooses, and the thought of the presence of God is never far from the heart's desire; but if one wishes to reach beyond the surface of the mind, a conscious effort has to be made. This effort consists of two parts, which are not really distinctly different. The first is to gain some insight, by concentrated thought, into the actuality of Divine Unity; the second is to hold the intellect in check and not to depict any particular aspect of this insight, but to see it in its totality.

What is required at first is more than ordinary thought; one has to attempt to give the idea substance in terms of the understanding. The difference is that, for most things, some sort of picture or image of what is thought about is sufficient; but, in this particular case, especially since there is no such easily grasped picture possible, we need to aspire to a certain clarity by eliminating wrong images. For instance, there is the image of God being located somewhere in the Heavens above, while I am a part of the earth below. The first idea then is to realize that God permeates all the world, and His glory fills all of existence.

There are two ways of viewing this concept of "His glory filling the earth." One can see it as children do, perhaps, as air filling all space, or as something all pervasive, like space itself. Or else, in penetrating into the philosophical nature of the problem, we touch on a certain Kabbalistic view by which the holy letters of the Torah are not the black designations of writing, but the white space surrounding them. It is like the drawings of certain painters (or the designs of gestalt psychologists), in which image and background change places depending on the viewer's emphasis. The world thus can be seen as an image against God Who is the background, or God can become the image against the background of the world. In either case, God is not to be found in some other world; He is somehow intrinsic to this world, constituting its very existence. Or possibly, the world manifests only the shadow of Divine existence. Like a film projected on a screen: What we see are only the shadows cast by the light thrown against a moving series of negative pictures. Thus, life as a whole can be justifiably called an illusion of passing shadows, which may hold us fascinated, but which has no more genuineness or reality than what we give them. Because "only He exists," and the world is not another reality in addition to Him; it is a shadow, or a small visible fragment of His infinity. God is not elsewhere, in Heaven or in some invisible spiritual realm of being; He is here and everywhere, filling all with that Divine essence which is being.

Thought is another analogy we may use to describe the close relationship between God and the world. On one hand, thoughts may seem to be independent forces, having a strong effect on the individual. On the other hand, they are clearly a product of a specific personality and of various random elements in life. They are an intrinsic part of the person who created them and of the one on whom they have such a decisive impact. Nevertheless, it is also true, as has been mentioned, that the origin of things, the beginning, is the thought, or the word.

To understand this paradox, let us examine the nature of the word before it is conceived even as a thought, when it is still in the nature of potential being. We may use the illustration of the sun and the light that issues from it. The strongest light is that which is closest to the surface of the sun; but it is so intense, so completely absorbed in the sun, that we cannot possibly see it. So, too, is the thought when it issues from God. Only gradually can we distinguish it as something separate.

Therefore, in praying, in trying to approach God with thoughts and words, the essential factor is nullification of self. Especially when one recites the Shema prayer, thoughts should be concentrated on the Divine oneness, not as contrasted to duality or multiplicity, but as His all-inclusive unity, in the sense that nothing else exists.

The thought of the Divine Unity is, therefore, the core of all contemplation. There is the story of the Chasid who, on a journey, stopped at an inn for the night. When he was asked if he desired to eat supper, he replied that he was far too tired and that all he wanted to do was go to bed at once, for he had to rise early. He was shown to his room, and there he briskly went about making his preparations for sleep. Among other things, as was his custom, he recited the bedtime prayers, and, at the right place, he concentrated on the greatness and the oneness of the Creator. In the morning, when the innkeeper came to wake him, he found the Chasid standing, with one foot on the floor, the other on the bed, still immersed in the thought of Divine Unity.

Of course, this contemplation need not be left to the moment before retiring, and it need not be so compelling that one forgets all else. On the other hand, it is not an abstract intellectual exercise. In the endless amplitude of meaning and shades of meaning it possesses for the individual, there is something to sustain every conceivable situation and every moment in life. Indeed, all that we read and study is only food for this one thought. And when it occupies the mind, there is no room for anything else.

In a word, what is being described here is the transformation of a single idea into the basis, not only of a life of contemplation, but of the constant presence of God. God is not a mental or moral entity; His nearness and support do not depend on whether one is good or deserving, or whether one is correctly observing Torah and mitzvot. God is always present, and He is closer than anything else.

The joy that follows from this knowledge is the joy of love that comes automatically with the recitation of the Shema prayer (". . . the Lord is One. And thou shalt love the Lord, thy God, with all thy heart, all thy soul, and all thy might").

To be sure, the nearness of God is not a matter of any measurable distance, just as approaching Him is not an act that is even approximately physical. He is always where I am. The question is whether I am here. To what extent am I conscious of God's presence? For instance, there are a great number of things in us that the mind is not aware of; we have to learn that they exist. For example, we begin to notice the heart only if it gives us trouble, and this in spite of the fact that it is quite noisy and physiologically involved with everything we do. Indeed, there doesn't seem to be any relation between the objective reality of anything—its vital necessity or even its nearness—to the fact of our being conscious of it. On the contrary, there seems to be a curious paradox about it all; what is close, so intimate as to be inseparable, often requires a greater amount of training and effort in order to get to know it.

In another context, it was said that of all the pleasures in the world, the greatest is the simple joy of living. But when does a person feel it? In rare moments—usually after emerging from a crisis—such as receiving a pardon from a death sentence or recuperating from a severe illness. As for the presence of God— it is closer to one's being than the joy of living, closer than the beating of one's heart. Because when one is conscious of it, all the rest is secondary, relatively unimportant.

God is present then, and He dwells within one, just as He dwells in the world as a whole. Except that I do not know of this Divine inner presence. As soon as I become conscious of it, however, I realize the purpose of Creation—"to be a dwelling place for Him in the world." God creates the world in such a manner that God, being invisible, cannot be taken for granted. He has to be sought out. There are aspects of Creation, like light, Divine light, which are self-evident. Other things, including the Divine Himself, must be looked for consciously. Like in the previous example of those inside–outside drawings, one can choose to see either the black picture against a white background or the white picture against a black background. The play of perception depends on one's own place, one's angle or point of view. Revelation is, thus, the sudden recognition of a reality that was overlooked, because it was considered background; it is the emergence of the essential image. It can occur in a moment, by a slight alteration of one's perspective or will, for example, by consenting to be a dwelling place for the Divine.

The difficulty for many of us is that we are separated from Him by a great abyss of terror. Who can dare to approach Him? Who can say that he has the right to be in any sort of relationship with God, much less to be a dwelling place for Him? The distance is indeed unbridgeably, immeasurably vast. No matter how tremendous one's efforts, or how great one becomes, one remains an insignificantly small creature.

That is only one aspect of the relation, however. The other is that God is always present and that one can be as near to Him as one chooses. If, however, one endeavors to approach Him by one's own efforts, it is hopelessly impossible. In relation to the Infinite, even moral and spiritual qualities have no meaning. It does not matter whether one is Moses, the Lawgiver, or an ordinary mortal—all stand at the same zero point before God. So that the great joy of the soul is savored when God comes to me, when the immeasurably great descends and fits Himself to my littleness. And the miracle is that God remains with one always; He becomes the one reality exceeding all else.

The faith that makes this possible is not something we necessarily have to achieve by ourselves. It is given to us as an inheritance. To be sure, for certain people it may be the end product of a lifetime of trial and error, thought and contemplation. But for the Jewish people, it is also a legacy from their forefathers. Therefore, the splendor of the Jewish heritage is the certainty that wherever and however one is situated, God is nearer than all else.

The recurrent question has always been: What is the key? And the answer that is always given is: "The righteous shall live by his faith." Because faith is the key that ensures the joy of life. And the joy of life is the same as the joy of existence itself. No matter what one's destiny, whether to be a sinner or a saint, rich or poor, happy or wretched, the one great and decisive factor is joy in the knowledge that God is present. And the more sincere this conviction, the more intense and alive one feels, because everyone lives by his faith.

It follows that when we have this knowledge of the constant presence of God, nothing else is needed. No matter how depressing or frustrating life becomes, no matter how dull the mind or sick the heart, one has only to think on the Divine Unity, on the oneness of His name, and the way is cleared for joy. True, an effort of will is needed to concentrate the thought and contemplate God's unity; but it is a minimal effort of guiding the mind, and it is less an effort than that which is equivalent to action. The thought keeps moving, no matter how we feel. To direct it in a certain way requires a certain amount of preparation beforehand. We need to have the tools, because it is not only a mental process. And there are any number of complex soul situations. Nevertheless, one is almost always compelled to think of oneself. And the thought "Who am I?" is hardly ever out of range. Who am I then that I dare to raise my head and share the life of the universe for a single moment? What am I and what is my life worth?

To this one responds, "My life is nothing, but God is here; He is with me."

Another aspect of faith is its power to resurrect the dead. For the soul of man can decline and even seem to disappear, and when it is restored to its proper place, it is in the nature of a resurrection. But God's presence can be established—and faith can be rooted firmly in one's life—only when one ceases to see oneself as the center of existence. The resultant joy can be described as the indwelling of God.

There is an anecdote about the Rabbi of Kotzk; he asked one of his disciples, "Where is God?" The disciple answered, "Why, of course, He is everywhere!" The Rabbi of Kotzk shook his head and said, "Not so. He is only there where He is allowed to enter." It may be concluded that the person who permits God to come into him is the one who is close to God. There is no need to draw and pull God to oneself or to climb and struggle to Him. One has only to allow Him to be present; or, at least, one's actions have to be such that God can participate in them.

Furthermore, the act of faith is a participation in the process of realizing the aims of existence, namely, to subdue the Sitra Achra and to transmute the darkness into light. What is this darkness? There is a specific darkness that belongs to the chain of one's past; it harbors a certain evil, issuing from a series of causes and effects. And there is a general darkness that is the darkness of the shells intrinsic to the material world. Indeed, the meaning of the shells, or Klipot, lies in the fact that they constitute whatever conceals the content so that one cannot perceive the Divine in all things. This concealment on the part of the shells will last until the end of days, when the world as we know it will be shattered.

Nevertheless, as it is written, "All flesh shall see," because God is in the world, whether He is visible or invisible, whether one believes or not. It is the shell of the Sitra Achra that shuts out the possibility of seeing the Divine. The testimony of an occasional relevation or miracle does not seem to alter much. If one is not inclined to believe, then even a miracle or a wondrous sign does not have much effect. Seeing is not necessarily believing. The Sitra Achra makes one unresponsive to anything outside of a very limited range of sensory stimuli. So that most people are quite fixed in their version of reality; they are held tightly confined within the darkness of their shell. And only when the shell is cracked, when this world will pass like a veil being lifted, only then will men behold the light of a new world.

The shells are more murky and more difficult to penetrate in the Diaspora. But even in the Holy Land, a person has to be in a condition of readiness in order to see the light. A person may come to the Holy Land from the Diaspora and bring with him all the shells of those other lands; and he may be so wrapped up in them that he cannot see anything. For the ability to see depends on one's purity of heart, and the ability to distinguish one place from another requires a certain readiness for change. Moving a dying man from a place of sadness to a place of merriment won't make much of a difference; he will still feel the gloom of his approaching end.

True light has an advantage over darkness. But not necessarily in terms of one against the other. Light is even superior when it issues from the darkness and includes the essence of the other. Light that comes as a resolution of darkness is usually, if not always, better and stronger. Genuine faith is just such a bursting through of light out of the obscurity; it is a power drawn from the hiddenness of the Divine at the core of the existence of the world, making it possible to declare: "God is with me!"

Two things may be said to happen when faith prevails as a matter of personal experience. There is the joyful personal factor of the one who feels the wondrous nearness of God. And there is the triumphal joy of God in the extrication of a person from his darkness and ignorance. The truth is that this wholly human concept of God's remoteness and inaccessibility is really another aspect of God's desire for man to come to Him. God puts a distance between Himself and man only in order to have man cross it. He conceals Himself so that man shall seek and find Him. And whenever man succeeds in crossing the apparent gap between them, then there is a creative joy on the part of both God and man. In man, the joy corresponds to the degree of his aspiration to bridge the gap. In God, it corresponds to the expectation that formed a barrier intended to be burst. Just as when a clever son is questioned by his proud father to ascertain the extent of the child's learning, he may answer one problem after another; but the joy of the father and of the child is greatest when the test is truly difficult.

It seems, indeed, that God poses before us the most difficult question of all—that of His Divine existence. And we have to grapple with a whole set of barriers and errors and confusions. But when we succeed in breaking through, then we not only feel the closeness of God, but we also delight in God's pride in us. There is a gladness in Heaven when man passes the trials and barriers of the Divine test.

Israel has its own special reason for rejoicing because it serves as a dwelling place for the Divine on earth. Altogether, Israel is one of the answers to the paradox of the world; it declares the presence of God in spite of the fact that He is hidden by His creation. It is Israel who bears witness, who proclaims, with the boundless joy of inner knowledge, that His glory fills the earth and His unity is simple and straightforward, beyond philosophy and mysticism.

Nevertheless, for all men, the world remains a public domain full of shells and Sitra Achra and blind forces of nature. A person living in the world feels as though he were located on the other side of the mountains of darkness, in an incoherent multiplicity of systems, rather than in a single stable universe. There is no purpose or direction; the public domain seems to be a rather wild, amoral, and chaotic place.

And it is in this public domain, with its mountains of

separation, dividing man from God, that one can be transformed into a private domain of light and unity. The very
struggle for existence is a gradual learning process in which one
discovers the singleness and the harmony behind the multiplicity and the disorder.

But the recognition of the unity, the faith that grows, is not
a belief that God is to be found somewhere or other. If God is
here or there, in the past or in some distant holy place, His
oneness becomes rather irrelevant. It doesn't really matter so
much whether He is one or two or three or more. Whereas, the
true unity of the Divine lies in the fact that there is nothing else.
There is no other force or reality or significance besides Him.
When a person tries to clarify this for himself, it becomes a
victory of the positive reality of the world over the otherwise
confusing hiddenness of the world behind the veil of Sitra
Achra. It is also a victory for God, for as we have seen, He
rejoices in one's success in overcoming the barrier to come to
Him.

Thus, when one becomes sure that God is, that He exists,
here and now, then the terror and the uncertainty are dissi-
pated, and one can join in the adventure, or the play, of finding
Him behind the partition. Even the certainty that He exists is
already a triumph of the highest order.

34

The Need for a Sanctuary

It is said that at the revelatory confrontation on Mount Sinai, the Divine presence was too much for the Children of Israel; they could not bear it. God, therefore, decided to have a sanctuary built, not only to serve Him as a dwelling, but also to protect the Israelites. Historically, this sanctuary, or the Ark of the Covenant, became the geographical place, or center, from which the Shechinah could emanate. But, of course, this is not to be understood in the sense of a physical source of light or energy. For the Shechinah is everywhere, and there is no existence, no reality, without the Shechinah. The emanation of the Shechinah should be understood rather as that which happens whenever there is a sharp consciousness of Divinity, whenever the Shechinah breaks through into life and awareness.

As for the inward presence, the Baal Shem Tov said that when the Shechinah pours down on someone, it may signify one of two things. Either the person is being used by God and made to act in a way that is beyond his control, as in the case of Nebuchadnezzar, the great king, who in the biblical account was called "my servant." Alternatively, one may be possessed by the Shechinah in the positive sense, and all one's actions and speech are natural expressions of oneself as well as of the Divine.

Similarly, when we say that the Shechinah departs, the meaning is that the specific manifestation has terminated, and everything returns to the normal state of affairs. Altogether, then, if the Shechinah is said to emanate, the meaning is that there is a perceptible revelation of the Divine unity; that is to say, there is an awareness of the universal harmony and God's omnipresence. The Holy Temple in Jerusalem was that spot where this was most pronounced. Since its destruction, God can no longer be said to be located at any one geographical point. Nor is it entirely correct to say that He is everywhere geographically. He has simply transferred His presence from geography altogether; He has made himself accessible, so to speak, within the confines of the Halachah. (The question of the proper use of the Halachah is something else—it is not the responsibility of the Halachah.) Torah and Halachah thus serve to designate what God wants of men and make it possible to get as close to Him as one can in this world.

The trouble arises when a person begins to reflect on the profound gap between the greatness of God and his own smallness. Recognizing his own incapacity to serve as a dwelling place for the Divine, he feels sure that he can never be like the patriarchs and the prophets, who did not have to enter a sanctuary or a Holy Temple in order to converse with God. Moreover, it becomes evident that in order to be any sort of vehicle, or Chariot, of the Shechinah, one needs to have a minimal level of intelligence and a certain knowledge of one's own Divine Soul. In the same way that a trained musician can read a musical score and hear the music, or a mathematician can enjoy the structure and harmony of a formula, so too is the concept of Divine Unity a source of inspiration and joy to those able to grasp it. It is a certain natural gift that has to be nurtured and developed. The important thing is that it is a potential that exists in every man, even though, as with most gifts, there are those who are more talented and those who are less so.

Those gifted ones, whom we call the great souls, have this extraordinary sensitivity for all that is holy. Others, and they may be very clever, learned, and even wise, will have much more difficulty in perceiving the Divine essence in anything, even in themselves. That capacity has to be fostered and trained; it cannot be coerced into being.

Nevertheless, even with the right combination of intelligence and soul, many persons tend to stop at some point in their lives and tell themselves that they cannot hope to ever make direct contact with the Divine. They feel that they cannot serve as a sanctuary; they have to enter some other, larger temple of God. This may be felt in spite of uplifting experiences (that come with greater or lesser frequency, such as in prayer or fasting). For many people do not know how to keep their entire lives centered around one thing. As the Chasidim of Kotzk used to say, "It is a matter of being absolutely straight," or all of one piece. In Chabad Chasidism, it used to be called getting to the point of the self where one was no longer subject to change — for one of the tests of truth is that it does not vary according to circumstances.

One of the results of feeling despair about ever making direct contact with God is the conviction that some kind of intermediary is needed. This is a mistaken notion, for it is possible to relate directly, and in any way one chooses, with God. There is no prohibition or barrier. The only restriction, according to the Sages, is the need to be clear and objective about one's capacities before coming to the conclusion that one is in the company of the patriarchs and the prophets.

Most people, then, have to rely on prayer and mitzvot to have opportunities for the encounter with the Divine essence. However, under the pressures of modern life, this may prove inadequate. The chance to be a vehicle of the Shechinah has to be grasped more deliberately. For example, the mitzvah to give charity prescribes certain minimums and maximums, and one can easily do what is proper. How different though if a person gives charity because he feels himself to be a vehicle of Divine mercy rather than a bestower of alms.

No matter how much or how little the charity that is offered up as a mitzvah or as a sacrifice, it represents the equivalent of the life force that has gone into the earning of the money. And according to the Scriptures, this fifth part of one's earnings, whatever one gives to charity, carries the other four parts with it straight to Heaven. In this way, the entire labor of a person is sanctified and made holy.

So, too, all that a person eats and drinks and enjoys can be transmuted into means of Divine worship. And if there are things in life that are not transformed by the direct power of the mitzvah, they can nonetheless be sanctified as utensils serving the holy—for instance, the ark or receptacle in which the Torah Scrolls are kept. In this way, almost all that is considered secular can be put at the service of the holy and made to assume a higher significance. It is a process of a heightening of consciousness, by which any person can make himself a dwelling place for the Divine.

What may prove disconcerting is the fact that liveliness and high spirits tend to bring a certain coarseness and vulgarity into life. And this in turn becomes a barrier between man and God, because the striving towards holiness is also a process of pulverizing the animal-self and the ego. The answer to this problem is that high spirits are essential, of course, but that true joy is something much deeper and consistent. If one becomes a dwelling place for the Divine by giving charity, it should not interfere with one's sense of proportion; it is no reason to cease self-disparagement or to feel that one "deserves a medal." On the contrary, a degree of prudence is called for: At the same time that a person feels himself to be in a blissful state of closeness to the holy, he may think and do things that create a barrier between himself and the holy.

Nevertheless, one generally has a pretty good idea of what one is. The famous statement by Hillel reflects this: "If I am not for myself, who is for me, and if I am for myself, what am I? . . ." One's nothingness is not so hard to recognize. What is hard is to reconcile it with one's potential for being a dwelling place for the Shechinah. Every man is a contradiction in this sense, a combination of the holy and the trivial. One has to integrate it all into some sort of workable unity—by building life as though it were an annex in the court of the Holy Temple, the inner chambers of which one can never be sure of entering.

Weeping is thus lodged in one side of the heart and joy in the other. Man lives with both. He knows the joy that sustains him in Divine worship; and, at the same time, he can be stricken with grief and a sense of profound inadequacy concerning his own life. In particular, the Benoni, the person of the middle way, lives out this contradiction on various levels all through the years of his earthly existence.

"It is well known that the Patriarchs themselves constitute the Chariot." They are the vehicle for the Divine. The Patriarchs are spoken of as the wheels or legs of the Chariot, in the sense that the Chariot is an implement used by God to get from one place to another. The personal essence of the Patriarchs has been used as an instrument to bring out the holiness of the world.

But in order for any man to serve as a Chariot of God, he has to become a pliant instrument, whether to bless or to curse, whether as a benign force or as a whip of Divine wrath. It is not a matter of being compliant in any particular situation; one's entire being has to become a tool in God's hands. One becomes another self, someone who may still be aware of oneself and of the closeness of God, but for whom this is no longer the chief reality; one has become a witness of oneself. And although the Patriarchs are said to be the Chariot (with David as the fourth wheel), theoretically, any person of Israel can reach such a level. There is no restriction; in fact, all men are challenged to become a Chariot of the Shechinah. What is involved is a nullification of self. One has to live one's whole life, sleeping and waking, consciously and unconsciously, as a serviceable instrument of the Shechinah.

There are a few persons who can act in this perfect serviceability when they are conscious; but when they are not conscious and alert, they lose the contact. However, when a person reaches the state of being a Chariot of the Shechinah, the contact is no longer dependent on the conscious mind or the will; it becomes a matter of existential reality and is no longer operative on its own terms. It has been said that there are two kinds of Tzadikim—those who do the will of God and those whose every act is the will of God.

The latter refers to those few persons whose every thought, word, or action—and even unconscious mind—are all vehicles of sanctity. Everything they do, even their errors, are instruments of Divine Will. It is in this sense that wisdom often appears in such unrecognizable terms that it is considered a mistake. Indeed, every person can become a vehicle of Divine utterance without even knowing it or wishing it. When such a thing happens—and only for the duration that it happens—all of that person's impulses and speech involuntarily exert an influence on the world, incalculably changing a large variety of things and people and events.

The holiness of Scripture is said to be in the letters, not because of any physical or magical quality, but because the prophets and others who were Chariots of the Shechinah not only transmitted the contents of Divine Truth, but also expressed holiness in their very modes of speech, phrases, spelling—no matter how personal this may have been. A prophet, by his very nature, cannot do otherwise.

This, perhaps, would be the meaning of Jeremiah's distinction between the prophet and the dreamer of dreams. He does not assume that the dreamer is necessarily a falsifier. On the contrary, a dreamer of dreams can have genuine prophetic dreams, as evidenced by several biblical accounts. The difference between the dreamer and the prophet lies in the fact that the prophet is in a state of Divine Unity and speaks and acts as a Chariot of God, whereas the dreamer, who may or may not have had a revelation, describes what he saw in his own terms. His dream necessarily contains elements of his own personality; and when he recounts his dream, no matter how faithful he is to its revelatory contents, his personality gets mixed up with it. As for the prophet, no matter how much his personality gets involved with the message, it retains the absolute ring of Divine Truth.

Thus, the Shechinah speaks through Moses, and there is no distinction between his private speaking and his prophetic utterances. Often a message of the Torah begins in the third person—as the word of God to Israel: "Thus saith the Lord"—and switches to the first person—"which I command you this day"—as though the barrier between Moses the man and the God Who addresses us through him were suddenly eliminated. This is, of course, the highest level of identification of which we have any knowledge.

As we have seen, however, the Divine essence fills everything. It is our mind that creates the barriers and forms separate existences. Prophets, like Moses, have simply broken down these fences and separations. At Mount Sinai, the Children of Israel could not endure this closeness to the Divine, and "their souls took flight," so that a sanctuary had to be built to preserve them.

The great problem of the Chariot, and of someone like Moses, heavy of speech and tongue-tied, is that Moses found it extremely difficult to be a man among men. In the Zohar, there is a description of such persons, declaring that they are like fish of the sea walking on land. Perhaps, then, the world of men is like the dry land, and the Divine essence is like the vast sea surrounding the land on all sides and occasionally flooding it.

35
Problems of Receiving the Shechinah

The central theme of the *Tanya* can be said to be the verse from Deuteronomy (30:14): "It is very nigh unto thee, on your lips and on your heart, to do it." And concerning this *doing it*, the question is asked: What is the way of the Benoni, the intermediate person who originally was a pure soul sent to dwell on the earth and cope with the insoluble problem of its contradictory existence? Should he struggle, knowing that the chances of a permanent victory (such as the incarnation in him of a saintly soul) are slim? Or should he try to reconcile himself to the persistence of the insoluble?

This does not even begin to answer the more fundamental question: *What for?* If, indeed, one is no more than a sample of "everyman," no matter how refined by idealization and effort, one knows that one is not among the Tzadikim, of whom there are said to be a thousand—at most, eighteen thousand—in any one generation. Or perhaps there are only two at any one time in the whole world. In any case, one can be fairly certain that one is not a Tzadik and, thus, the problems of life and existence will never be overcome. All the advice and help one

236

may obtain from men and books can make this more endurable, perhaps. But there is no way of evading it: The pain and sorrow remain.

In fact, as one grows older, they increase. With maturity, the evil impulse has a greater field for action, even if there is a change in form. As it is said, there are three things that divert a person from eternal life: envy, lust, and honor. And they seem to correspond to the three stages of life. A child is provoked by rivalry and jealousy to exert and develop himself; a young adult is driven by the passionate desires of mind and body; an older person becomes the victim of his own pride—without entirely losing the former incentives of jealousy and lust.

The only difference between a Benoni, the intermediate person, and the wicked one is no more than that the Benoni does not allow himself to become a vehicle for evil to express itself. Essentially, he is the same. And he has to keep himself in a state of tension, of conscious effort, in order not to act like the wicked. He is not unlike a soldier holding a live hand grenade with the pin pulled; he cannot ever let go. If he should relax his self-discipline, he will soon find himself overwhelmed by the same appetites and cravings as the wicked.

Why then, it is asked, have the souls of the Benoni descended into this world to labor in vain, God forbid, to wage war all their lives against the evil inclinations which they cannot vanquish? What is the point of this futile struggle? All the goodness and integrity of the Benoni seem to be rather pointless. It is as though the whole of a man's freedom were whittled down to a simple choice between living as a Benoni or as a wicked person, since he cannot hope to become a Tzadik. It is like the choice given to most men in the realm of learning—one can choose to study or one can choose not to study; one cannot choose to be a genius. In any event, this is true for all but a very few exceptional cases. Because there are individuals who can change the essence of themselves and of the world. And they, too, have a choice: to be or not to be a Tzadik or a genius. But for the vast majority of men, the option remains fairly limited: to work or not to work on oneself. This brings us back to the reason for the enormous effort involved in being a Benoni. What can gladden the heart in spite of the futility of the conflict?

The traditional answer is that even if one cannot be happy about one's personal lot, one can rejoice in the nearness of God. What is suggested here is that the deliberate search for faith and tranquility of soul, for the bliss of Divine Unity, is rather absurd. Because, aside from the very exceptional case, an ordinary man does not ever achieve it. Even the most faithful pursuit of righteous living and the fulfillment of the commandments will not necessarily bring one to this tranquility of soul. On the contrary, as we have said before, the Benoni lives in a state of constant tension. He cannot afford to relax the taut quality of his existence. If he does, he will find himself sliding into a dullness of the heart, and thence, into a certain boredom and sin. An apparent serenity of mind, with the comforting thought that all is well and there is nothing more to be done, can be the most dangerous state of being. If one does not rise by conscious effort, one slides back and falls. The struggle is constant and unrelenting.

In the Chasidic story of Rabbi Simcha Bunim, he explained that every person should visualize evil as though the devil were standing over him with an ax, ready to chop off his head. Upon hearing this, one of the disciples asked: "And what if a person cannot see himself that way?" Rabbi Simcha replied: "That is a clear sign that the devil has already chopped off his head."

In other words, the man of God is someone who is constantly struggling. The one who does not struggle but only does not harm anyone—not being one of the wicked—is not a servant of God. Faith then, is not of itself a solution to the agony of the soul; it does not necessarily bring peace and tranquility. On the contrary, for the great majority of men, the way of piety and scrupulous keeping of the commandments is a way of perpetual conflict and ever-increasing effort.

What does faith offer in return for the struggle and the effort? It gives the presence of God, but not always the sense of God's presence. A person studying the Talmud portion about the ox that gored a neighbor's cow will not necessarily achieve religious ecstasy. That is not what is promised—which is not to say that there is no relation whatever. What is proferred to the one who occupies himself with Torah and the mitzvot is that he will be objectively nearer to God, even if he does not feel that nearness. Therefore, one has to decide what one really wants – the actual presence of God or the feeling that one is close to Him. If one wants to feel as though he is close to God, there are many ways, from drugs to the rapture induced by some technique or other. One can actually be in the presence of God, however, without having any ecstatic experience and without even knowing what is happening, that is, without any sort of great joy or enlightenment. The bliss either comes or does not come. But no matter how one is privileged to receive a revelation, it should be viewed as a special gift.

The problem, however, in a life of steady devotion and sincere worship, lies in the fact that habit makes the tension slack. Piety can become a comfortable state of being, in which one is afraid of change. When arriving at such a stage, the sincere worshipper of God has to assume an additional burden – tighten the tension – otherwise, he will slip into a state of gradual spiritual decline.

All of this is rather a grim prospect, and the question we are putting to ourselves is not answered. Where is the joy or the personal satisfaction in serving God? Especially if it involves such unmitigated struggling and tension. As an aside, before proceeding further, it may be noted that we are living in an age of psychological values. Everything is measured by the effect on one's subjective thoughts and feelings. Does it inspire one? Does it depress one? And the spiritual life has also become dominated by the same shallow standard of measure. It is very like the confusion in estimating simple things like eating – one may or may not enjoy one's food – it has nothing to do with the need to eat in order to live.

So, too, is the Benoni concerned with serving God; he fulfills his obligations as best he can; he works incessantly on himself; he changes the world for the better by his religious actions. In spite of this, he may or may not be happy.

The important thing, as it is written in Ecclesiastes 2:14 and quoted by the Zohar (Balak III, 187a), is that "the wise man's eyes are in his head, but the fool walks in the dark." That is, the

Shechinah, or the source of light, is on the head. Which may explain, incidentally, why covering the head is a necessary protection for Jews. The uncovered head is a sign of freedom from restraint, and the covered head is a sign of the feeling that the Shechinah is everywhere, and one thereby expresses one's subordination to it.

The wise man whose eyes are in his head is in a constant state of contemplation and wakeful consciousness of this relationship between the Shechinah and himself. He has also to act accordingly, to make sure the oil of good deeds flows to the flame of his soul, knowing that neither the oil nor the wick, of itself, could provide any light. Man's function is to be a medium for good deeds, for those actions or events that would not have any meaning without man. At the same time, it has nothing to do with the personality of the person; it is not a matter of subjective problems and thoughts. As long as the lamp keeps burning and the soul is alive, the wick, or the physical being of a person, may suffer or be consumed to a greater or lesser degree; it doesn't make much difference.

The individual joys and sorrows are private matters; what is vital is the light that comes forth from the person. And if there are 600,000 wicks burning—the number of souls that received the Torah and continue to be reincarnated as the Jewish people—what is called the "Pure Lamp," the light of the world, is kindled, and this is the purpose of existence.

If the soul is holy and the light of the Shechinah is all that is desired of existence, what then is the need of good deeds and physical actions? Why is not the love of God sufficient? But even for the most holy of saints, the man for whom the Divine presence is all, the one who is constantly consumed by love for God to the extent that he is unable to sleep at night, so agonized is he by the fear of losing conscious contact with the Beloved—even for such a one, the separation remains a hideous fact. The "I" is still there, and there is no unification. For the ultimate desire of the Tzadik is to be made null and void in the Divine and not to keep loving and yearning for Him, even in the paradise beyond the Garden of Eden, where the love of God reaches unimaginable heights of bliss.

The point is that the very existence of a separate self is an obstacle, for it is written (Deuteronomy 5:5) that "I" stood between the Lord and you. It is not a matter of being on a higher or on a lower level. As long as man is man, there is a barrier. The very greatest love and fear of God are themselves only expressions of this abysmal gap between the human and the Divine. It is the same fact as that which categorically states: "For no man shall see me and live" (Exodus 33:20). If I am I, I cannot be He. And all the experiences of the self, no matter how sublime, serve only to emphasize this truth.

On the other hand, the mitzvot are holy in themselves; they are not dependent on man. Because the mitzvot are the will of God, it is possible by performing them to realize a Divine union that effects the desired nullification of self. To be sure, it may be said that the whole world is an expression of His will; but the world is by definition "something else"; it is that which is other than God; it veils divinity. For Creation was an act of contraction and concealment of the Divine face. Whereas the mitzvot are a revelation of the Divine Will.

Revelation is not necesarily a phenomenon of thunder and lightning and the sounding of trumpets. It may be seen as a constellation of forces, an unforeseen combination of things. God indicates a way which consists of a simple integration of certain elements: specific objects, times, and places, more or less defined actions, words, and thoughts, which, when combined, serve to produce inestimable effects. Whether one is aware of these effects, or whether one feels any lofty sentiment or satisfaction, is irrelevant. In point of fact, the performance of the mitzvah may lie beyond one's understanding, so that one feels a certain strangeness and incompatibility. It doesn't make any difference. For the mitzvah does not rely on thoughts or feelings; its point of departure is relationships. The Divine code is not easily given to comprehension, but one can do the mitzvah as best one can, in the way one transmits a message in code, trying to avoid mistakes or distortion, clinging faithfully to whatever contact one has with the source.

In short, the true connection between the world and God cannot be made by the world, because the world is always "else." It can only be made by means of signs or signals that God Himself provides. He creates the means of communication with Himself. And this mode of contact is, in turn, not dependent on one's small human self; it is dependent on the Divine. The whole essence of revelation is an opening up, a making possible of genuine contact, of being able to talk to God. And it is important to talk to God in one's own language, which means doing things with one's mind and body. And, at the same time, contact of this sort is genuine in the sense that it doesn't depend on oneself; it depends on God.

Insofar as one speaks to God only in the language of inner experience, it may be beneficial and pleasant to oneself. It does not make the connection with that which is beyond self, with the greater reality reaching out to the endless. In order for real speech to take place, one has to talk in a language that is also spoken by the other. And the language of the other is given to one, and it is not something one determines by oneself. Torah and mitzvot are the language provided by the Divine to enable us to talk to Him. It is also the ultimate mode of communication between the world and God.

The question was asked: Why can't one reach a state of union with the Shechinah by means of intense devotion? Why is it not possible through love, profound awe, ecstasy, or any other subjective manifestation of the soul? And the answer was that it does not depend on any personal feelings or thoughts, but on certain actions or situations in which the person becomes a vessel for the Shechinah.

The difficulty for most men is that one's very humanity seems to make it impossible to be an abiding place for the Shechinah. Because, although the outward sign of such an indwelling is the Divine light, the inner consequences are that the one in whom the Shechinah abides ceases to be an individual self. To be sure, all creatures are instruments of the Divine, but one cannot say that the Shechinah dwells in them. For that in which the Shechinah abides becomes null and void of any being of its own. And that which retains anything of its own being cannot manifest the Divine light.

From this, it seems that this deeply desired unity with God cannot be reached so easily, either by passionate devotion or by certain duly performed steps or actions. Not that man should ever cease to progress and strive for an ever higher degree of love and awe of God. And there are always higher and ever higher levels of being. Even Tzadikim are said to be restless men. As one of them put it: That level, which yesterday was the Heaven above, has to be made into the ground on which one walks today; otherwise, one has not reached the dimension of his humanity; he does not have anything to do in the world.

Is it at all possible, then, to achieve this unity called Devekut? The answer is that it is not achieved through human effort, but by virtue of Divine revelation—as when God gives the Torah or the mitzvah. And the efficacy of Torah does not depend on the degree of penetration into its content or meaning, or even on the purification of one's mind and actions in relation to the ethical ramifications of doing good or combatting evil. Even the social benefits, no matter how great, are incidental and peripheral. The essential fact about the Torah is the way it comes to man, across the abyss of the infinite, as a communication of God's will, God's thought. And the more external reasons and justifications a person gives for living according to Torah, the more scaffolding and superstructure he adds to the essential revelation. True, there are many people who need these reasons, for a while or for all their lives. One circumcises his son because it is hygienic or traditional, and one eats kosher because it is healthy, and so forth. No matter how subtle and sublime the rationalizations, it does not change the fact that, ultimately, one is not doing the mitzvah because it is good or pleasant or beneficial but because God has said, "I want it." And since one cannot establish a communication with God on one's own level, within the world one lives or in the language one understands, one has to use this code, this way of getting to Him as experienced in revelation. This revelation does provide a certain system of words, actions, forms, and situations—namely, the mitzvot of the Torah. This is the given area where contact can be made.

God descends on Mount Sinai with great noise and thunder; and what, after all, does He say? If one holds up these messages to careful scrutiny, one finds them to be at best no more than a few succinct injunctions that were fairly well known and necessary in the ancient world: Thou shalt not steal, thou shalt not commit murder, thou shalt not commit adultery, and so forth. Does God have to descend from Heaven just to instruct a fugitive tribe about things they could learn by themselves if they took the trouble? The point is that what God says is unique and special, not in terms of content, but because it is God Himself who says it. Included are the ethical formulas, "thou shalt not do" or "thou shalt do" this or that, which are all part of the human structure. But when the same injunction is part of a Divine communication, it acquires another dimension of power and meaning. As, for example, in music, the intervals and emphasis are just as important as the notes themselves. The silence around the sound is what gives it meaning, like the space around a shape. So that the mitzvah may be regarded as no more than an exteriorization of social ritual, a human act, while the Torah, which revealed the mitzvah, is what makes this mitzvah a vehicle for Divine Unity. Not only because it is what God wants but because He has extended His hand across the abyss of the world, saying, in effect, that whoever grabs hold can reach the other side.

It may be appropriate to recollect a Chasidic commentary on the Kabbalah indicating that Divine unification is not possible unless it comes through Wisdom. And Wisdom (Chochmah) is also Koach Mah, which may be interpreted as the capacity to listen, to fully absorb what is given. In itself Wisdom is, perhaps, nothing; its efficacy comes from the fact that it is a point of reception, the focus, attracting and absorbing what comes from above. By which it is clearly suggested that the secret of wisdom is self-nullification, not being there to block the reception. Thus, for example, it is said that wisdom may best be learned from babies, from anything that is a perfect receptacle.

All of this only serves to explain, in a variety of ways, why the complete bliss of Divine Union is not to be attained through great love, mystical meditation, or ecstatic prayer. Why a soul cannot burn, like a wick, by itself, why fuel is so necessary, the oil of correct action.

Pursuing this line of argument, it is presumed that when a person occupies himself totally with Torah, the Shechinah abides with him. And it does not matter what the subject of the study or perusal may be—the very experience of being absorbed in Torah is enough. A certain flow or circuit is created. The Torah itself does not do anything in the world; it has to pass through the medium of the person reading or hearing it. The quality of that participation is another matter, because the body and the animal-soul create their own defensive measures against comprehending what is happening. In a certain sense, this is the paradox of our existence, justifying the structural combination of body and spirit. If our animal-soul were ever to catch a glimpse of what it was up to when absorbed in Torah, it would burst. Our ability to sit quietly and learn a few pages of Talmud depends on this dense barrier, on this relative unconsciousness of the physical in relation to the spiritual experience of edification.

An interesting insight into the nature of Chasidism may be inserted here. The friend and relation of Rabbi Schneur Zalman of Liadi was Rabbi Levi Yitzchak of Berditchev, a saintly man of ecstatic temperament. According to a certain easy stereotyping, Rabbi Schneur Zalman was classified as a cold intellectual, like the Gaon of Vilna; Rabbi Levi Yitzchak was considered a highly emotional type like the Besht. The truth of the matter is very far from this all too simple arrangement. Just as Rabbi Levi Yitzchak was an extremely profound thinker and intellectual as well as being given to outbursts of spiritual emotion, so too was Rabbi Schneur Zalman, the intellectual founder of Chabad, a man of vast emotional depths, capable of feeling faint with exhaustion in the throes of spiritual experience. Like others of this kind of genius, Maimonides, for example, the cold clarity of Rabbi Schneur Zalman's thinking was not at all an indication of lack of concern; it was, rather, the direct expression of a profound inner struggle, of magnificent control and discipline. The extraordinary emotions of the religious life of Torah were invariably present. The impersonal writing was an effort to give classical form to inner experience, believing that this objective intellectual clarity was necessary as well as appropriate. Necessary because unrestrained emotional and spiritual expression is dangerous.

As Rabbi Levi Yitzchak once said: If someone were to enter

the Garden of Eden with the *tzitzit* physically intact, the whole of Paradise would be consumed, unable to bear the fierce light coming from the *tzitzit*. Why then can a human being wear the *tzitzit* and not be consumed? Because the human being is protected by the permanent structure of Divine hiddenness. Being made up of body and spirit, he has the advantage of being able to penetrate into realms of holiness that a pure soul—without a body—would be unable to approach. The physical may be seen as a kind of counterbalance as well as a protective or sheltering factor. To make any real contact with the holy a human being has to develop a certain immunity or armor against the "blinding" light. The trouble is that this armor is often overdone to the extent that a high degree of density becomes natural.

Deuteronomy 32:18 states: "Of the Rock that begat thee thou art unmindful and hast forgotten God that formed thee." Concerning this verse, it has been remarked that God provides man with the capacity to forget (the world) as well as to know (the Lord), but man often chooses the opposite, distorting his freedom. To be sure, a certain balance is necessary. The angel who has no freedom and no capacity to perform a mitzvah may be closer to God. But to what extent can a person be aware of the Shechinah dwelling in him and still continue to perform his duties in the world?

And the answer given is that the sanctity of the mitzvah as deed involves thought, word, and action. Through the mitzvah, with the participation of the body, unity is possible. Because then, the animal-soul, which is of Klipat Nogah and does not belong to the realm of holiness, can be transformed. For the moment, at least, the person is united with his Divine Soul. In other words, the physical body, which is not ordinarily under the control of the Infinite in any form, not even in the form of the Divine Soul, can be influenced or changed by the intelligent, vital aspect of the animal-soul. And this is what happens in the performance of the mitzvah. All the different parts of the being coalesce at that moment of contact with the light of the Infinite, the vital soul is transformed, and even the material forces that nurtured it are raised to a higher level.

Nevertheless, as we have said before, the person is not

transformed; even if, at the moment of the mitzvah, a certain connection is made between the world and God, the doer of the mitzvah is not necessarily changed. Which brings us back to the subject of the nature of the Benoni, the one who does only good, but who knows that if he lets go, evil may overwhelm him. No change occurs in him, even with the most punctilious performance of the mitzvah. What is this holy temple one builds for the Shechinah, if all around it, and even inside, all manner of unholy forces continue to flourish? Even if they remain on the margin of life, even if the person is not acutely aware of them, they are there—these personal and impersonal forces of darkness. So that even if, for a moment, one has been a vessel for the Shechinah, immediately afterwards one may easily become a medium for pettiness or corruption.

It seems to be an insoluble problem for most people. And indeed, men tend to keep the abomination of it well covered up, as though the only thing to do is not to admit it or see it. However, it is important to draw it out into the open and examine what is taking place.

First of all, the various parts of the body and soul that have participated in the mitzvah have consented to it, even if not entirely of their free will. The negative aspects have been subjugated to the higher aspects and have been put into a state of inaction. For that moment, at least, a person can say that his soul is a light of God.

The light is an encompassing light, that which is given from without, an influence that is not of one's own making. One cannot reach it physically at all, and in fact, one will probably not even be aware of it. Nevertheless, there is some sort of personal participation—even if sometimes of a tragic order, with a candle burning on one's head, and the darkness within not illuminated by it at all. Indeed, a person may forever be lighting candles and lamps while his house remains in darkness. The one who performs the mitzvah shakes the world and touches the Divine somewhere with a great spark; but the fact is that he himself may not feel it that way.

36

God in the World

According to the Sages, the purpose of Creation is to establish a place for God to live in the world. As a certain folk story described it: Whatever for? Why should the Almighty ever want to dwell in this nether world? And the answer is that like so many other desires and cravings, it should not be inquired into. True, the philosophers have not added much to this half-joking explanation, but it may be appropriate to investigate it a little further.

First, there is a certain technical difficulty to be overcome. If we say that God wishes to live here on earth, it may imply that He is actually somewhere else. Thus, we are confronted with the paradox of above and below, because for the Infinite there can be no such thing—neither place nor time nor difference in dimension. Even though there is a matter of levels in relation to Divine essence, higher and lower levels, we are still baffled by the fact that He occupies all places and levels equally.

Before He created the world, only God may be said to have existed, without limits or distinct forms, and there was nothing else. But nothing actually changed in this respect by virtue of Creation. He is still everywhere. And the relationship with His creatures is a one-way relationship. Even the person who claims to have seen the Divine essence can be said to be looking into a dark glass that does not transmit light; the only possible exception is Moses, who is said to have seen God in a "luminous (transparent) glass." Nevertheless, the general truth holds fast that no man may see God and live. For the "luminous glass" is also a transparent window through which one "looks" and is looked at by oneself. Thus the prophets, in peering into this "glass," were able to see only as much as the dazzling luminosity permitted—the less light there was, the more they could see. In any event, this is a most complex matter in itself. For our purposes, suffice it to say that those who receive anything of the Divine essence are invariably caught in the paradox of seeing and of not seeing, of being confronted with a one-way concealment in which they are themselves made transparent and yet are unable to penetrate beyond a certain depth.

Even the angels may not see God; no one and nothing can pierce the veil of Divine hiddenness. What can be observed is an unfolding of worlds, a process of descent, or generation, which creates that which we call a lower world, a world of levels that are ever more dense, more wrapped in the Divine hiddenness and less exposed to God. Even in individuals on earth one may detect such differences of density or "concealment."

The lower world, created by the process of Divine emanation, is physical and of substance, and, in certain respects, it is also an end product of the Divine Will. That is to say, it is a world that can be measured, and it has distinctiveness and form; it can be touched. Man, too, is a part of this world of matter, and no small part of man's struggle in life consists of the effort to gain release from the physical limitations of his being. It is not only a question of making contact with genuine holiness; it is also a question of freeing oneself from images and pictures, from the sense of touch and the bondage that comes from the attachment to that which is of substance.

Moreover, there is still another part of this world, even lower than all the rest, containing shells of imagined independence; that is to say, they are so far removed from God that they can even deny Him. Just as at the highest level of this lower world of ours there are those with minimal wrappings separating them from God; so too, at the lowest level of this lower world, there are those who claim individual independence; that is, they do not acknowledge their own creatureliness, their status as a product of Creation. This lowest level is the source of evil as opposed to good and is recognized when a person says: "I and none else." There are, thus, two poles of being. One admits that there is God in the world and that alongside Him, throughout the whole world, nothing else can exist. And there is the other, which does not only fail to see God everywhere, but which sees itself as the basis for everything, the beginning and the end of all existence. In other words, the shell, as a category, is merely a matter of level of existence between these two poles. Anyone, whether man or angel, who says "I and God" or "God and I" includes the shell in his being.

The question here is: What nourishes the shell and sustains its existence? And the answer is: God Himself, even at the extremity of the shell's impudence, when the shell is allowed to repudiate God. The greater the gap, the harder it is to see the direct connection between Creation and the world; one sees only the links. As Maimonides said, all idolatry is a degeneration of one's faith in the unity of the linked system of Creation. The first step in this degeneration of faith is to consider the desirability of establishing some relation with these links, channels, or instruments of Divine power, in order to ensure their proper functioning for one's own benefit. And as happens whenever one learns to deal with the lesser officials of government and forgets that there is a sovereign power who is really in charge, one begins to depend on oneself. The slogan of "I and none other" steals its way into the soul.

All of this explains what is meant by above and below, upper and lower—the "lower" being not what is further removed from God but what is less open to the knowledge of the fact that God is present within it. The upper worlds are open to Divine influence and transmit everything easily, without taking or gaining anything for themselves. The ultimate purpose seems to be the worlds below, the lower levels of being. If this is true, then this world of ours has two essences built into its very structure. It is the lowest of the low. It is also charged with a purpose—to reach a certain level of consciousness, so that it is sufficiently able to receive the Infinite light. When this is achieved, the very depths of darkness and the Sitra Achra will shine and radiate more powerfully and brightly than the upper worlds. For the light of the upper worlds is still clothed and hidden somewhat—being, of necessity, separate from the Divine and not altogether nullified in Him. The point is that God and the world are, in essence, opposites; they are contradictions in terms of being. They can exist together only when there is a state of ignorance, when the world does not know the Divine essence and cannot even recognize its presence. Because as soon as the world feels God, it cannot continue to be anything, much less itself. That is to say, all the world lives on the basis of the fiction that it has some sort of independent being. Where there is a knowledge of the truth, the world ceases to exist.

Our world is no more than a variety of such false relations; and although it may feel the absurdity of its position, it does not suffer unduly from the urge to nullify itself before the absolute Divine light. To be sure, there have been instances of men who experienced the rapture of the kiss of death, uniting with the Divine essence. It is told of Rabbi Moshe Zechut (HaRamaz), for instance, that in a state of religious ecstasy, he crumpled to earth and ceased to breathe. The fact is that, throughout history, there have been many more such instances than are known, even until fairly recent times.

All of this readiness for self-nullification does not, however, characterize the World of Action as it does the higher worlds. In fact, our world is characterized by grossness and evil, and is, therefore, very different from the many thousands of spiritual worlds. Nevertheless, this becomes an advantage in that it enables one to reach Divine consciousness by following a certain path in life without the risk of self-nullification in the Infinite light. The very fact that it is so structured, based on gross matter, which is relatively impervious to the Divine, makes it possible to become a vessel to contain the Divine light. The spiritual worlds have no such covering or protection; they remain one-dimensional. Nevertheless, we may well wonder why we have to struggle against grossness, cruelty, and insensitivity. As Rabbi Nachman said: "People maintain that this world exists, and I am quite willing to believe it; but from what we can all see, it looks more like Hell." The point is that we somehow manage to live in this world because, notwithstanding all its horrors, it has the capacity to absorb what the higher worlds cannot assimilate.

Our world is, therefore, the place where the ultimate Divine revelation will occur, precisely because of its limitations and restrictions. Without delving into the matter deeply, we may say that the theory behind this is the process of generation or involution (as opposed to evolution). Among other things, it explains the descent of God in terms of levels, and further explains His withdrawal as whatever makes it possible for something that is not God (Divine absence) to exist. It does not explain the development of matter. And ultimately, the whole process of physical creation seems to point to a lower frontier, the edge of existence. Only the infinite power of the Divine can create matter which is finite, which puts a limit to God, and this contrast has its emotional implications. We tend to relate to matter and spirit as two levels or degrees of the same thing, with matter, since it is more dense, being of lower value. But the truth is that matter is simply what is more hidden or concealed from Divine light; it is not necessarily of lesser or lower value.

Furthermore, matter can be a vessel to contain the Infinite, which the spirit, with its greater vulnerability, cannot be. That is to say, the physical Torah is a way to achieve a certain Divine love and unity, while pure love of God and ecstatic experiences are not able to contain the Infinite because of their human personal limitations. In other words, the Divine hiddenness is not seriously affected by the presence of God in matter, whereas in the realm of the spiritual, it is difficult, if not impossible, for Divine hiddenness to be maintained. It is only at the end of days that the revelation of God will eliminate all the barriers marking His hiddenness in the world. It will be the end of the Divine experiment that began with Creation—could a world exist in the light of God without the protection afforded by His hiddenness.

This brings us to the problem of the resurrection of the dead.

In contrast to Maimonides, the Baal HaTanya maintains that it is impossible to achieve a complete spiritual union of the human with the Divine; thus, the ultimate revelation cannot take place in Paradise; it has to be realized through and within the physical world. Therefore, there has to be a physical body, because the body can undergo all sorts of modifications. We cannot conceive of all the possible transmutations that can occur in the body as a result of the mutual relations between body and soul. The existence of the body, or of matter, is a part, not only of reward and punishment, but also of that which makes it possible to experience a true revelation and to see God in spite of the fact that "no man shall see Me and live." Moreover, it is said: "Eye to eye will they see God." All of this is, perhaps, to be interpreted to mean that God cannot be seen now, when man has to divest himself of his outer (physical) garments in order to approach God, a state in which there is no desire for life and no possibility for life to continue. On the other hand, in the time of God's revelation, there will be a transformation in all the world—the change toward which we aspire.

All our efforts to serve and worship Him are intended to bring about the upheaval involved in Divine revelation, beyond anything that was or could be in the past. Indeed, the whole world was created for that purpose. And life after that, the life of immortality, is thus the aim of this life. It is appropriate to mention that the ultimate reward will be given in the seventh millennium, within the reality of this world, and not in Paradise. That is to say, Paradise and Hell are no more than stations along the way. A person lives a certain span, doing his share of good and evil. If the evil predominates, his soul is corrupted, and he needs purification and correction. He is therefore sent for a while to some such place where this can be done for him. Another person, who does not require such a transition period and special corrective conditions for the purification of the soul, is sent somewhere else, according to his level of being. Such a one, according to the Baal HaTanya, is not yet seated with the righteous and the saintly in blissful enjoyment of Heaven: he simply waits for the end of days, which is a real time in the concrete history of man; during this period, his entire being has to pass through a great modification.

A precedent for this may be seen in the experience of the giving of the Torah (Matan Torah), which was a revelation of God, a breaking of all the barriers and concealments, while at the same time sustaining the world intact. The Almighty said, "I am that I am," and added, "and the world may also be." The people were brought into contact with the reality of Divine existence; it was not a matter of intellectual proof or even signs and miracles; their very senses apprehended God. His voice filled all of one's being. The Revelation at Sinai left no part of a person separate from the utterance "I am." There could be no such thing as hesitation or doubt.

The Revelation at Sinai was thus a manifestation of the innermost light, and for this reason, it was said: "We, the people, were nullified and then, by God, revived." It was a momentary bursting of all normal bounds, an intimation of the sublime reality of the end of days. Yet, what is being described is speech, the words of the Ten Commandments, hewn in the stone of the tablets. And the Hebrew word for "hewn" is similar to the root of the word for freedom, *cherut*, freedom from the angel of death. As it is said of the end of days, "And death shall be swallowed forever" (Isaiah 25:8). At a certain moment in history, the end of history came and went, and this was the flash of revelation.

However—and this seems to be the point of the dissertation—this was in part necessary only because the people did not yet have the Torah—they did not possess the means of protecting themselves from the Divine light and were, therefore, unable to know God in any other way than by the miracle of His descent. The Torah, among other things, provides man with the tools to experience the Divine, even if, at times, in a very rudimentary fashion. As some Chasidim used to say: "We study the secret lore, learn about the existence of other worlds, angels, seraphs, and heavenly beings; but I don't see any angels or heavenly beings, and I don't believe that anyone who studies more is able to see more. Nevertheless, the difference between the one who studies and the one who does not study is that, in the future, when these things are made manifest, the one who studies will be able to recognize them better, to relate them to what he has learned."

This hints at a concept of what is to be expected in the ultimate time. It will not be a total nullification of matter, but a purification of matter, a metamorphosis of all physical density making it transparent. Matter is now the densest and heaviest of all the forms of existence. At the End of Days it will become purified and luminous; the reality of the world will become transparent, completely receptive to the Divine light.

It is written in Isaiah 60:2: "For though darkness covers the earth and dark night the nations, the Lord shall shine upon you and over you shall His glory appear; and the nations shall march towards your light and their kings to your sunrise." This is possible because the Torah is a structure that the soul can aspire to and attain; it is a code of the spirit, a many-layered message concerning the manner of relating to the highest holiness. This relation is something we build up for generations, constructing and tearing down and continually striving to form something lasting. When we do reach some kind of closeness with God, when we begin to make proper use of the code—in Torah, in mitzvot, or in deeds—much of what had been secret wisdom and hidden lore becomes something that reveals Him. As Rabbi Nachman of Bratslav saw it: The whole of Torah and mitzvot may be apprehended as a new arrangement of the world, making the world into a means of communication between God and man; and it is one's task in the world to make the necessary changes that are integral to this new arrangement, changes that transform a disorderly world into an orderly one.

This can be illustrated in various other realms of existence where human intervention is crucial—like in the magnetization of iron—all man does is place a particular substance in certain positions and thereby he induces movement; and the innate force in the substance, the atoms and the molecular structure of its reality, arrange themselves in a new order, augmenting the nature of the substance and transforming it. It is a process of creating some order out of the ordinary lack of order which is chance. As it is described by the modern science of communications: The world is full of sounds and all we have to do is put these sounds together in some coherent fashion. What does God say? What does the Divine want to communicate by this or that "noise?" When we sort out the sounds, we can begin to understand and eventually to respond. The basic element of experience, which is made up of matter and the combinations of matter, is not a fundamental creation; it only points to something else that is not apparent to us, which, with the proper grasp, can become an instrument for our own use. It is like a problem to be solved, a puzzle to be clearly worked out; the change one introduces makes it into a vessel for something that is needed. In this respect, Torah can be conceived of as that which changes the world by means of wisdom, speech, and actions; it enables life to achieve a higher level of communication, thereby allowing light to enter. "For My mouth has spoken."

37

On the Essence of Torah Study

$\mathbf{A}$s has already been said, there are many sides to the performance of the mitzvot. First, the individual soul does not need the mitzvot for itself; it needs them only to correct or elevate the world. That is, the function of man and his soul is to raise the level of reality in the world, not to raise himself, or rather, his soul. Because that other part of himself, his flesh and blood, is actually a part of the world and not of himself.

This brings us to the saying that charity is weighed against all the other mitzvot. True, it has been said of other mitzvot as well that they are weighed against all the others; and this has to be considered in the context of the understanding that all the mitzvot together constitute a whole, that each and every one has something that is not to be found in any other. Charity, for example, is considered one of the three supporting pillars of the world: Torah, Worship, and Kindness. To be sure, kindness may be reckoned as a broader concept than charity; nevertheless, for our purposes here, they are identical. This is reflected in the inner development of the Jewish people for whom, in the passage of time, the concept of a mitzvah became the performance of an act of kindness or charity. For this is the

257

essence of the act of the positive mitzvah—it raises the world, corrects it, or remedies its hurt. When one performs a mitzvah, one is venturing into the realm of shadow and obscurity, the twilight shell between light and dark, between holiness and abomination; and one is redeeming something from that realm, taking it out of its misplacement and carrying it over to another dimension of existence, more appropriate to it. Charity does this and more because the substance of charity is not the money itself, but the life force that a person has invested in order to earn this money. That is, the life force is a more significant factor than pious intention. And even the enthusiasm and passion of an ordinary mitzvah, like *tefillin* or *lulav* and *etrog*, cannot really be compared with the time and effort involved in the earning of a sum of money for charity.

The saying that Talmud Torah, the study of the Torah, is also weighed against all the other mitzvot, indicates only that, in contrast to charity and other meritorious actions, the one who studies Torah has a higher contact with holiness. Charity, on the other hand, is on a relatively low level of holiness, a more elementary, even a primordial level, a giving of the material self rather than an offering of the mind and soul. It is only when one speaks of charity as self-sacrifice that a comparison can be made in terms of a higher contact.

To be sure, when one gives charity, one is really acting as an extension of the hand of God, as it is written, "You open your hand and satisfy the desires of all living creatures" (Psalms 145:16). Along the same line of thought, when one studies Torah, one's mind is bound up at a very definite point with holiness, that is, with the higher Sefirot of Intelligence and Understanding, and not with the lower Sefirot of Chesed, Gevurah, Tiferet, and the others.

To clarify this a little, let us make the observation that when a person reaches a level of real love for the Creator, this is a function of the Divine Soul, namely of the higher Sefirot (Chochmah, Binah, Daat). At the same time, the Divine Soul is acting through the medium of other agencies such as the animal-soul, or the mind of man, which is also a physical instrument of emotion and experiences, or what is generally called the natural part of man. This part, the heart's desire of ordinary man, and of the Benoni as well, does not undergo any change. It does not alter its course or its essence; it continues to be connected with the objects of attention determined by the body. However, when a person is under the influence of his love for or fear of God, these human passions tend to be subdued. That is, when a person loves God, he cannot at the same time give himself to any other love; his lusts are blunted. Only the Tzadik undergoes a significant transformation—a sort of mutation—in which the naturally desired objects of the soul change and the soul aspires to different modes of being. The Benoni does not experience this. In him, the animal-soul is not transformed. It is modified and influenced, but it remains what it was. Thus, for instance, the most devout Benoni may find that his mind wanders even in prayer and his thoughts suddenly dwell on something extraneous, showing that there is an internal struggle between varying forces and desires. From this it is again concluded that even the Benoni cannot break out of the physical life altogether and transform the essence of his soul. Nevertheless, when anyone is immersed in the study of Torah, he causes something to happen to the essence of his Divine Soul dominated by the higher Sefirot. The Torah itself becomes an object of desire.

The Benoni is, thus, not only the one who has the potential of being a righteous person; he is also able to use his will to think only holy thoughts. Thereby, all the rest of his being can only develop in a certain fashion. For action follows thought, and by a consistent effort of self-education and self-control a person can reach a condition of living in holiness all the time. The same person, of course, may not be able to control his dreams, which are a different part of him and reflect all the hidden desires which conscious thought cannot eradicate. Nevertheless, his conscious world is a very definite one and has its human breadth and range; and although the method of conscious control has its difficulties, it enables the one who practices it to prevent the undesirable and to bring himself into a state of freedom of choice between doing and not doing, between abandoning himself to desire or relinquishing fulfillment.

However, if a person is occupied with Torah, he is, at that

moment, in another realm of thoughts, and his whole being responds accordingly. The question that arises is why one cannot transpose this benign influence of the higher intellectual Sefirot to the lower emotional ones. The problem is far more profound and is connected with the central fact of the "Breaking of the Vessels" and the resultant polarity of good and evil, which is different for each of the Sefirot. Thus, in the Sefirah of Chochmah (Wisdom), there is no such shattering as in the others; in any case, it is a relatively external process, while in Chesed, Gevurah, Tiferet, and the other low Sefirot, there is a more total breaking of the vessels. This creates the situation we know—that the mind is far more pure than the lower nature with its desires and emotions. Of course, consciousness cannot exist without its emotional component; there is no completely isolated realm of wisdom, and there is no absolute objectivity. This partially explains the existence of sin and its relation to the Tree of Knowledge—that one cannot know without relating emotionally to one's knowledge. An inner involvement of some kind is inevitable. As it was once described: A Chasid wished to observe the naked reality of evil in order to be able to avoid sin; but inasmuch as this could not be done at a sufficient distance and with proper objectivity, that is, without any perilous involvement, the wish could not be granted.

Consciousness is, therefore, itself a form of involvement, with varying depths and intensities of influence. As soon as one knows something, there is always danger of contagion, even when one is ostensibly unaffected. All the same, in a very general way, consciousness is itself neutral; it does not belong to any special realm. Thus, by involving consciousness in the holy, in studying Torah, the mind and the objects of the mind are united. This experience does not necessarily evaporate when one ceases to study; it remains in the memory at least— if not as a lingering substance in wakefulness. Therefore, when one learns a single chapter of Scripture—"In the beginning . . ."—at that instance, his soul is no longer a part of a known objective reality, but becomes a part of the spiritual reality of what is being made known to him "in the beginning." And this knowledge, becoming part of his soul, has something of holiness in it. It is possible that the same person may be a great sinner, but no matter how hard he tries he cannot erase from his being this fragment of holiness absorbed into himself by the study of Torah, the knowledge that "in the beginning. . . ."

Another reason for the study of Torah lies in the fact that the positive mitzvot can be seen to be like the 248 "organs" of the Divine; thus, when one performs a commandment, one is making it possible for something that was a part of the world to become a part of God. True, every organ, in man as in God, has its own level of vitality; there is a basic difference between one's head and one's feet. As an aside, it may be mentioned that, according to Halachah, the heart is not considered to be an organ—just as the brain or the liver are not organs—an "organ" has flesh and sinews and bones of its own. From this point of view, it is argued that since prayer is like the heart, it is not really a mitzvah. Even if the heart is not an organ, it is what gives vitality to the body's organs. In the same way, there is a difference between Talmud Torah (study of Torah), and Yediat HaTorah (Knowledge of the Torah). Talmud Torah is the physical act of saying holy things with one's mouth. The Yediah, or knowledge of Torah, is not the same mitzvah as a definite action. One may, for example, perform the act of studying Torah without getting to know Torah, and one can know Torah without performing the physical act of studying it. The mitzvah of study is a physical mitzvah involving eye, brain, and speech, and is structured accordingly. We are thus able to make a distinction between the light of the positive mitzvot and the inner light of the Torah itself. Each is at its own level. Just as the mind of the most foolish of men is at a higher level of spiritual vitality than the arm of the wisest of men. So too is the mitzvah to know Torah on a very high level, even if the one who does it is himself on a relatively low level of being.

No one can be said to reach the wisdom of God; at best one attains an understanding of a portion of His Torah—concerning an ox that gores a cow, that the *tzitzit* should have four threads, and so forth. This, even if it is not Divine light, may be said to be useful as illumination. One has acquired what one needs to live meaningfully. In the same way, the ancient Egyptians, although they never developed Euclidean geometry, were aware that the square of the sides of a right triangle were always proportional according to a fixed formula; thus, they were able to lay out their buildings without any difficulty. They did not have to know more for their purpose; perhaps, it was enough to have a guiding formula in any given situation. So too, in terms of wisdom, it may be sufficient for each person to know as much as he can absorb—the level of one's knowledge is a secondary matter.

Nonetheless, it is maintained by the sages that "not learning, but doing, is the essential thing" (Pirkei Avot 1:17) and "this day to do it" (Deuteronomy 7:11). The emphasis is on the present, on here and now. Even if one's study of Torah is on a very high intellectual and spiritual plane, when confronted with the need to perform a positive mitzvah (something that only you can do, like prayer, or showing someone the way), then one is obliged to cease from study and to do the required mitzvah or action. To be sure, if it is something that another can perform just as well, then one may exercise some discretion. On the whole, however, although the study of Torah is among the most noble of all the mitzvot—and weighed against them all—it has to be abrogated when faced with the demand to fulfill any positive precept.

For this, it appears, is the purpose of Creation and of man—to provide God, the Creator, with an abode here below. God, it seems, wishes to live in the world below, "where darkness can be turned into light, so that the glory of the Lord shall fill all of this material world . . . and all flesh shall see it together." That is, the glory should be in the physical world of substance and not necessarily in the heavens. The wish is here expressed, for all flesh to see the Divine glory, not the soul, but the flesh itself.

To be sure, all of the Torah can be said to be an explanation of the mitzvot—and one can find in any one of the mitzvot, or even a part of it, enough spiritual nourishment for a life time. For the Torah is, as it were, the "Chabad" of the Ain Sof (Infinite), and engagement in any part of it draws unto oneself the Divine splendor. This brings us to the question of quantity—of observing any one part against observing the whole, and the problem of doing a kindness as opposed to studying

Torah. One person will maintain that he can do no more than devote himself to intellectual pursuits of Torah; another, that he is busy with good deeds. To this the Talmud answers that for such persons, it would be better had they not been born, because any separation of a single mitzvah from the totality of Divine worship separates it from holiness and causes a cleavage in the person. An act of sanctity is meaningful only within a framework that is holy. When one is so wholly occupied with one thing that one criminally neglects another, one is losing touch with the essential, and that which occupies one becomes an intellectual game. There is a story told in the Jerusalem Talmud of Rabbi Avihu, who lived in Caesarea and had sent his son to study in Tiberias with the great teachers. Upon meeting someone from Tiberias, Rabbi Avihu asked what his son was doing. The other told him that the young man was occupied with deeds of kindness, especially with burying the dead. Rabbi Avihu said that this was indeed a great mitzvah for which few volunteered; but when he came home, he wrote a letter to his son saying: "Are there not enough dead in Caesarea that I sent you to Tiberias?"

The point here is that when there are others who can perform a necessary task, one is free of the obligation to perform it. On the other hand, there is another Talmud passage that lists the priorities of mitzvot, those which can be abrogated in the urgency of another: Work is abrogated before Talmud Torah, Talmud Torah before burying the dead, and so forth. Certain mitzvot take precedence or are considered more important than others. The essential point is that, although every mitzvah is its own joy, the study of Torah is that special joy of direct contact, the relationship of union with the Divine.

True, every mitzvah contains the possibility of such union with God; as it was said, when a person gives charity, he is acting as the hand of God. And this goes beyond the joys of contemplation and meditation. But Torah is a level of joy that is more open and vulnerable to the soul. When one is occupied with Torah, one is calling upon God, even though there is no apparent emotional involvement. It is more like a spontaneous exclamation, unconsidered and genuine, and a true expression of something with which a person may not even be totally identified, but which exists, nonetheless, in his essence. It is like crying out, "Father, father!" or like the saying, "All ye who are thirsty, come and drink!" and there is no water but Torah. The thirst is the thirst for God, and only Torah will quench it. It is like saying I do not desire a great abundance of experience, but I desire to come closer to the source, and for that I need to get to water. What is being expressed here is the idea that the Torah is not an intellectual exercise; it is the word of God, and it is the way to approach Him. Occupying oneself with Torah, therefore, has to be done in a state of "fear and trembling."

38
Intention

According to Halachah, meditating on a word or idea is not the same as saying it. Even concentrating with *kavanah*, or spiritual alignment, does not release one from reciting the words of a prayer or blessing. On the other hand, if one does say the words but does not manage to align oneself spiritually, one has fulfilled one's obligations. To be sure, the religious demand is for both outer and inner participation; but—aside from the recitation of the first verse of the Shema prayer and the first benediction of the Amidah prayer—one does not have to repeat the prayer even if it was recited without proper *kavanah*, intention or directed concentration.

All of this may seem rather unspiritual, that is, for prayer to suffice with an external expression rather than with an inner intensity of purpose. The explanation is that the soul does not really need to do exercises, expressing love of God, and so forth; but the physical body does. Every mitzvah has its material component, an outer action in the world. The other components—mostly spiritual in essence—are not considered as having the same importance in terms of doing. Not that the spiritual components are without value; they simply have a different task or function.

For, as we are well aware, nothing in the world of action can be accomplished only by good intentions. Man has been given a garden to cultivate, and no matter how sublime his thoughts about the plants (and even the possible beneficial effect these thoughts may have on the plants), yet it still seems to be necessary to do some hoeing, planting, and weeding. In other words, the task of man is connected with the essence of the world of substance, with those things that his soul cannot deal with in the abstract. Acknowledging this connection, we are stopped short by the paradox that there doesn't seem to be any need for the soul. Good thoughts and good intentions are ultimately no more than the scaffolding of the structure and not the structure itself.

On the other hand, as a Kabbalistic image puts it, the spiritual qualities of love and fear of God are like the two wings which enable every act to fly; without them, one remains bound to the earth. True, it is the purpose of man to descend and correct or repair the inadequacies of matter; but the lower the material problem, the higher he can rise in solving it, in effecting its Tikun. Ultimately, this may be reduced to the simple performance of mitzvot—the recitation of each of the letters of the Shema, the actual performance of certain basic actions, like offering a penny to charity, and so forth.

Now, it is known that God sustains the souls of all living things, giving to each its specific form and vitality. For all things possess a "soul" of some sort, having been given their existence by God. Nevertheless, the light of the Divine Soul in man is something else entirely.

The difference between the two kinds of soul lies in the degree of hiddenness of the light in the physical and in the whole process of being clothed in matter. Just as there are various stages of mental being—the first, of total concealment of light (the ignorant man), the second, where God is still hidden but is clothed or outwardly manifested in some definite shape (the humanist-atheist), and the third, which is the rational world of the philosophers, sufficing with systems and explanations of reality and leaving no room for God—so too, and how much more so, in terms of the soul, do the stages of the knowledge of God range from extreme darkness to light.

In any case, God is inevitably present, whether in nature or man, whether in body or in soul. One of the qualitative differences in the various forms of existence is in the capacity to sin. A more common classification, not necessarily qualitative, of the forms of existence includes: (1) nonconsciousness (inorganic), (2) life (plant and animal), and (3) speech (man), where the difference is in the degree of life force in them. True, there is no relation between these two kinds of difference; something of no value in terms of good and evil may have considerable significance in terms of its potential for holiness and vice versa.

In mathematics, one can speak of an absolute number; besides this, one can determine the power or size of a specific number by adding zeroes or by giving the specific number a root or power sign. So too, in the moral life, one can relate to each action by itself—either it is a transgression or a mitzvah—and its power or significance is something that is measured by oneself, by what one gives to it in terms of intention, inner effort, joy, or participation. In performing an act of charity, for example, it is a matter of what it has cost one to obtain the money, the quality of the spiritual accompaniment to the act, and so forth. The differences between the levels of charity are far more than in the value of the money; the coin remains the same; it is a matter of the smile or the groan with which it is given. Thus, there is a meaningful distinction between body and soul, between intention and act.

Nevertheless, there is no contradiction between this and the fact that the physical performance of the mitzvah is paramount. Therefore, to return to a previous distinction, the body and the soul can be on the same level in terms of holiness (good and evil), but in terms of life force, the soul has infinitely more power than the body. There is more life in the spiritual soul than in any physical body, more "power" and potency. As for intellectual activity, its importance lies in that it accompanies the body. But a body that has a living soul in it lives far more intensely than one that has no soul. On the whole then, a mitzvah performed by someone with knowledge and understanding is a holy action and very different from one performed in ignorance.

This brings us back to the intention of the mitzvah, which gives the mitzvah wings and enables it to rise. The more love and fear of God involved in the act, the higher the level of the performance—ranging from a mitzvah that remains in the World of Action and changes something in the realm of good and evil to the mitzvah that rises above the world of matter and causes a shifting of things in the higher worlds.

Since the aim of human life on earth is precisely that—to redeem this world by bringing it up to some level of contact with the Divine—aspiring to higher levels by proper intention is a vital aspect of this process of Tikun or correction. Thus, if a person has the opportunity to perform a mitzvah, either he chooses to do it only with his body, with its circumscribed field of force and of life, or he chooses to harness it to the power of his thought and feeling, giving it a certain orientation and additional potency. Like any act which one may perform—such as digging with one's hands or digging with a tractor—the action is the same, but its power is different. So too, the mitzvah, whether it is giving charity or reciting a blessing, is always itself; its strength and capacity depend on the life force one puts into it, and this is mainly a matter of the heart's intention and the thoughts of the knowledgeable mind. True, the intention without the body can have no effect whatsoever; but together with the physical act, it can effect a crucial change in the essence of the world.

39

The Dilemma of Habit

The "place" of a soul is a way of designating its level of holiness in Paradise. The souls of men who serve God with the natural love and fear of a devout Jew are located on the World of Formation (Yetzirah), which is the world of the angels. (For the angels also serve God naturally; indeed that is their very essence.) While the souls of Tzadikim who serve God with a love that is conscious and freely chosen, who comprehend and grasp their position, are located in the World of Creation (Briah), which is the realm of the Throne and of intellectual Understanding (Binah).

This does not have anything to do with the person's actual achievements in life or his religious practice. There is a difference between the soul itself and the works of the soul. To be sure, when the soul creates something or when it is engaged in Torah study or performing a mitzvah, it is already higher than the person who is doing these things. But it is the mitzvah that links up with the Infinite light of the Ten Sefirot. It does so by first uniting with Sefirot of its own particular world. At the same time, the Ten Sefirot of a particular world or realm of being are not identical with the realm itself; they are the Divine pattern, the framework, and the driving force in each realm.

Even though the Sefirot are in a particular world, they belong to another level of existence; they manifest the Divine in that particular realm. They do not manifest the realm around them, but the Divine force which illuminates the realm. What is more, the Ten Sefirot of the World of Emanation, the highest world, are contained in the Sefirot of all the lower worlds. Thus, when one performs a mitzvah, the contact is made with Divine Unity through the Sefirot of the realm in which one is working.

From this aspect, the Divine power gives life to all the worlds, even though it becomes more heavily veiled as it descends from one world to another. There are many varied forms to this covering or veiling of the Divine light. Nevertheless, it is the same Divine light that gives life to all. As it has been said: there may be some differences in terms of the experience—a person can touch the King's hand itself or through His sleeve—it does not matter; the contact takes place whenever a person is engaged in Torah and mitzvot. For the mitzvah is the vehicle of Divine contact. However, the soul of the person performing the mitzvah remains at the level of the realm in which it takes place; even in Paradise it is still not wholly united with the Divine and keeps to its own place. To be sure, the soul is at a higher level than the ordinary consciousness; it belongs to the realms or Worlds of Creation and Formation and enjoys the glory of the Divine countenance; but it does not become a part of the Shechinah. For the soul is not necessarily of the same essence as the Shechinah; it is a part of the particular realm of its existence. The mitzvah, however, does unite with the Divine through the Sefirot.

What is special about the relation of the Ten Sefirot of Creation and Formation to the soul is the spiritual light of Torah and Divine worship. Because Torah is the Wisdom of God, and the mitzvah is the expression of God's Will; thus, when the mitzvah is manifested in a world higher than our own, it returns and makes contact with the person; and the person then delights in the mitzvah which he performed because he is bound to it, and through it, he senses the Divine glory. For the mitzvah is in itself a blessing; and, as it is said, the reward for a mitzvah is a mitzvah; that is to say, the reward comes from the higher worlds, and the person enjoys the light of the Shechinah that comes back to him through the mitzvah he has performed.

This, therefore, belongs to the Worlds in which the soul is found and not to the World of Emanation, which is higher than all the soul can ever know. For the soul remains a creaturely thing, while the World of Emanation is where the Infinite Wisdom dwells; it is the place of Divine Unity beyond measure. Even though in the World of Creation (Briah), there is a revelation of Divine Wisdom, Understanding, and Knowledge (Chochmah, Binah, and Daat), it does not compare with what is manifested in the World of Emanation. For in the World of Creation, there is a certain contraction of the Divine Wisdom. Even though it appears as a maximum revelation in that World, where Wisdom is the very ground of its reality, it is still not the essence of Divine Wisdom itself because it cannot absorb more than a certain amount. In order for the lower worlds to receive from the higher, there has to be a contraction of the Divine power. The vessels of the created world are not adequate; they have their limitations and would be shattered by the influx of the Infinite. If the created minds of men would ever hear more than they should, if they received too much, glimpsed something from the other side of the "veil," they would cease to be creatures, products of Creation, and would be unable to relate to reality as it is. In order for a person to see reality, he has to restrict his view; a more comprehensive view would eliminate that which was specific, and not only would external reality evade him, so would his own existence. So that from the aspect of consciousness, the knowledge that "there is nothing besides Him" cannot be grasped; there has to be a created world to enable the mind of man to sense God or even to be aware of the reality around him.

The World of Emanation is a realm without any such limitations; it is not restricted in any way, as it is written in the Kabbalah, and there are no veils hiding the Divine glory. In any case, the knowledge that "there is nothing besides Him" is the very nature of consciousness in the World of Emanation. To be sure, created minds cannot usually grasp anything of this. Just as human vision is limited to a relatively small range of light waves, and any other light is beyond perception; the World of

Emanation remains as if in darkness, even though there may be experimental proof of the existence of such unseen light. Nevertheless, the World of Emanation can somehow be known by the most subtle illuminations of the great Tzadikim. It is available to the select few whose work, over the centuries, went far beyond the range of ordinary human intelligence.

The achievements of these great saints and Tzadikim were thus a vehicle, or a Chariot, to the Infinite, blessed be He. Their achievements consisted also of a process of self-nullification, a negation of one's existence in this world, and a desire to be absorbed in the Divine light by adhering to Torah and mitzvot. So that the World of Emanation is the world of the Tzadik who has removed himself from existence. By nullifying his essence, he becomes a Chariot for the Shechinah and an instrument in the hands of God.

It should be evident that those great Tzadikim or saints who reach the level where contact is made with the World of Emanation are very few indeed; they are "Chariots" of the spirit. Lesser men, however, perhaps even the vast majority of people, can also reach a very high level of spiritual being. It is possible, even within the confines of the available, overt tradition. A person has simply to worship God with love and fear.

The difficulty arises in regard to the validity of this love and fear. Is the emotion one of a vivid awakening to the reality of the Divine presence, or is it merely a self-induced feeling of uprightness? And a person may, indeed, be full of sublime thoughts, feel himself on the verge of some heartfelt revelation, and still be expressing only his "natural" love and fear. Such natural feeling is usually not more than a personal experience and belongs to the realm of the World of Formation; it does not even reach the level of conscious contemplation of the Divine essence, which belongs to the World of Creation.

Admittedly, in both of these instances, there is some sort of genuine emotion accompanied by a proportional shift to a higher level. What happens, however, when a heart fails to express the love and fear that is contained within it, when the act of worship is performed as a habit, mechanically, or simply without any inner awareness whatsoever? As the Baal Ha-Tanya says: "It remains below in the world of separateness, called the externality of the worlds, having no power to rise and be absorbed in His blessed Unity in the holy Ten Sefirot." This is so, even if the action is not of the category of transgression, even if it is routinely accepted and conventional.

The point is that the act was not performed for its own sake. A mitzvah done for its own sake is done for the sake of God and not for one's self, and it is inevitably accompanied by a certain uplifting feeling. It is like doing something for someone else—there is usually a reason, some kind of emotional involvement—whether it is because one likes the other or one is afraid of what he will say. So too, it is almost impossible to do something for the sake of God without it being related to one's latent love and fear of God.

Even if behind the habitual act there is a genuine wish to serve God, a certain combination of love and fear is needed in the moment of the act. Love without fear (of God) is often an agreeable state of mind, and a mitzvah may be performed because it is pleasant or appropriate. But if it does not quicken the spiritual emotions, even those lower forms like respect, it does not rise.

On the other hand, a worthy action done out of self-love or self-esteem or for any reason other than "for its own sake" belongs to the Nogah Shell and is, therefore, not entirely evil. To be sure, it is also not holy. It belongs to the Sitra Achra and has to remain in the shell of life until repentance is made, and it becomes subject to the process of healing. Because, whereas ordinary healing is the correction of some injury, the healing of repentance is the correction of the whole person and not only of the injury. Not only does the penitent himself return to God, but his worship and his Torah also return with him. For this reason the Sages have said that a person should continue to occupy himself with Torah and mitzvot even if it is not for its own sake, because out of the action "not for its own sake" will come the action "for its own sake." That is to say, when a person repents, whatever belonged to the Nogah Shell (not the

Shell of Uncleanness, but of the inbetween region) is nurtured by the holiness in which he is now engaged, by the Torah for its own sake, and it is raised up to a higher level.

It is like the eating and drinking in which a person has indulged before repentance; it may be classified as belonging to the Nogah Shell; however, because it enabled the person to live and turn to God, it is transformed into a higher category of existence. Similarly, a person who studies Torah in order to further his personal ambitions, and not for the sake of Torah, may find that his efforts are spiritually rewarded only after repentance, when what was gained for the wrong reason can be gainfully used for the right reason.

This is important because it is indeed difficult for a person to maintain a proper spiritual tension throughout the routine of the religious life; prayer tends to become repetitive, actions become mechanical and, without being aware of it, the "intention" sags. If a prayer is uttered with the fullness of intention, for its own sake, even once or twice in a year, or even once or twice in a lifetime, it somehow gathers up all the other prayers which were spoken out of dull habit, and they are integrated into the experience of genuine love and fear of God and are raised to a level of holiness.

40
Torah for Its Own Sake

"A person should always oc-
cupy himself with Torah, even if not for its own sake, for from
motives of self-interest he will come to study it for its own
sake" (Pesachim 50b, Nazir 23b). This is explained as follows: If
a person studies for his own sake, he has to repent in order for
his Torah to be received in Heaven. When he does finally study
for the sake of Torah, he thereby raises all the studying he has
done previously to a requisite level.

The Sefirot are expressions of the Divine force or Godliness
in the various levels of existence. However, as long as a person
performs any mitzvah, like prayer or study, without any
conscious spiritual force, his mitzvah does not ascend even to
the Ten Sefirot of the World of Formation or even of Action.
Any self-centered action, undirected to sanctity, has no way of
connecting with the Divine. Without love and fear of God,
even a mitzvah cannot rise up to Heaven.

This brings us back to the matter of the essential difference
between good and evil, mitzvah and transgression, beyond the
usual distinctions of cause and effect, or of well-intended and
ill-intended actions. A mitzvah or a good deed creates something that is holy; and this is so even on a low level of intention

when the mitzvah is performed without any inner content whatsoever. Thus, when a person studies Torah on the level of an intellectual exercise, as preparation for matriculation, for instance, the mitzvah cannot be said to rise; nevertheless, it remains a mitzvah, and it cannot be erased. Indeed, no action or thought can be erased as though it had never been. What comes into existence creates a certain indisputable reality.

What remains belongs to another realm of existence: Every mitzvah becomes an angel, pleading one's cause, and every transgression becomes a force of indictment. It isn't that all actions are recorded for or against a person, but rather that the action itself becomes an angelic being of one kind or another, good or bad. This is so because the mitzvot and the transgressions each have their own essence; they are very definite segments of reality. And in spite of its having substance and form, the essence is something else, beyond the physical elements that constitute it. Therefore, it can easily be transmuted into another expression of the same essence, such as an angel. This is possible because the thought behind the mental conception and the physical deed, the true content, was a part of some genuine spiritual existence.

The idea is not inconsistent with modern thinking, which admits to the law of the conservation of energy and of matter, and recognizes that there is no end to the forms that existence may take. Thus, an action does not just vanish into nothingness. Everything is conserved. Not only are there material consequences and residues, there is also a certain transformation of subtle energies and thought contents; new forms are assumed, and there is movement into another frame of reference, such as the spiritual. For there is also a law of the conservation of spiritual essences. And the spiritual contents of a human action are subject to alteration and can become something very definite, such as a being of the angelic order.

In other words, the spiritual essence of a mitzvah, its inner content, constitutes a certain existence which becomes a force seeking its own level and framework of expression. It has to be retained somehow in the structure of things that are real. It is not a matter of instruments or means to an end; it is simply that one's actions remain and cling to one's life. The angels, or the demonic creatures I create, swarm about me and cry: "Father, you are the one who brought us into existence." I cannot, therefore, cast my life away from myself, out of sight behind my back. Only the process of repentance can change things and erase some of the past—or at least, to cut the connection with certain actions or states of mind of the past. But this too is often doubtful.

In any case, when a person studies Torah, he creates an angel and becomes a creature that has connections with a higher order of existence. Any attempt to picture this spiritual essence has its limitations; nevertheless, it is of an experiential order; that is, it is something that happens. The physical pronunciation of holy words is a reality that transforms, and the sanctified essence thus created is connected to the person who created it.

There is also a dimension of substance and form, or as it is called in the esoteric philosophy, "lights and instruments" (*orot v'kelim*). In fact, almost everything in the world has a degree of substance and form—even thought, or spirit—in the sense that every phenomenon has a specific frame of reference and contents. The framework that contains a phenomenon and gives it its uniqueness may be said to be its substance, while that which vitalizes it may be called its form.

In a way, there is such a relationship between all essences in the world, including entities such as ideas, for example. An idea is built out of the formal elements that are its genesis and its environmental source and from the inner contents that such structures possess. There are instances where the distinction between substance and form is quite clear—such as in a literary work, where it is possible to see the same contents or substances reappearing in any number of combinations or forms, the same idea expressed in several different modes of expression. The relationship, of course, is always a little different, and there is always a certain interaction between form and content; the vessel and what it contains do have some influence on one another.

This relationship between substance and form exists in all things. In man, it is manifest as body and soul, the soul being quite unable, for the most part, to act beyond the provisions of the body. That is to say, even though the body is apparently matter, and the soul is spirit, their need to function together necessarily influences them profoundly. Thus, the soul will respond in a certain way to one particular body and in another way to another body. There is an unmistakable relationship, even if extremely subtle, between a particular body and a particular soul.

This may be extended to the realm of thought as well. For example, what happens when we translate? Apparently the content is the same, but it has been given another form; it is different not only by virtue of being clothed differently but because the clothes have an influence on the substance. This also explains the uniqueness of a holy tongue. As it would seem, language should be able to say everything. Nevertheless, there is a now-almost-forgotten fast day in Jewish tradition, the eighth day of Tevet, when the Torah was translated into Greek. And this in spite of the fact that the Sages spoke in praise of this translation, which enabled many Jews and non-Jews to read the Torah. Notwithstanding this, the fast was kept for many generations as an expression of lamentation for the loss of the original Hebrew "vestment" of the Torah.

This is only to emphasize that the problem of substance and form is not merely that of materiality and spirituality. Thus, when we say that angels have their own substance and form, we mean that they are beings composed of a certain formal configuration and of the contents of this configuration. The two together also comprise the essence of thought. They still are not holiness, but they are a structure, an existence in the world, belonging to that which is good. As it is said, a book of the Bible is also an existence belonging to the good, and it is also built according to the same scheme of substance and form, even if uniquely so.

Naturally, substance and form keep changing, and beyond a certain limit, things cease to be what they are and become something else. Nevertheless, the angel who is the consequence of a certain action is restricted to a definite range of being. What belongs to one person, as the result of a good or bad deed, does not belong to another. This does not contradict the multiplicity of categories of angelic beings—some of them universal and others limited to a particular kind of person. It is like the assumption made in the medical science of immunology, namely, that the body repels or accepts according to what is in itself.

The rule that everyone gets what he gives is according to the law of correspondences; certain classes of things belong to each other. A person who sins acquires one prosecutor after another, and there is no way of getting rid of them; they move into the house and begin to belong to one's self. For one cannot so easily send one's transgressions to Hell and slip out of there oneself. Hence, incidentally, the need for a day like Yom Kippur.

What is more, there seems to be a balancing system in the spiritual world by which parasitic elements are disposed of—otherwise they would overwhelm us. One of the counterforces is suffering, which casts out the iniquity. Another is regret—and it is well known that the wicked are full of vexation and remorse. Indeed, the whole experience of repentance is an endeavor to separate oneself from the things one has done.

One seems to be surrounded then by myriad creatures of one's own creation—good and bad. If one could see them, it would make life impossible, of course. Nevertheless, there are a few descriptions. They are scarce, not only because of the reluctance in Jewish tradition to make pictures of angels and demons, but also because of a real absence of interest. What is the face of envy, greed, lust, and so forth? The descriptions are almost all agreed that the demons reflect something in oneself. As the Bible expresses it in God's words to Cain: "If you do well, you shall be lifted up, and if you do not, sin crouches at the door, and unto you is its desire, but you may rule over it" (Genesis 4:7). The relationship is thus a complex and ambivalent one: The demon I have created loves me, but alas, seeks to destroy me. It has a need to express itself within me, and this is precisely what chokes the life out of both of us. All that I have done wrong is there to torment and kill me. On the other hand, the good that a person does also accompanies him. Thus, there are descriptions of the ministering angels who join a man on the eve of Sabbath, for example.

Repentance is a matter of trying to disconnect oneself from—

or, at least, to weaken the connection with—these creatures of one's past. However, the highest level of repentance is the transformation of one's sinful deeds, making them accomplish something meritorious by changing the course of their consequences. Because to a degree, the significance of an action may be measured not only by its intrinsic morality, but also by its ultimate consequences. But this is a very high level of Tikun and belongs to the way of holiness. Where a person can effect such transformation (of his sins), it becomes a powerful lever, raising him to heights otherwise unattainable.

Studying Torah for any other reason than for its own sake— even if the reason may be praiseworthy, such as a sincere wish to gain knowledge, or to teach, and the like—still remains below, on the level of the Klipot (shells). It does not ascend. This would seem to put the Torah in the same category as any other occupation. Indeed, "what profit has a man of all his toil which he labors under the sun" (Ecclesiastes 1:3), if even his Torah cannot be taken with him when he leaves this life. For, just as one cannot take one's cloak, or one's bank account, or one's social position with one when life ends on earth; and just as all these things are no longer relevant, so too is the learning acquired for the wrong reason irrelevant. On the other hand, it is said in Heaven: "Blessed is the one who comes here with his holy studies in his hand."

Can the words of Torah be considered like any other words in the world, either related to and concretized or rejected and just left behind on earth? The answer is that just as Torah and Godliness are one and God fills the world entirely, nevertheless, not all places and things are equally holy. What is more, the worlds are not all of the same category. The higher worlds receive an infinitely greater radiance than the lower, and they receive it without as many "garments" and "screens" as the lower. And this world of ours is the lowest, where the radiance is most contracted.

The essential distinction between higher worlds and lower worlds is not a matter of height, of course; it is a matter of differences in their scope and their clarity. The higher worlds are infinite and much wider in their capacity to receive, and their scope is measureless; but, in terms of texture or density, whatever they make part of themselves is immeasurably clearer and more transparent. In life, these two aspects of the higher worlds are reflected in peculiar ways: One person grasps ideas on a high spiritual level; another absorbs great quantities of information; and yet another person understands only what is demonstrable in practical terms.

For example, one person may have enormous intellectual powers and be able to manipulate great ideas with ease, and yet be unclear about what good and evil are in his life, while another person may be limited in his conceptual grasp, and yet be very precise and sure in his ability to discriminate between good and evil, right and wrong.

Altogether our world is indeed like some backward pupil— grasping things in their smallest detail, but being unable to see much beyond them. Even the relations between good and evil, holy and unholy, are very problematic for most men. True, this is also the result of the Divine hiddenness. However, since the Torah teaches us through the vehicle of this world, as it were, cloaked and masked, liberation is attained only by intensifying the relationship between man, his soul, and the mitzvah. Where this relationship is lacking, or where it is a negative relationship, the Torah remains just another book which, even if it is considered holy, does not necessarily belong to higher worlds. It has no "wings." Without any means of taking off from the earth, for as long as the thought of the Torah remains human, the Torah does not have any more effect on one than anything else does in the world—whether book, object, or idea. In short, the spiritual consciousness, or the holy intention, is decisive.

This brings us back to the whole idea of the mitzvah. Although the intention of the mitzvah is not its most important aspect, it is, nevertheless, an essential factor in enabling the mitzvah to emerge from the flow of action in the confines of matter. For this to occur, there must be a point of contact between man and God. A closing of the circle. As it is often repeated: What does God ask of you but love and fear and the performance of the mitzvot? The problem is: How much? How much love and fear? What is expressed in terms of real action? For the performance of the mitzvot should provide coherence and meaning in addition to specifying the minimum required of a man.

To be sure, there are scales of devotion and levels of holiness. As has been noted in the various instructions on repentance, it is important to know the penances for different transgressions—for example, how much fasting one must do for an outburst of anger. These questions also asked: Can everything be connected? And is there no other way? The answer is that it depends on what level one strives to repent, to return to God. And the simplest level is only the firm resolve to disconnect oneself from the transgression.

Similarly, in order for the mitzvah to be valid it needs a minimum of inner relationship, the same sort of minimum which functions in repentance saying, "No more!" This is only a beginning point—to love and fear God and do His command.

41

Awe and Fear of God

We have spoken of the extremely complex relationship between the mitzvah and the love and fear of God. On the one hand, the accompanying love and fear of God are not an essential part of the mitzvah as such; that is, the mitzvah remains a mitzvah irrespective of how it is performed. On the other hand, without love and fear, the mitzvah is a mutilated or defective act that cannot rise or take off.

What, then, is the very primary factor, the point of departure? Is it not the commandment to relate with a certain awe, respect, and fear to Divinity and to recognize that the fear of God is the root of deliverance from evil? Love is the basis of good deeds; the love of God in one induces actions, such as mitzvot, that will bring one closer to Him. While the awe and fear of God, the dread of being separated from Him, is more than enough motivation for one to avoid transgression. Love is, therefore, not enough; there has to be a stirring of the natural apprehension in the heart of man, a fear of rebelling against the Almighty. Indeed, love without fear remains incomplete, unfinished and even crippled. For there has to be a certain distance between me and God, a real gap, in order for love to

283

be a union with that which is "other." There has to be a vivid
coming together and not some sentimental or intellectual play
with oneself; far more should happen than just a pleasant
sensation emerging from a self-induced frame of mind. And
unfortunately, without the element of obligation, a certain
amount of such illusory play of ideas and feelings does creep
into one's relationship with God.

The obligation is a matter of the specific mitzvah and its
components, awe of God and the necessity to do the deed
correctly. True, every person will exhibit a different amount of
awe in his performance of the mitzvot; and one can hardly
expect from an ordinary person the ultimate fear, which is like
the fear of the angels. As the Psalmist says: "All my bones shall
speak," and all of my being trembles. Nevertheless, one may
achieve at least the minimum fear of being aware that one is
only human, the feeling of veneration that is indigenous to
every Jew. This feeling draws upon the basic uncertainty of
a ground, or rather an absolute, in existence. Sometimes, it
can become a revelation-like experience, an opening of mind
or heart, in response to some extraordinary event. Even if it
never warms up sufficiently to become an experience of the
love of God, this awe is still intrinsic to everyone. The
difference here between the exoteric and the esoteric, the
known and the hidden, lies in the extent to which a person is
stimulated or spiritually moved by things. If someone needs to
have extraordinary things happen to him in order to be moved,
such things are likely to occur; but, however it comes about,
one can easily become conscious of the innate fear of God,
whether it is as a solemn dread or just a vague intimation of His
presence.

But the more profound fear of God is the result of conscious
contemplation. The feeling of awe thus aroused is as tangible as
any other emotion, and it confronts one in no uncertain terms.
Of course, through meditation one is able to actualize almost
anything, but here we are expanding on an innate conviction.
We are being urged to contemplate the greatness of the blessed
Ain Sof and His majesty, which extends throughout all worlds,
both higher and lower, and to focus on the thought that "He
fills all worlds and encompasses all worlds." And then, after
acknowledging the greatness of God, one should meditate on

the uniqueness of Israel, which was chosen by God, and on oneself, the person of Israel, who is now contemplating God. As a result, a person will exclaim: "For my sake was the world created." In other words, there is something in thought that is not only an expression of one's human egoism, but is also a part of the process of worshipping God. When one perceives oneself to be at the center of the universe, there is more than one way to react: The world can revolve around me on any number of axes and in many possible directions. I myself somehow remain at the core of experience and worlds; I can see it all as happy for my sake, or I can feel responsible for it all. Thus, if I am at the hub of the world in the mature sense, I am also brought to an awareness of the consequences of my thoughts and actions; the good and the evil I do seem to effect a reality beyond anything immediate. Even if I am conscious of other people at the center of their worlds—more or less important than my own—the consciousness of my own centeredness carries a certain amount of sobriety and responsibility.

Israel as a people is really an abstraction, because the reality is a matter of specific persons. In terms of responsibility to God and doing His will through mitzvot, the concept of Israel means, first of all, myself. When one recites in prayer, "Who chooses His people Israel with love," one is not thinking of the Chief Rabbi, but of oneself. When one says, "You alone will we worship with awe and reverence," one is also not thinking of any official body at the head of the community, but, again, of oneself. In other words, when one says "we" in this context, or "we Jews," or "we, the people of Israel," one means "I," or, at least, primarily "I." As it was once expressed by a Tzadik: "A person should pray in the synagogue as though he were in a forest, with a tree here and a tree there, and feel that he alone is communicating with God in worship." Not that the others are not praying similarly, but that they have no significant effect on one's own prayer. One is immersed in one's own solitude, making the reckoning of the world with God at the center point which is "I."

Therefore, it is written "And behold God stands over him" (Genesis 28:13) and "the whole world is full of His glory" (Isaiah 6:3) and "He looks upon him and searches his mind and

heart (Jeremiah 11:20). Essentially, one's own self is before
God. One must do what should be done, irrespective of what
others do—whether they are good or bad, whether they even
exist. Considering that, from a certain point of view, the whole
world is only a peripheral background for one's own self; and,
at the present moment, one must be God's faithful servant in
the world. And the world itself is dependent on me, because I
am its focus.

There is always a still higher fear and awe, level above level;
and there are levels of response, extremely subtle and pure,
beyond almost all human discernment. But without getting so
far into the spiritual triumphs of ethical realizations, let us
relate to the most immediate level of the fear of God. Like all
else that is basic and fundamental, it is very simple. At this first
level of reality, God stands over one. Yes, at this moment, He
has left all the worlds; He is not concerned with the fate of the
myriad other forms of existence; He is concerned with this one
thing, with me. And the earth is filled with His glory, and He
stands over me. He is not there in the higher planes, unseen
and unseeing; He is actually looking at me, and I am here. We
look at one another, and He sees not only what I do, but my
very heart and liver are exposed to His gaze; He is aware of all
of me.

The essential point of awe is, therefore, the basic confrontation between oneself and God, His being here and now. It is a
matter of God and me, and all the rest are shadows cast to the
side. And I cannot extricate myself from it in any manner; I
cannot run away or practice some deception. It is no longer a
matter of what I think of myself or what my neighbors think of
me. It is something unnervingly straight and simple and very
basic.

This then is the situation: I am here and God is here. What
is one to do, especially since He knows, not only my innermost
thoughts, but also how I will act them out? Incidentally,
whether one practices such meditation or not, for a Jew, seeing
himself thus, standing before God, is a subject for constant
reflection.

Clearly, there can be no uniform technique or rigid form to
this contemplation, just as there is no single channel in which

thought can be made to flow. What we can say, however, is that, on the one hand, it is a striving to deepen the thought, entering further into it and penetrating it with the whole of one's being. On the other hand, it is also an effort to expand the thought, repeating it and seeking additional sides to it, finding new aspects to its possible manifestation. One may thus call it a kind of creative meditation (in contrast to the mainly passive meditation practices in certain Eastern traditions).

To be sure, there are also many differences in the actual way this is done inside and outside Chabad circles. It is largely a matter of capacity, of intellectual grasp. Not everyone can proceed in depth intellectually—especially without the aid of esoteric training such as Kabbalah. At the same time, everyone is certainly able to contemplate an idea and hold it before his awareness with whatever intelligence he can bring to bear on it. And what is of considerable importance—according to one's capacity to give time to it. A contemplation of three minutes is very different from a repeated return to the same subject, allowing it to proliferate. Theoretically, such a rumination can continue for a long time. As an old story tells of a Tzadik who was asked why he began his morning prayers so late. He answered: "It is all because of 'Modeh Ani' (I hereby give thanks), the first words I utter when I awake. It seems that just as I begin to dwell on what I am saying, to reflect on who I am, to recognize Who is before me and to acknowledge to Whom I am grateful—before I know it, a half a day has already passed." This Tzadik was essentially no different from many an ordinary Jew in this respect. A person whose spiritual experience is not unique is thus requested to expand and deepen his reflections on God. And when a person does this, he is liable to sink more heavily than he intended. Consequently, there is a certain amount of instruction given as to when this is advisable: "Before one occupies oneself with Torah or a commandment, such as putting on *tallit* or *tefillin*." That is to say, upon undertaking the performance of a mitzvah, even a very ordinary, routine action, like prayer, a Jew is advised to take time to prepare himself by reflecting on God, by being aware of the awe and trembling of his being before the Divine presence. And then, as he draws the prayer shawl over his shoulders or dons the phylacteries, he should also be conscious of drawing the Divine light over himself.

There are then two parts to the mitzvah; the first is the awareness of God's presence; the second is the action itself, performed as a Divine revelation. This may be the reason why certain mitzvot, like honoring one's parents or doing acts of charity, do not require the preliminary benediction, lest the conscious act of reciting a blessing put the person into such a deeply contemplative state that he would not get around to actually doing what he intended to do. For every mitzvah, whether it is important or trivial, has an element of revelation about it, for it attracts the Divine light and has the potential of being a mystical union. The mitzvot may be likened to the vertebrae of the spine; even if only one is slightly damaged or shifted out of place, it may cause enormous disruption and trouble; but when each functions properly, each as a link in the unity, they constitute a working harmony. Every mitzvah is a part of a whole. And I, as a man, merely join them together, as one joins water pipes or electric wire to allow the passage of whatever it is that flows. I myself do not create the current; I merely make it possible for it to flow, with greater or lesser freedom. At one end, there is the Infinite light and, at the other, the speck of soul, which is both myself and a spark of the Divine. As it is written in Ecclesiastes 12:2, "Until the silver cord be cut." This silver cord has been mystically likened to the spine, and every mitzvah to a link in it, through which the Divine light flows.

Similarly, the phylacteries have been compared to a current "to subdue the heart and brain" to Divine service. The Torah passages in the *tefillin* correspond to Wisdom and Understanding (head) and Love and Severity (arm), and the person who prays with them creates a mode of connection that is an example of the meditation exercise prior to the performance of the mitzvot. Concerning such meditation, there are two levels. On the first level of meditation, a person does not know the significance of a mitzvah and suffices with a general intention of acting as a channel for the Divine current to flow. On the second level of meditation, a person is conscious of the specific meaning of a mitzvah and can direct the flow in the desired direction.

To be sure, every mitzvah establishes a connection between one's soul and the Infinite light, whether one is aware of it or not. The *kavanot*, or right intentions, serve to enhance this unity, and the more one is conscious of the factors involved, the greater the intensity and efficacy of the mitzvah. Thus, every mitzvah has its own *kavanot*, its accompanying thoughts before and during the actual performance. The first part is a reflection on the fact of being in the Divine Presence, of His standing over me; the second part is the creation of contact between myself and the Infinite light.

In this process, a person can become so frightened and awestruck that he is rendered unable to continue to perform the mitzvah. It is, therefore, important also to see the value of ignorance, of not knowing the higher meaning of the mitzvah. For if one penetrates and probes too deeply and becomes too acutely aware of the details of one's words or actions in the awesomeness of standing before God, it can become dangerous in many ways. However, if a person is sensitive enough and intelligently aware of what is happening to him, if one truly seeks God as the highest value, then the true fear of God can be understood. The one who says: "Well, I tried and didn't succeed" is not being sincere. For the degree of effort one invests in seeking God is not to be measured in the same way as ordinary occupations. One cannot equate the worthwhileness of meditation before performing a mitzvah with the worthwhileness of making a particular purchase in the grocery store. Thus, when speaking of the meditation process involved in the mitzvah, it is quite impossible to say much more than that it depends on the person himself.

There is a story told about a Chasid who was an enthusiastic disciple of the founder of the Chabad movement. He was a rather simple Jew who had considerable difficulty in understanding the intellectual subtleties of his rabbi. Although at that time, this great teacher was trying to expound a more popular version of the Torah to make it available to all, the disciple, nevertheless, began to despair of ever reaching the level of his own fellow disciples. He would repeat the lessons in vain; he just could not grasp their meaning; finally, in utter despair, he made the long journey to the rabbi in order to ask what he should do. The rabbi told him, more or less, that everything can be learned with the right amount of effort, which was different for each person. A clever person could do it in less time, a simple person required more time and more effort. The disciple went home, wound up all his affairs, and returned to the rabbi in order to devote all his time to Torah. He plunged into meditation and study, working hard to attain both under-standing and a capacity for right contemplation. In other words, he concentrated on the ability to put all else aside and to focus his attention on one single thought, until this fragment of an idea became clear to him from every possible angle. Thus he sat for many months. Sometime later, one of the grandsons of the rabbi related that the man never became more than a mediocre scholar, but his understanding of Chasidism was beyond compare; this was due in no small measure to his self-taught capacity to concentrate on one single subject for many hours on end. Nothing could disturb him, and when he had completed his contemplation, he could explain the matter with great clarity. As an indication of the regard he was able to earn, one of the rabbi's sons dedicated one of his writings to him, a work that was both complex and technically involved.

This is an example of what is meant by "If by effort you have found something, believe it." The point is that every person has the capacity to learn. Moreover, every Jew can experience the fear of God; but in order for it to be significant, it has to be developed by reflection and meditation. Then, too, will the actions of such a person become "perfect service," without significant blemish. Even when a person is not naturally conscious of his innate awe and fear, he may somehow be aware of the need for it, and this feeling can be enough to give wings to a sincere and stubborn effort.

42

The Higher Fear of God

Evidently, there are different kinds of souls: the more sensitive and the less sensitive to holiness, higher and lower in some basic fashion according to their essence. A soul that is less sensitive may have to labor more in order to reach certain levels of being that are natural to a higher soul. But every person can attain a minimal spiritual level, a "lower" fear of God. As the Sages have maintained: If someone says, "I have struggled and found," one should believe him. Thus, if a person claims that he has not found (God), it means that he has not labored hard or long enough. Like buried treasure that can only be recovered by digging deep enough, the fear of Heaven is usually hidden in the depths of the heart, and considerable effort is needed to draw it forth.

Thus, the attribute of Understanding, associated with awe or Divine fear in the heart of man, is not bestowed on one (except for the exceptional instance); rather, it is a function of time and effort. The time factor varies of course, and is in itself quite mysterious for each person. It belongs to a different dimension of reality. In order for the fear of God to penetrate the soul in the realm of action, in order for it to become a dread of sin and not just an abstract fear of the transcendent, it has to become a

part of one's conscience, beyond time, and yet, not disconnected from the specific conditions of one's life.

In short, a thought that goes beyond thinking and becomes
action, a soul potential that is realized in life as a result of
struggle, has inestimable spiritual significance. Depart from
evil and do good in thought, word, and deed because God sees
and hears and observes and understands all the slightest
movements of your being. Even when one is aware of being
observed by another person, one's tendency to sin is curtailed;
how much more so when there is consciousness of God's
presence. It is not merely that there is an eye that sees or an ear
that hears from above; it is more like the consciousness a
person has of his own body, an intimate sense of what is
happening to one's own organs and limbs, from within. For
God knows us as a part of Himself, and we are not separate
from Him.

At the same time, the kind of identification the soul has with
the body, reacting to its needs and pains, proud of its order and
beauty, is not representative of God's concern for the world.
For God can scarcely be said to react to the world at all in that
way. He gives life to everything and knows what is happening,
so to speak, but He does not marvel at the wondrousness of it
all, nor is He repelled by the foulness of anything. There is both
Divine involvement and Divine separation in all that occurs in
the created worlds.

And if any person, wise or ignorant, great or small, will
concentrate on the thought that God really fills all that exists in
Heaven and earth with His glory and sees the inwardness of
man—his liver and heart, his thoughts and actions—then a kind
of awareness of oneself is built up. The smaller the soul, the
harder it will have to work at it. But if a person reflects on this
each day of his life, deliberately taking an hour to do so, it will
become engraved in his being and have a permanent effect.

This amounts to a process of a self-education, although it
consists of no more than regular contemplation on the greatness and glory of God. The spiritual fear—which is really no
more than a certain wonder or awe following on the recognition of the reality of God—strikes at the very core of one's
being, and there is no longer any need to find reasons for

avoiding evil and doing good in thought, word, and deed. The time spent in such concentrated meditation is also cumulative in power, and whatever is gained becomes a firm basis for further insight; indeed, it is often sufficient just to recollect an experience in order to reawaken its spiritual significance for oneself.

Rabban Yochanan ben Zakkai told his pupils that he hoped they would experience fear of Heaven in the same way they experienced fear of man; that is, the experience should be vivid physically, emotionally, and intellectually. It is not only a deep inner conviction but something that compels appropriate action. One cannot fear God as a witness, as one who merely looks on. One fears God because one feels Him, both within oneself and without. He is "here" and my life as a whole reacts accordingly.

All of this is still a "lower" fear (Yirah Tatah) and not a "higher" fear (Yirah Ilah). It is based on an awareness of the presence of God, but it is not the same as a true contact with God, which is Knowledge (Daat). As the esoteric wisdom of the Kabbalah teaches, the task of Daat in the tree of Sefirot is to be a connection between the hidden and the revealed aspects of Divinity, between the Binah, which is beyond human intelligence, and the human, comprehensible aspects of living. It is called the dimension of Moses, the intermediary between God and man.

For just as one is awed by the presence of a king of flesh and blood and impressed by his royal garments and retinue, indeed, by the whole external manifestation of his sovereignty, so are we impressed, in the lower fear, with God's world. It is, to begin with, an intellectual recognition. We surmise the king's power through what is external; we do not actually stand in awe before the garments themselves when they do not clothe the king, nor do we even fear the king's physical body or his court—it is his unseen power that impresses us. Similarly, we are impressed by God's world; we are overwhelmed by the way the whole of the universe bows to the one Divine Will.

The universe is thus the garments of the King; and it is only when one realizes that it is the King Himself, the Holy One blessed be He, to Whom we turn in prayer, that knowledge comes to us. But it is a matter of the practice of faith—and in Hebrew, the root word for both practice and faith is the same— to gain faith (*emunah*) one must practice (*imun*) and thereby acquire ever increasing proficiency.

In addition, this knowledge leads to a certain identification with what is known and a willingness to assume the burden of the Kingdom of Heaven. This burden, or yoke, is thus also a responsibility, and it requires discipline and vigilance. God ties up all of His Kingdom into a bundle and places it upon us. God is also called My Rock, King of Israel, and Redeemer of Israel. This means that we receive the burden of His Kingdom at the point of union with Him, which is equivalent to Knowledge (Daat). This is expressed, not only by the verbal declaration in the prayer of the Shema, but also by the symbolic prostration of the self at the places indicated in the recitation of the Eighteen Benedictions. This symbolic prostration signifies the fact that we willingly assume the burden of responsibility in actual living for the Kingdom of Heaven on earth. It is an ongoing process, beginning with an acceptance of the discipline and the obedience involved, and rising without end. That is to say, the practice of this discipline brings one to ever more meaningful emotional and spiritual levels of experience.

43

The Higher Fear and the Great Love

The "lower" fear of God is the first rung or the first step toward Wisdom. For it leads to an acceptance of Divine authority as expressed through Torah. It is lower only because it is external; but it has many levels of genuine spirituality, reaching up to a contemplation of the very utmost breadth and height of God's presence. Even then, even in contemplation of the vastness and universal omniscience of God, the relationship is primarily external because the contemplation is focused on the garments of the King and not on the King; it does not try to know God himself.

Trying to know God evokes the "higher" fear of God, which is a more inward state, and probes into the Divine essence which gives life to all the worlds. The relationship to Wisdom is more profound here. For Wisdom begins with the repudiation of self, a nullification process at the end of which one is equated with "nothing." And in contemplation of this nothing, Wisdom grows by watching the way all things are born out of the nothing. For it is by the powers of the Divine word, the breath of the Blessed One, that the world comes into being. And since all reality in the universe is a product of the spirit of God as expressed by His word, then reality is also nothing in

295

itself, and can be nullified by His spirit. Just as the life-giving
rays of the sun are produced by the sun and are nullified in the
sun itself. Man may thus surmise that the reality perceived by
his senses is only an unstable wrapping or exteriorization of the
Divine spirit. God speaks in terms of the substantive; this
world of substance not only changes all the time, but it
becomes null and void in the light of the Divine being. This
does not mean that all the world is nothing except for myself.
I myself am also part of nothing; my body and soul and spirit
are also nullified in God, like everything else. One of the
external signs of this higher fear of God, incidentally, is the
sense of shame; one is not afraid of God, but one becomes
ashamed of one's creatureliness.

The only reality then is God. And this is the beginning of
Wisdom. It is attained both by the "higher" fear of the Divine
presence and the "lower" fear. Indeed the lower fear is absolutely necessary for the higher, providing as it does a firm base
for Wisdom in a life of disciplined action based on Torah. But
it is the fear and love that are the components of the relationship to God.

In the love of God there are also two grades or phases of
being: Great Love (Ahavah Rabah) and "World Love" or Love
in the World (Ahavat Olam). Great Love is an ecstatic love, "a
fiery flame that rises of itself." It is securely embedded in
delight, not mixed with the pain of longing or the convulsions
of desire; it is a sense of not being able to wish for more than
feeling good in the nearness of God. A person cannot make it
happen, and no amount of nurturing or manipulation is of any
use; it comes of itself, from above, as a gift, so to speak, to the
one who is perfect in his fear. This Great Love of delight is the
blessedness bestowed on the one who has gone through the
vicissitudes of the fear of God and, in certain respects, it is a
portion of the next world made available in this world.

As it has been said by the Sages, the way of a man is to court
a woman, to be pulled by that part of his nature. So, too, does
the Great Love follow after the Fear of God; the right Sefirah of
Chesed is attracted to the left Sefirah of Gevurah. One does not
necessarily precede the other. Nevertheless, it may be said that
the Great Love comes from the World of Emanation (Atzilut);

it is always a gift from a higher realm of being and is extremely rare. The experience of love that is not dependent on any worldly thing whatsoever is not common in our world. Only in the World of Emanation, where there is no real separation between the Sefirot, can such perfection be attained.

At the same time, the desire for such a fulfilling love lies at the core of every human desire; no earthly object of love, no thing or person or idea can fill the heart. Thus, we experience the lower grade of love, the love in the world, as a substitute for the Great Love or as a way to it. To be sure, God does pervade all the worlds, and He surrounds or contains all the worlds, as it is written, "and all that exists is nothing but the product of His word." And if one contemplates the world properly, one cannot help but enter into the intimate experience of love for the Creator. Indeed, the soul has within it a certain measure of limitless love, which expresses itself as an attachment to objects of various kinds. Nevertheless, every person chooses from this abundance of inner and outer things in his life those which he fears and those which he loves.

The point is that man clutches at the specific delights of worldly love, even when he knows that it is all derived from God. He distinguishes his desires and has his preferences. He proceeds from minor cravings to great yearning and covetousness, forever finding things that are more beautiful in his eyes, abandoning one love for another. In a single lifetime, man may pass from an intense attachment to toys and modes of sensual gratification to passionate love for people, from an intellectual fervor for ideas to a recognition of his ultimate need for God's nearness. The phases of love are familiar enough; what is worthy of consideration is the way they are superseded, one by another, and how the core of each love persists in terms of feeling or sentiment. It is not that a person compares them, weighing the smaller against the greater. There is simply a recognition, at some stage, of the worthlessness of a certain object of desire, and basically it is a shadow of the knowledge that all things are insignificant and bereft of value when compared to the ultimate object of love, the one God.

World love is, therefore, an education in love. It is an education in which a person teaches his innermost emotions to

relate to objects worthy of love. Thus, it moves from the small
objects to which a child clings, the playthings, the trivial and
the sentimental, to the more complex things of adulthood,
which also have to be identified as playthings in the light of the
Divine essence which gradually enters consciousness. Even
someone who is deprived, for whatever reason, of the delights
of this world and does not experience any of the usual
attachments and loves of this life—a grim and cold person who
knows pain and suffering more than joy—can train his soul to
reach for Divine love by reflecting on the same question. What
are these transient experiences but preparation for the Truth,
for the ultimate reality itself? Thus, the potential love in his soul
may be kindled in him for the first time.

The difference between the two grades of love is that Great
Love is quite indifferent to this world and to any of the
wondrous things, people, or places in it; it is absorbed entirely
in the relationship between man and God; all else is of no real
interest to it. The one who loves in this way will, therefore,
tend to isolate himself from other people, self-sufficient in his
bliss. World Love, however, draws upon its relationship with
the world in order to go beyond the world. It also precedes the
fear of God, just as Great Love comes after fear. For the Love
of Delights, the Great Love, is not attained unless a person
goes through the levels of fear of God, from lower to higher.
World Love, on the other hand, occurs before the fear of God;
it then has to proceed through Knowledge or Daat, for it is from
Daat, Knowledge, that the real emotions issue. Otherwise,
they are merely expressions of physical reactions. That is to
say, if two people observe the same object, for one it may
arouse emotions of admiration and wonder; for the other, it
may be uninteresting or even repulsive. The difference depends on the measure of Knowledge in each of the observers;
that determines their attitudes. Daat includes Chesed and
Gevurah, so that the same experience can make one person
react with love while another reacts with fear. It depends on
which takes precedence in the mind.

For one person the greatness of God causes terror and
dismay; for another it brings a yearning to be absorbed in His
love. Since it is possible to make the transition from fear to

love, and the way to repentance is always open. Then, too, the tradition has always insisted on the combined way of both love and fear, because of their mutual dependence on Knowledge. For each person the particular path is different: Sometimes knowledge has to evoke love before fear, and sometimes it is the other way around.

Thus, a person who is not on a high spiritual level may attain a certain level of love before he reaches a level of fear, primarily as a result of a certain awakening in contemplation. However, if it is not tempered by fear, by the maintenance of a proper distance, it is not really love. It is more like the satisfaction of an appetite—a pouncing upon the desired object without restraint—and woe unto those people who love or who are loved in this way. At every stage of love, there has to be an aspect of keeping one's distance as well as a craving for union.

It is considered dangerous for a person to be awakened to a true love of God before he has reached a level of knowledge and spirituality that enables him to contain it. When the attribute of Fear is inadequate, there isn't enough dread of sin or fear of doing something against God's will, even in ignorance. On the other hand, the sublime feeling of being close to the Great Love may be genuine enough.

This, however, is a unique case and is not the way for most people. The proper order of Divine worship is to begin with the lower fear and to relate to the small things in life, to depart from evil and to do good. Through this practice of correct action, one reaches a higher level of fear, not necessarily a fear of punishment, but a knowledge of limitations and a sense of the prohibited. This fear is needed in order for the soul to be illuminated, in order to fill the soul so that its awakening will be meaningful and soundly rooted in life. Contemplation by itself is not enough. Only after having known fear can the light of love enter the soul in order to dwell therein. In gematria the words "and thou shalt love" (*v'ahavta*) have a numerical equivalent that is twice that of light (*or*), and in the esoteric wisdom, twice light is the light of love plus the light of fear. In other words, the true "and thou shalt love" is the combination of love and fear.

Thus, the experience of mystical love may turn out to be no

more than an exultant state of mind that passes. For love to be true love, it requires a certain frame of light around life as a whole; and in order for this to happen, and for the love to endure, it has to have its proper measure of the fear of God.

44

Two Ways of Loving God

W̶e have inherited two kinds of love from our fathers, and both kinds can therefore be considered a natural part of us in the sense that everyone can experience them, given the incentive and the guidance. The first of these loves is Ahavah Rabah (Great Love), which is indeed vast and superior in every way. Its greatness is such that it is beyond description; all one may venture to say is that it exceeds all other love. It is so totally superior that it is not dependent on anything external—as all our earthly loves are—and can only be known by the act of inwardness, of meditative action. By persevering reflection on the word of God and the acts of the Creator, one rises to a level where it is possible to apprehend Divine love and fear. This level of love opens one up to a growing awareness of some degree of inner identity with Divinity. It is a wholly inner experience, deeper, wider, and more sublime than any other.

On the other hand, one may justifiably wonder whether this sublime love is necessary for one's immediate welfare; why can't one just love God with the second love, simply and naturally, like a son loves his father? Why can one not simply confess to the soul's dependence on and yearning for God and leave the intellectual search for His greatness to those better qualified to do so? After all, the simple, natural love is given to all men. Whereas the intellectual inquiry and meditative comprehension of the Divine requires a higher level of connection, attained by only a few.

On the other hand, if a son can become conscious of the greatness of his father, learn to appreciate his virtues and capabilities, this would serve to increase his love, enrich it, and give it a breadth and power it may otherwise lack. The simple love emerges from its irrational, natural, and personal confines and becomes something that greatly enhances one's capacity to live in the world of God, the Father of us all. It is as though one were to say: Even if God were not my own King and Father, I could not help loving Him in every way. The relationship gains another dimension.

The two loves are thus not on the same plane. Natural or World Love is on the level of the young child's need for a parent. Great Love is more like the love that develops when a child matures and gets to know what his parents really are, when he can relate to them realistically. And just as one may not always be able to make sharp distinctions of love in relation to one's father as one grows up, nevertheless, there is no doubt that new aspects and new dimensions of love can always be added within the framework of human emotions. So too, love for God is enhanced and enriched without end by meditating on the nature of the Divinity as the Creator, the Sustainer, and the Provider of life—until "it reaches a stage of fiery intensity, like glowing coals and flames that rise upward."

What is the relation between these two kinds of love: Ahavah Rabah (Great Love) and Ahavat Olam (World Love)? Great Love is essentially a love that satisfies itself, for it has no need of anything further. But it is said in the Song of Songs: "My sister, my beloved. . . ." This implies that there are two loves—the kind of love one has for a sister and the aspect of the love one has for a lover. From a certain point of view, the love for a sister is a kind of self-love because it is a relation of essence, not necessarily dependent on who the sister is. On the other hand, the beloved as lover is something else entirely. It is a relationship that is chosen and developed; it has an intensity far sharper and more poignant than love for a sister. Thus, there is the distinction between the love relationship of choice and that of destiny and birth. The first love for the bride and the beloved is a Great Love, whereas World Love, for the sister, is an Eternal Love, a quiet and consistent love, without outbursts of passion. It satisfies itself and makes no demands. The chosen love of the beloved is more personal and specific; it is the Great Love, and it manifests itself as the feeling of being betrothed forever. The love of bride and bridegroom is like that between man and God; it is one of mutual choice, of having fallen in love, as opposed to the natural aspect of love that comes from one's birth. The former is intense and burning; and when combined with the latter, it is so powerful that "many waters cannot extinguish it, nor rivers quench it" (Song of Songs 8:7).

There is the intense love that comes from understanding and knowing the greatness of God, and there is the simple love of man for God the Creator within oneself. As it is written: "There is the advantage of gold over silver; silver belongs to the Sefirah of Chesed because of its color and for other reasons; and gold belongs to Gevurah because it is reddish and exciting." The advantage of gold over silver is like the advantage of choice in a relationship over a relationship destined from birth. Even though the aspect of choice of God is, perhaps, not on the same level of freedom as other choices, it is a higher level of contact. And on this subject, there is an article written by a famous rabbi, which questioned the difference between the levels of Divine worship in the period of earthly exile and in the period of Redemption. The answer was that in the world to come, worship will be higher, although the worship of God in this world is dearer or more joyous. That is to say, the relationship that is not dependent on anything may be on a higher level; but it is not as precious as the one that is chosen. Thus, the desirability of blending the two, the gold and the silver, is obvious.

In short, the knowledge of the greatness of God enhances the love for Him and is an aim in itself. It is also a mitzvah, for such is the purpose of man, to know the glory of God and the splendor of His greatness. For this, man and the world were created. Even on the level of worshipping Him with a full and eager heart, a certain degree of knowledge is required. Thus, the traditional emphasis on learning of Scripture and the study of secret wisdom—to "know God your Father." What is more, this mitzvah, although not on the same level as the mitzvah to love God, provides man with unique joys of discovery and enables him to experience the delights of knowing himself as a conscious entity.

45

On Pity and Compassion

Abraham is associated with Chesed, the attribute of love, and Isaac with Gevurah, awe and fear of God, while Rachamim, or compassion, is considered the attribute of Jacob. This is a third, and yet another way of worshipping God—a straight path (Yeshurun and Yisrael may be derived from the same root as the word "straight") in contrast to the wandering and twisted inclinations of the human heart.

True, there are people who reach higher levels of spirit by way of the crooked path of trial and error and sinful indulgence. There are those who deliberately choose to pursue the idolatrous roads of the world out of a need to learn for themselves. Thus, the straight path may have many interpretations, corresponding as it does with the attribute of pity and compassion, as well as harmony and justice. The Sefirah of Jacob, Rachamim, poses a number of problems of its own. One may readily comprehend the desirability of loving God, and of feeling the awe and fear of God; but how is one to experience compassion for God?

One feels pity for God because He has to bear the shame and mortification of man, because He descends to all the lowest

305

places of human degradation. There, where the love and fear of God cannot even penetrate, places where men are unable to look up in any worshipful manner to God, there it is still possible for the Divine spark of mercy and compassion to enter. One feels sorrow for oneself and for God who has to share one's humiliation.

This contingency emerges, not only on the lower levels of sin and idolatry, but also in the higher levels of consciousness. To better grasp this, it may be relevant to indicate the difference between Love (Chesed) and Compassion (Rachamim).

Love is granted by choice to those who deserve it. Compassion does not have to be deserved; anyone who is wretched enough can stir our pity. In this respect, compassion is the central pillar of existence; from the top to the bottom of creaturely existence, all are in need of mercy—man, perhaps, even more so. Indeed, there is a certain aspect of compassion that applies to all that was ever created—including the very angels—based on the failure of all the Divine sparks to go endlessly upward. As the story in the Midrash puts it: A rich merchant was to marry the king's daughter. Everything he gave her, however, was somehow inadequate and inappropriate—for she was born a princess—and he could never be rid of the feeling of obligation to her. The soul too is a princess and can never be recompensed sufficiently; it is a spark of the Divine, and no matter what one does or says or strives to accomplish, it is hardly ever enough. Hence, the attribute of compassion is necessary to bridge the gap. God hides Himself, even within the body of man, amidst all the body's grossness and problems; His glory fills even the limited space of one's physical self. At the same time, the Divine in us is the innocent one whom we compel to accompany us in our transgressions. It is thus that He is deserving of pity. This Divine spark in one needs to be redeemed, and the whole system of Torah and mitzvot may be considered a means to this end. How shall I restore the Divine spark to its source? How can I save the princess and bring her home?

Even the person who does not sin at all is still composed of gross matter, and within it something of the Infinite light is encased. And since this matter is not only dense, but is also shamefully inclined to corruption, every human being has good reason to sadly consider his deeds and his thoughts and to recognize the bondage in which he holds the King. One's mind runs about with the King woefully tied at the other end. One descends into the depths of the turgid imagination, carrying the Holy One within one's being. For all one's life is from Him, and even in transgression "He is with me." He binds me with a spiritual umbilical cord that sustains all that I am. I may move on, and even think of separating myself—but in vain. I may aspire to do the impossible and to burst through all the fences and restrictions; the cord simply moves with me from one order of things to another.

Another way of understanding the deeper aspects of compassion is the Kabbalistic view of Rachel as Knesset Yisrael, or the human community of Israel. Jacob, who is Divine mercy or compassion, loves Rachel. Their meeting in life is described by the phrase "And Jacob kissed Rachel and lifted up his voice and wept" (Genesis 29:11). In esoteric terms, the aspect of Compassion (Rachamim) is the highest level of love, for it is written, "His mercy (compassion) is upon all his creations" (Psalms 145:9), not necessarily on one or another, but on all. For all beings are in need of His mercy, even the angels in Heaven, even the souls of the just. All need to be pitied, because everything needs God's mercy to continue to exist. Hence this aspect is called the "Father of mercies," and it is used in prayer only on the most solemn occasions (as distinct from the usual phrase "merciful Father"), only when there is some sort of revelation of Divine plenty. Jacob, then, raises his voice, in order to arouse the Divine compassion for Rachel and her children, the community of man—and in order to lift them up and to unify them with God. How is this done? By the Kiss of Love that Jacob gives Rachel. Here, the use of the verb "to kiss" means the touching of spirit and spirit. As it is written, "And he kissed me with the kisses of his mouth" (Song of Songs 1:2), or the meeting of the word of man with the word of God (Halachah).

The question remains: How shall Jacob, who is the higher compassion, touch with such intimacy Knesset Yisrael or the human congregation? The answer is: When a person is engaged in Torah. This is the Kiss of the Divine, mouth to mouth, for Torah is the word of His mouth, and my mouth repeats it. The Kiss, as meeting of spirit with spirit, is also a union with God. I think His thoughts, I speak His words.

In the realm of action, the performance of the mitzvah is contact with the Divine, especially in acts of charity and lovingkindness. In such deeds a person embraces God, so to speak. Moreover, mitzvot are connected with mercy—one has pity on something that rolls randomly in the universe; and one performs a mitzvah to redeem it, which is an act of lovingkindness. One has thereby lifted this thing to a higher plane as an expression of pity for the lost sparks of the void.

There have been Jews who were so sensitive to this matter of the mitzvot as an act of redeeming kindness and compassion for all of existence that it qualified their entire lives. There is a great deal in Kabbalah concerning the metaphysical aspects of this same relation—the waters of the sky above and the waters of the earth below must flow into one another in order for the world to exist. The nether sky weeps cloud upon cloud wishing to be higher up, nearer to the Heavens. The earthly waters say, "Why must we remain below while the higher waters are so wonderfully posed on high?"—and they are always evaporating. Then there is the secret of the feminine waters, the mysterious seeping into the ground of the lower waters and their subsequent issue as the fountains of the earth. The time of the Sukkot festival is the end of weeping and the time of joy, when the lower waters rise joyfully and are poured on the Heavenly altar, and the higher waters descend with the first rains of the season. It is also a process of eliminating sorrow and rising in joy through compassionate performance of the mitzvah and the recital of the blessing, "Blessed is He who has compassion on the community of man."

That is to say, when man has mercy on earth and community, he makes contact with God in the form of an embrace, like Jacob, who cannot bear to see the world crying and thus kisses Rachel and lifts his voice and weeps. One is also feeling compassion for one's own soul, for the God in one, Who is compelled to go along with one's sojourn on earth. Therefore, all of a man's deeds should ultimately be the result of compassion for God, even more, perhaps, than being motivated by the love or fear of God. For one cannot bear to see the world in tears—one must do something. This level of compassion may thus be considered higher than love. Unlike love, which chooses its object according to one's own criteria of admiration and affection, compassion has no criteria for its expression, except, perhaps, that its object should indeed be wretched. To love, there must be some sort of higher emotional consciousness; in order to feel pity, all that is needed is something or someone in a sorry state. And, since the world is quite full of such objects of pity, the attribute of compassion is more readily available to one. Even when one is unable to love God or to fear Him, especially when in a state of desolation, one may, nevertheless, know His compassion by feeling it in oneself and for oneself and the world.

The lowest of the low, therefore, are able to know some degree of pity, even those who seem to have no feelings at all for God or other people; even if it is only for a dog or for one's own wretched self, but one is bound to feel sorry for any of God's creatures in distress. It may be the very last shred of humanity left to a person, hidden away behind a habitual toughness and hardness. At this last and lowest level of humanity, which may be called the Valley of the Shadow of Death, the Psalmist cries out, "Thou art with me" (Psalms 23:4). It is only when a person does not know that he is in the Valley of the Shadow of Death, when pity is totally barred, that God cannot save him.

Compassion or Mercy is thus the attribute of Jacob, the Sefirah at the center of the Kabbalistic tree, connected to almost all the other attributes and therefore able to awaken responses in every aspect of existence.

It may even be considered a more spiritually powerful factor than love (Chesed) because if a person does good deeds and studies Torah only out of a love of God, he may lose interest in the outer life and in other people and fail to realize the more profound precepts of Torah. Whereas Rachamim, or compassion, awakens the "greater love" of people through the understanding of the heart; it is that which reaches from the highest to the lowest in spiritual and creaturely existence. Called "the straight path that man shall take" after Jacob, who is also known as Yeshurun, the straight, it constitutes the core of the Tree of Life.

46
The Need for Gratitude and Knowledge

As has been mentioned, the love of God implanted in every Jew makes it possible to suggest ways of Divine worship that are already intrinsic and do not have to be concocted out of mysterious or extraneous elements. That is to say, there are certain quite basic ideas and relations that are common to all men; we need only to provide the key to unlock the spiritual possibilities they contain and thereby enable a person to develop beyond the hitherto anticipated limitations.

The demand is of the highest, namely, to attain a blissful relationship with the object of worship. But we wish to achieve this in an age when it is sufficient to refrain from defiant transgression in order to be considered something akin to a saint. Therefore, the urge to strive for the highest may seem exaggerated.

Nevertheless, there is firm ground for believing that it is possible as well as desirable. The important thing is the sincerity of the endeavor, that the action be performed with all one's heart, from the depths of one's being, and in genuine truth. For the fact is a person can attain happiness or even ecstasy in many ways, through relatively external, emotional,

311

aesthetic, or even social stimuli. But in the end, it would be proven not to be the soul that is awakened, but some physiological-mental combination in the personality.

In that case, the response is usually to intensify one's efforts, to deepen the pleasure, to make it more refined, and to feel it more soulfully, so to speak. There is also the effort to experience exultation through careful religious observance, not only in the performance of the right actions, but also in emotional love and fear of God. What then would be lacking in such efforts? The Talmud satirically describes seven types of pious persons, including the good man who says, "What I have to do, I accomplish," or another who is so full of loving devotion to God that his love becomes a habit, or a third, who kisses the *tzitziot* four times instead of the prescribed three, and so on.

The point, then, is not the ordinary religious way of conventional faith, which was once common to all the Jews. The demand is to do so "from the depths of the heart, in absolute truth." To begin with, there is the need to genuinely love God; otherwise, it is all sham and hypocrisy. Then there is the problem of growth—with prayer as one of the chief components in the daily spiritual practice. No two persons pray the same way, even if they repeat precisely the same words. There are passages that speak secretly to one and other passages that ignite the soul of another. At the same time, the order of prayer is a movement in a certain direction, a rising up of one's whole inner being. The central factor seems to be the intimate personal relationship with God.

Just as, in standing water, one sees his own face reflected back, so too is the heart of man reflected in the heart of another. As I relate to my companion, so will he relate to me. There are two aspects to this: the hidden feeling and the retrieval of what one thought was hidden. Even when one cannot quite depict the nature of another's relationship to oneself, the automatic response is usually an accurate one. It is not dissimilar from those responses in us which are not entirely under our control—like the contagiousness of yawns and laughter. In certain people, who are especially sensitive to the social environment, there is a capacity for understanding one another which is beyond natural explanation. As an example of such simple natural responsiveness, one may mention gratitude—a virtue which one does not learn from books, and which, if lacking, may be considered a sickness of soul. In the same way, if one feels loved, it is almost impossible to remain indifferent; it arouses a similar feeling in response.

In speaking of the dangers of this, the sages mentioned how close it was to bribery. If one receives a gift, one is no longer objective in one's judgment, even if the judge likes to think otherwise. Thus, the concept of a face reflected in water, of a heart reflecting a heart, can be distorted by the suspicion of bribery. Thus, there were judges of religious courts who would refuse to even look at the people who were engaged in dispute in order to avoid letting personal preferences creep into their judgment. There was an avoidance even of unconscious influences.

In short, if someone loves me, or goes out of his way to do me good, it is difficult to avoid responding positively. It is one of the most natural things in human nature. How much more so if the other is a great and mighty King who bends down to exalt a lowly person like myself and showers me with tenderness and affection. Besides the automatic response of great love, there is boundless gratitude because I know how unworthy I am.

Thus our relation to God should include such a simple human emotion as being unreservedly grateful to Him who gave us all we possess. But we are not thankful, in contrast to animals and children for instance, who are on the whole far more inclined to show gratitude. This stubborn distortion in the heart, this inability to respond in a simple, natural manner to Divine love and goodness is, perhaps, our worst infirmity.

It can only be partly explained by a lack of intelligence or learning: The King brings one into His chamber, but one may fail to comprehend what is happening. Only he who has reached a certain level of understanding will appreciate it. As one of the many allegories puts it: A king went out into the fields, and a certain farmer, not knowing who the king was, offended him. The courtiers wanted to have the farmer executed on the spot, but the king said that such punishment was not equal to the crime. Instead, he suggested bringing the man

to the royal palace and educating him until he became aware of
the enormity of what he had done.

In order to appreciate what God has given one, there has to
be a certain level of awareness of the world and one's place in
it, of Divine transcendence and human creatureliness. To
awaken this awareness requires a process of education and
inner growth.

As any reader of the first books of the Bible cannot help but
observe, the Children of Israel were an ungrateful lot: God had
delivered them from bondage in Egypt, had divided the Red
Sea for them to pass through, had given them manna to eat,
and more; but, nevertheless, they complained and acted un-
graciously at the least provocation. The explanation is that a
proper understanding of what is happening to one requires
distance, a proper perspective, and adequate tools. When a
person is too strongly loved and too quickly rescued from a
predicament, it may be difficult to respond suitably. One may
need a thousand years or more in order to begin to grasp the
wonder of one's deliverance. In any situation of a miraculous
nature, the participants may be hard put to realize what is
happening to them, and the response will often come only
much later.

Altogether, the capacity to grasp any aspect of Divinity is
quite limited, and the explanation adapted to the human
understanding of a certain generation may sound absurd to
another generation. Therefore, it is only an act of humility to
refrain from being too critical of the expressions used by the
teachers of the past, who after all, were only endeavoring to
impress their audiences with the greatness of God by using
figures of speech, images, and symbols appropriate to their
time. What is important is that there always was an attempt to
bring the Divine into the range of the people's grasp, even to
the simplest of men. The mere fact of saying that there are
numberless "mansions" containing numberless worlds and
that each world is infinitely greater than our own is not enough
to do more than freeze us intellectually, thereby canceling the
importance of our existence. The question that follows, however, immediately restores meaning: "Where is the place of His

glory?" The angels answer: "The whole earth is full of His glory!" And it is experienced by His people Israel. It is here, among His people Israel, that Divine glory becomes tangible.

A parable relates the story of a man of the people, who came to one of the Tzadikim, crying bitterly: "I have such awful pains, headaches, and worries. I can neither pray nor study. What will be the end of me?" The Tzadik answered: "You are greatly mistaken. You think that God needs your prayers and your studies? If He had any such need He would place a few thousand angels to pray and study for Him. God needs your particular pains and your headache and your worries. For this He cannot get angelic or human help. Only you can supply it."

Or else there is the story of the man who was able to penetrate the palace of the king. He looked with wonderment at the various beasts and animals in the stables and at the innumerable servants, the many courtiers, and the men of talent—poets, minstrels, and the like—in the rooms. In the king's inner chamber, he found a golden cage with a parrot which could utter a few garrulous phrases. The man asked in amazement: "With all these splendid specimens of their kind, and with all the poets and men of letters about, why do you need the parrot in the inner chamber? Can he talk better than they?" And the answer given was: "Certainly not; the parrot cannot talk better than they; but the wonder of it is that in spite of being a bird and not a man, still the parrot speaks." In His great love for us God pays attention to us, not because we are any more qualified than the angels to sing His praises or carry out His wishes, but because, as He says: "See this wretched man I have created, with all his troubles and pains and worries; in spite of it all, he stands up and prays to me." Therefore, we humans are brought by Him to the inner chamber.

The concept of the inner chamber is derived from the imagery of the great intimacy between God and Israel, as expressed in the Song of Songs and in the statement that He Himself descended and brought Israel out of Egypt. God also divulged to Israel His plans and secrets; thus, when a Jew studies Torah, when he thinks in terms of Scripture, he is in close contact with God, conversing with Him about these intimate Divine thoughts. And when a Jew performs the mitzvot with his body, when he prays with his mouth, a true unity is established, as it were, of "kisses and embraces."

These intimacies may be divided into three categories—right, left, and center of the Kabbalistic tree—Chesed, Gevurah, and Rachamim (Lovingkindness, stern Justice, and merciful Compassion). This expresses, in part, not only the relationship of a single man to God, but it also represents the relationship of the children of Israel to God, beginning from the time of bondage in Egypt when Israel was probably even worse than it is today, having been allowed to wallow in the filth and corruption of that world without any knowledge of Torah. Therefore, a proper understanding of what happened then, the intervention of God, His raising up of the degraded soul, can bring about an inspired urge to turn to Him in worshipful love.

The threefold way of Love, Fear, and Compassion leads to specific modes of communication with God. It is something that is given to a person, allowing the heart to reach out to the Divine with a love that is natural and inherited. The greater the knowledge and understanding, the more that is learned of the actions of God, His words and His thoughts, the more it is possible to have one's eyes opened and the heart awakened to His presence.

47

Intimacy with God

We have said that the inti-
macy into which God, through His great compassion, brings
man, in spite of man's degradation, may be attained by human
efforts such as study of Torah, performance of mitzvot, and so
forth. This has been called a kiss of mouth to mouth since the
Divine name is uttered with the mouth, and there is a union of
spirit with spirit. When one thinks only thoughts of Torah,
contemplating the thoughts of God, so to speak, there is union.
Even if one is obviously not on any conceivable level of equality
with the Divine spirit, the thought itself becomes the link. And
the performance of a mitzvah is an act of embracing, for as it is
written, the 248 positive ordinances are the 248 (physical)
organs of the King.

The positive mitzvot (as "body" of the King) may be divided
according to the Kabbalistic tree into right, center, and left.
There are mitzvot that are essentially of the right, namely those
of giving (Chesed); others of the left, restraint or severity
(Gevurah), include acts of ritual, judgment, worship, and art;
and those of the center, Tiferet (Harmony and Mercy), are
expressed by study and enlightenment, feeling, and physical
love (the central core of the torso). This makes the embrace of

317

the mitzvah an action of the most intimate contact with God,
like when man and wife become one flesh. Thus, the act of
sanctification in mitzvot is compared to the sacrament of
marriage.

From this it may be deduced that mystical union, as it is
known in other cultures, is expressed in Judaism directly by the
mitzvot. For example, in the ritual act of *tefillin*, the prayer for
binding the phylacteries is an oath of betrothal. So too, the
Song of Songs is a love poem between God and Israel. And
there are the many spontaneous outpourings by individual
Chasidim and expressions by even ordinary people in music,
dance, poetry, prose, and simple ejaculations of love for God.

Another aspect of being sanctified by His commandments,
besides that of God descending to gladden His chosen people
like a groom coming to the bride, is that of actually being raised
up to holiness. He makes us holy with the higher sanctity; that
is, we are brought to a point of contact with the Divine, which
is higher than all our connections with the world. It separates
us from all else. By being sanctified, we are made more like
Him: "Be Holy, for I am Holy."

The contact with God, then, which is holiness, means
separation from, or, at least, experiencing something distinc-
tively different from, the world. God is apart from the world by
virtue of His quality of "encompassing all worlds." Thus, our
use of the concept "to sanctify" loses meaning when it is
applied to human actions, because holiness belongs only to
God and cannot even be properly defined by men. All we can
do is recognize that something is holy. Its inner meaning,
besides that of being separate from all that is not holy, from
everything that is in the world, is in fact beyond our grasp. At
the same time, God does come down and sanctify us. We are
made holy; that is, we are made separate from all else, and we
relate only to Him. But separation is not a partition cutting us
off entirely from the other nations of the world; it is more of a
distinguishing factor making us His. Contact with God makes
for holiness, and holiness connects one with whatever is
beyond the frontiers of ordinary existence, but it does not
disconnect one from life and ordinary existence.

I am His—but this does not mean that God becomes "mine"

in the same way as anything else can be possessed. First of all, to say "My God" does not imply possessiveness. It is more like the expression "My Lord," which conveys something more in the nature of a relationship. Nevertheless, the regular performance of mitzvot does create a special kind of relationship, which may warrant the possessive adjective. Anyone can say "My God," but the one who also works and strives and suffers for the actualization of Divinity in his life manages to achieve a more intimate and real union. The separation is overcome. God is no longer beyond reach and separated from one. The problem is whether one is making a connection with God or with something else that is lodged in one's imagination. To answer it requires a profound sincerity, a recognition of the fact that it is only God who can make the connection.

Hence we repeat the phrase, "God of our fathers, Abraham, Isaac, and Jacob," because they were so completely His vehicles of expression. If then we are able to say, "The Lord is our God," it is because, in keeping the mitzvot, in doing His will, we too become a Divine vehicle, a chariot of the Lord. The difference is that the Patriarchs were personally conscious of their life roles, whereas we are participants in no more than isolated actions, involved only for the moment of the mitzvah.

Thus the well-worn expression, "our God Who sanctifies us . . ." scarcely approximates the relationship for most of an ordinary person's life, with the exception of the time of prayer and blessing. This is why all Jews, and even scholars, used to stand up respectfully before the performance of a mitzvah— because at that moment, at least, the Divine presence was a perceptible reality.

The difference between this sort of union and the mystical experience is that the one who performs the mitzvah does not necessarily feel the Divine presence as a subjective exaltation. In contrast to the Patriarchs, an ordinary person does not feel the Shechinah's action within himself. He can, of course, attain acute responsiveness if he manages to refine and purify himself sufficiently. But this requires a certain capacity or potential that is comparatively rare and depends on two things: a very considerable amount of hard work and an inborn spiritual talent. The Patriarchs were able to experience the next world in this life, which we acknowledge as fact in the Grace after meals: "May we be blessed as were our forefathers in everything and by everything." This latter phrase points to a state of being that manifests the great gift of knowing God's presence within oneself. The ordinary person's vision is blocked by the physicality of his own existence; to achieve anything spiritually meaningful, a person has to have reached a certain rung or level of consciousness beyond the physical. Otherwise, there is simply no possibility of making the contact that could enable one to understand what he is experiencing. Just as children, and even many adults, can grasp only so much of a work of art and no more, especially if they are untrained. They can come into physical proximity with it, see or hear it, and respond according to their individual levels of understanding. Just as recent experiments on the process of observation in animals disclosed that they distinguish only moving objects. Not that an animal fails to see an object that doesn't move, it is simply alerted only by the exterior stimulus. And so it is for all creatures; the ability to grasp the reality of a situation depends on the level of consciousness of the one experiencing it.

As human beings, we are unable to perceive various spiritual entities, and only by the performance of the mitzvot, or its equivalent, is a relationship established. Whether one will feel this relationship with the spiritually invisible depends on one's level of consciousness. An ordinary person is usually unable to do so beyond a limited extent.

Thus, for example, it is maintained that in the Land of Israel there is a greater concentration of holiness. If, as not infrequently happens, someone complains that he is not aware of any more holiness in Israel than elsewhere, the answer is that he himself is to blame—not the Holy Land—that he should work on himself and repent and try to make himself a more effective receptacle of spirit. The perception of holiness belongs to the perceiver as well as to that which is perceived. Just as the same book can be profoundly meaningful to one reader and be utterly meaningless to another, the same place can be holy to one person and commonplace to another.

Nevertheless, when a person performs a mitzvah, it may be assumed that he knows what he is doing in the sense, at least, of providing a certain emotional accompaniment to the action. He should feel a degree of fear and awe, and love as well, coming from the sparks of Divine light stirred up by the mitzvah. In theory, at least, since one is a vehicle of Divine will for that moment, one should be carried away, so to speak, by the mitzvah. Angels and holy seraphs should bear one up. But ignorance and unknowingness are so pervasive that one remains "like a beast before Thee" (Psalms 73:22). Just as an animal may be brought to a palace and be fed before the king, it will still proceed to eat like the animal it is; so too, one may enter the synagogue and commence the performance of a mitzvah, insensitive, like an animal, to the possibilities of the situation.

This does not alter the objective truth that "I am with thee always." It is physical matter that prevents one from knowing it. And yet, there is mercy in the ignorance as well. If one had to carry a load of dangerous explosives on one's back, it could be very unsettling; if one were to put the load on the back of a donkey, it would be borne without any fuss, the beast being blissfully unaware of what he was carrying. So too, the ignorance of holiness can simply be a merciful device to enable one to carry it on one's back without strain.

Infinite light fills all the worlds; it was not only so in the past, but it is so in the present as well; even the greatest darkness cannot obscure it. Indeed, light and darkness are the same in this respect; the one who knows and the one who does not know are at the same distance from the source, except that the one who knows feels the enormous burden of resistance, and the one who does not know skips along in carefree ignorance.

The point being made here concerns the nature of Divine union. When one performs a mitzvah, one is in a state of firm connection, which can be called union with God, even if one is not entirely conscious of it. And, to a degree, this ignorance may be a protection, for the awareness of the Divine presence may be so perturbing a factor that one is unable to act at all.

Few indeed have the double capacity: to know what they are doing and to do it as though they did not know what they are doing. It is said of Aaron the High Priest, for example, that he was able to go about his duties with a firm hand and eye, precise and tranquil in all his movements, fully aware not only of the terrible holiness, but also of the immense significance of what he was doing. Other men, not necessarily more sensitive men of God, would have become far too emotionally involved and would have been unable to maintain the control and poise. Aaron simply obeyed—he did not let himself be moved personally. For there is a stage of development in which a person can know the meaning of what he is doing and can be acutely sensitive to what he is doing and can still continue to live in the world as an intrinsic part of it. To be sure, this is a very high degree of being and turns into a practical problem for only a few in each generation. To feel deeply as a result of knowledge and, nevertheless, to be like all other men in the world is not something that can be done easily, even by those who rise up to confront the possibility. However, there were those who, like some of the Tzadikim, were able to speak for all of "Knesset Yisrael," the soul of the people, saying, "I am ignorant and do not know, like a beast am I before thee," and yet to maintain, "Nevertheless, I am always with thee, even though I do not know." It is in this sense that we speak of the mitzvot as being objective, as having the capacity to bestow Divine union without necessarily providing mystical rapture.

To better understand the special logic of sanctity, we may observe what happens when it is not recognized at all. What is the punishment meted out to one who desecrates the Sabbath or who eats bread on Passover? Whether the trespasser is aware of the law or not, whether learned in the way of holiness or altogether untutored, the punishment is the same: *karet*—to be cut off from life in the community of men. To be sure, there is a great difference, subjectively, between the Sabbath of a Tzadik and that of an abysmally ignorant Jew; but objectively the Sabbath remains the same for all. Its essential holiness does not depend on anyone's subjective feeling; desecration is as objective a fact as sanctification. There is one law, one Torah, for all. We are all equally receptive to the higher sanctity of the mitzvah, irrespective of the measure of our feeling for holiness or of our knowledge of the meaning of the action.

It has been said: "With Wisdom have You (God) made it." This implies that Wisdom is not God's way of thinking but his tool for doing things, like a hoe. In man's world, wisdom is sharply distinguished from the physical senses and is viewed as that which gives the senses meaning and direction; it is considered higher than the senses. Whereas in God's world, the difference is quite insignificant; indeed, the highest of human wisdom probably belongs more to the creaturely world of material essences than to the Divine essence. Similarly, God is available to all men. As far as God is concerned, it makes no great difference; all men, whether they be saints and sages or average persons, are equal to Him. Even light and darkness are not separate realms for Him, indeed the whole universe still belongs to the nether world, below that of Emanation. Above this highest of known worlds, the Sages still speak of the Behemah Rabah (the Great Beast), the fountain of being prior to the existence of the world, the hidden intelligence without the idea, the primordial ignorance. That is to say, there is no difference between worlds as far as God is concerned. For many clever men, the difficulty that is an obstacle to understanding Him comes not from His greatness but from a basic misunderstanding of His greatness. The person who thinks that God is justifiably concerned with the vast affairs of the galaxy and is not concerned so much about my reciting a blessing before eating a chocolate bar does not really see the greatness of God. To the Divine Omniscience, there is no large or small, significant or insignificant detail in the infinity of the universe.

This is the justification for man's saying: "I am ignorant and do not know" (like a beast); but as with all the other creatures of the world, God replies, "I am with thee always."

48

Encompassing Light and
Pervading Light

Any serious reflection on the greatness of God and His boundless mercy will lead to the realization that there is no end and no purpose to His light. This light also remains unchanged and constant in its emanation from the Divine and it never imposes a limit in any of its manifestations. In contrast to a numerical (or any other) infinity, with its severe limitations in all directions but one, the infinite light of God has no limit in any direction or form.

The world itself is necessarily bounded on all sides—even when we reckon distances in terms of light years, or as an old Jewish tradition has put it, in terms of the 500 years between heaven and earth and between one firmament and the next; the universe is still finite, no matter how vast. And one should keep in mind that the law of limitations holds for all creation, for the next world as well as for this one. It is true for the Paradise of the highest saints and for the realms of the angels. To be sure, the nature of the boundaries imposed on higher beings is not the same as those applicable to a tree or to a political entity like a country or a province. Thus, even that which we call spiritual in the highest sense is restricted to a definite domain of being and purpose. God provides to each domain what it requires—no more. But even if spiritual entities are without size or weight or even duration, being constructed differently, they are, nevertheless, restricted to a prescribed range of being and of power to act. There is even a limit to their enjoyment of the light of the Shechinah. For example, those souls who rest in Paradise receive only as much as they are able to receive of the bliss and joy available there. Because all creatures, earthly and Heavenly, can bear only so much of Divinity and no more. To be sure, the Divine light given to higher beings is so far beyond our capacity to conceive it that we tend to think of it as measureless; nevertheless, like all else that exists, it is limited and finite. This is the necessary conclusion from the Kabbalistic interpretation of Creation as a Divine contraction, a process whereby God deliberately hides Himself, retracts His infinite radiance to allow finite worlds of all sorts to come into existence.

The essence of this contraction is that the transition between prime cause and that which is brought into being, between giver and receiver of plenty, is not direct. There is no direct transmission. The receiver does not get more than he is able to absorb, and, of course, this is very little, infinitesimally little, no matter what the size or the nature of the created being. The point is that the transition from infinite light to finite existence is accomplished by contraction, by a Divine withdrawal. In order for a created thing to have meaning, it has to be separated from the origin of creation. Just as in our capacity to imagine quantities, the number one can have a value in relation to a thousand or a million; it gets obscured as one proceeds into hundreds of millions or trillions, and it has no meaning at all when related to infinity. Indeed, any number divided by infinity equals zero.

Infinite light is thus beyond reality because it is not revealed in reality. That is, reality draws its existence from a limited or contracted light, and there can be no relation at all between this light—which is the essence of all worlds and things—and God, because the Infinite nullifies anything that is particular, no matter how big or marvelous it may be, and it is impossible to make any connection with it.

Nevertheless, we do relate to it. The infinite light that

surrounds and contains all reality is known as that which
"encompasses all worlds." To be sure, this term should not be
taken literally as something that spatially circumscribes all
reality. It is simply the opposite of that which "pervades all
worlds," a term that indicates that God is within reality in all its
minutest detail. While the transcendental essence of God,
being beyond reality as we know it, is called that which
"encompasses all worlds." For it is only too easy for the mind
to make pictures and diagrams of anything that is close; and
only something explicitly outside—far beyond the idea of some
Divine being in the heavens at such and such a removal from
the earth—can be expected to check this impulse.

The spiritual concept of place, or of being located, is altogether different from anything spatial or temporal. The terms
"Encompassing Light" and "Pervading Light" are intended to
describe modes of influence on reality as well as angles of
perception, the ways in which ultimate cause works. Indeed,
they are really technical terms serving as diagrams or tools by
which we can continue to worship God and to inquire into His
manifestations. Revelation in the deeper sense is His influence
in the very life of reality, and in certain Jewish writings, it has
been called the way God clothes Himself in the world. The
specific existence of all things is determined by the way they
wrap themselves in His influence, to contain and be contained
in Him. Thus, an object traveling at a certain speed is
"wrapped" in the energy of its motion; the object includes the
energy in itself, even though it is not "burnt up" by it. Most
influences, even those that are direct, will not be revealed or
made known to the object itself, because they are hidden. Light
that is shed on reality from outside and beyond, and not from
within itself, is not to be grasped; it cannot be included in itself
and cannot be understood. For all understanding means that,
to some degree, the subject is encompassed, is contained in the
mind. But there are things that cannot be contained because
they are beyond us. We, therefore, call them that which
encompasses or surrounds us.

The emphasis is on infinity as the basic essence—that which
cannot be anything else and which clothes itself and is revealed
in the finite. The revelation, however, is very minute; only a

very little is manifested—just enough to give form and substance to a reality and to provide it with its own specific boundaries and purpose and meaning.

The basic idea is that the infinite light cannot reveal itself as it is in the finite, for the finite could not possibly contain it. Hence, we have the distance, as far as man is concerned, between that which "encompasses all worlds" and that which "pervades all worlds."

As an illustration, let us take the biblical saying "the whole earth is full of His glory." This means that His blessedness fills the finite world; it does not mean that the material of the earth is illuminated by His light or radiance. For, even though God is in everything, Heaven and earth, and He contains and is contained in all that is, nevertheless, He cannot be felt inwardly or known coherently by His creatures. All things of substance, whether spiritual or material, cannot hold the Infinite within themselves.

"That which encompasses all worlds" is, therefore, beyond our inward comprehension; it points to an essence that exists outside us and not in us. It has nothing to do with the spatial separation between things, but rather indicates the difference, or separation, of fragments of essential being, each from the other and all from their source.

49

Man as the Purpose of Creation

The Kabbalah of the Ari has outlined for us an enormously complicated and even detailed scheme of Creation. Without going into the complexities of this system, we may note that "there are three levels of powerful and comprehensive 'contractions,' giving rise to three comprehensive worlds. These are the Worlds of Briah (Creation), Yetzirah (Formation), and Asiyah (Action). The fourth known World of Atzilut (Emanation), which is higher than these, is Godliness itself." To be sure, there are myriads of contractions within each world itself, levels upon levels of potential that have to make room for realities of all kinds. The fourth and highest of the worlds, Atzilut, is not included in the above because it is beyond our grasp. Even the World of Briah, which is the world of the spirit, of angels, and of higher beings, is accessible to us only with difficulty. Nevertheless, something of this world is available in some degree at least, because the angelic orders function through the Sefirot of Chochmah (Wisdom), Binah (Understanding), and Daat (Knowledge), and these man can contact at his own highest level.

It should be remembered, too, that the contractions between one world and the next are so great that, for all intents and purposes, they are infinite. Not only is this true for the transition from the totally transparent world of Atzilut, which is the Godhead, to the world of Briah, but it is also true for the transition from Briah to Yetzirah and from Yetzirah to our own world of Asiyah. Thus, even the smallest particle of light that comes down from Atzilut to Briah is of the nature of the infinite, and this is similar for each world. There is something so unfathomable and wondrous about anything that descends from an upper world that it cannot be absorbed; it is virtually "infinite."

What is most incredible about all this is the role of man. Placed at the end of the series of contractions, together with gross matter and the evil impulse, man is also the purpose of it all. Having been granted a Divine Soul in a material body, man stands between light and darkness, between good and evil; and in choosing the light and the good, he raises himself to holiness. By doing so he justifies the emanation of all the worlds; he gives the creative process a meaning. Because in themselves, the higher worlds are, to a large degree, totally dependent on God; they are built and are made to function, according to set laws of Divine unfolding. Only man has the freedom to choose and to change the otherwise fixed course of events. It is in this respect, then, that we can be guided by the saying, "As water mirrors the reflection of a face." We surmise that God has put aside His infinite light and concealed it, so to speak, in the three great contractions that brought forth the knowable worlds; and He did this out of a love for man and in order to bring man to a knowledge of God. Thus, all the contractions and withdrawals were meant to provide a place for man in this world, and he is, therefore, the purpose of it all. For the existence of man is possible only if the Divine light is hidden, because His love transcends all flesh, and we could not survive in its effulgence. It is as though God pushes Himself aside in order to make room for man to exist. So does man, in response, have to go toward God and even to abandon all else in order to cleave to Him—"as water mirrors the reflection of a face."

In other words, in response to God's unremitting graciousness to man, His reduction of Himself to enable man to grow freely, man should abandon all else and hold fast to whatever he knows of Divine reality. Nothing should prevent him from devoting himself to God. Neither body nor soul, neither inner nor outer forces should interfere with his acts of gratitude to God; even one's wife and children, money and honor should be regarded as having no value in themselves, compared to that which is God.

With this in mind, it may be possible to appreciate the profound insight exhibited by the Sages who fixed the order of prayer before and after the daily recitation of the Shema (Hear oh Israel, the Lord is our God, the Lord is One). The first of the blessings before the recitation is an expression of thanksgiving for the creation of the world, to Him who created light and made darkness. But somehow neither this nor the next blessing seems to have any direct relation to the Shema. There doesn't appear to be a connection, as there is in most blessings, before a mitzvah is performed. Nevertheless, we do feel that it is an intrinsic part of the recitation, because the principal part of the prayer following the Shema lies in the statement, "And thou shalt love the Lord thy God with all thy heart and all thy soul and all thy being." As the Sages have explained: "With all thy heart" means with all of your impulses and desires, with all your capacity to love, which includes the love of wife and children, the strongest of the impulses of the heart. The peripheral loves of a man are easily given away to God; the truly important and central ones, those to which the heart of man is bound by nature and his very life, like wife and children, are surrendered only with much difficulty and are, therefore, more significant. Similarly, "all thy soul and all thy being" means to offer up one's very life force and money and livelihood to God.

Everything, then, has to be given to the Divine, life and love, well-being and wealth. The obvious objection is that it is too much to ask of material man. This may help to explain the preceding blessings, addressed to Him who creates the light, and so forth. They provide the necessary background, including, as they do, the passages on the angelic orders who proclaim the glory of God, and who at the same time nullify themselves in His light. "In dread and awe they all do the bidding of their Lord, and they open their mouth in holiness and purity with song and psalm, and they bless and praise and glorify and declare the power and holiness and majesty of the name of God."

In other words, the angels do not see God as close to them but at some distance, as "filling the earth with His glory." And what is that which fills the earth with glory if not man, or Knesset Yisrael, the Divine Soul in the body of the Jewish person? This interpretation of the declaration "Holy, holy, holy, the whole earth is filled with His glory" intimates that for the angels, the seraphs, and the holy creatures on high, God is a transcendental being. His glory is not necessarily in them, but it fills the earth, the nether world of material substance, where God saw fit to place Israel, and from where Israel communes with Him. Hence the angelic orders say: "Blessed is the glory of His name from His place." Why from His place? Because the angels do not know, nor do they have access to, His place. They praise Him and His glory wherever it may be, in whatever place. As it is written: "He alone is great and holy." He is beyond all that can be perceived, even by the higher spiritual beings. At the same time, it is in us (human beings) and between us, that God dwells.

The second of the blessings preceding the recitation of the Shema emphasizes the theme of "great and abundant compassion with which you have loved us, O Lord our God. . . ." It is a love that exceeds "the nearness of God" in relation to all the hosts above who proclaim His glory aloud with reverence, in unison. God thus confers His holy spirit on man, who is thereby able to say "our God," the God who is ours, just as we say the God of Abraham, Isaac, and Jacob. This mode of address betokens a state of belonging, and God, it seems, allows us to assume this possessive attitude and to say "our God" and not the God of the angels.

The love of God for man, and for Israel in particular, like all love which overcomes the flesh, has the capacity of superseding the self of the lover. So that the Divine contracts His light; His boundless love is brought down to the dimensions of man in order to include Israel in the blessedness of His unity and oneness. The very words of the blessing bring attention to this overwhelming compassion—the word "Yetzirah" describing it indicates "more" than the great and abundant love for all created things and points to the fact that "You have chosen us." Israel is chosen as a physical entity as well as a spiritual one, "to render homage to God and with love to be in union with Him."

If one stops to consider this thoughtfully, to meditate on it ever more deeply, it becomes apparent that the blessings were meant to be more than verbal utterances of readiness for the Shema recitation. They are expressions of the "reflection of a face in water," the urge of a soul to respond to God in like manner to His infinite graciousness and to cleave to Him and to be at one with His light. This urge is manifested as a longing for His embrace like that of lovers, of mouth to mouth, of spirit to spirit. The further expressions of this love in the following passages express the readiness to render to God all that one is and all that one possesses: "And thou shalt love the lord thy God with all thy heart and all thy soul and all thy being."

What is behind such an exorbitant declaration? Is it more than a manner or speaking? How is it to be done? For there is no doubt about the sincerity of the urge to cleave to God, to unite with Him in love, spirit to spirit. The answer is given immediately after: "And these words which I command you this day shall be in your heart. And you shall teach them diligently to your children and you shall speak of them when you sit in your house and when you walk by the way, when you lie down and when you rise up" (Deuteronomy 6:5-7).

As it is written in the book, *Etz HaChaim*, this loving embrace is accomplished by the union of the Divine Chochmah, Binah, and Daat with the corresponding Chabad in a person; and this means the study of Torah. For man cannot otherwise unite with the Divine Wisdom, Understanding, and Knowledge. This is what is intimated by the phrase "mouth to mouth, and spirit to spirit." For from the mouth the spirit comes forth and is articulated in words; words of Torah that speak of God and with God. Thus is accomplished, insofar as man is able, the Divine union. For "man shall live by every word that proceedeth out of the mouth of God" (Deuteronomy 8:3), and when spirit meets spirit in this manner, it is called the kiss of Divine love.

However, this is still not the realization of man's life on earth; it does not yet fulfill the final phase of the many contractions of God and His worlds. In order for man to keep the flow going, he has to make his physical body participate in it: The mineral and vegetable substances which he consumes as food and become his body and life force have to be raised to the Divine. "And the glory of God shall be revealed, and all flesh shall see it together" (Isaiah 40:5). The purpose of Creation is the revelation of His glory and that "all flesh shall see it." The emphasis is on filling this earth of ours with His glory, to "change darkness into light and bitterness into sweetness." This is the direction given to man's labors, to help draw the infinite light down. And this can only be done by first raising the "feminine waters," of receptivity, by offering up his own soul and his whole being to God. Thus, the purpose of all Divine worship is not the expression of human desires and needs, nor even the uplifting of man himself; rather, it is the drawing down, or extension, of Divine glory into the world. This is the final goal of spiritual work, even though this work cannot be done without raising the "feminine waters." That is, if man does not make his effort to raise and rise, he cannot make the connection. The contact must be established properly in order for the Divine light to flow. But the essence of the matter and the purpose of man's labors is really to be a channel for the Divine light, that through man this light should be able to illuminate all of the reality of the physical and the spiritual world.

50

The Love That Excels

The various levels and manifestations of love hitherto described have, for the most part, been those of Chesed; they belong to the right side of the tree of life and are considered to be characteristic of the role of the Priest. On the whole, it is a love that is best expressed as a longing for the holy, a yearning (*kesef* or silver) for the beloved that is relatively gentle and firm and full of a quiet, inner joy.

But there is also another kind of love that belongs to the left side of the tree of life, that of Gevurah. It characterizes the role of the Levite, who sings and plays rapturously before the Lord. It is a love that excels all other loves, being like flames of burning fire in its intensity. It glows bright and red like gold, and like gold, it is superior to all other substances including silver (or longing). Unlike the sweet yearnings and the deep gladness of the love that is Chesed, the love that comes from Gevurah is stormy and fervent. But it is not the emotionalism that accompanies an outburst of human passion; it is rather the steady burning of the soul with a love that leaps up to God, and it is like the flames that seek to separate themselves from the fire.

We have here another kind of ardor for Divine essence, one

that can take a person out of his sane and orderly existence and break the wall of inhibitions that circumscribe his world. With the force of such a fervent love, a person can sooner reach the borders of a higher world; the reinforced intensity of fiery love propels the soul toward God with far greater force than that supplied by any other kind of devotion.

It can also be likened to a great thirst for God, as it is written: "My soul thirsteth for thee" (Psalms 63:2). In practical living, this may be expressed as a "lovesickness," as such an inexplicable weakness of mind and body that one feels as though "my soul expireth" with longing. Or else it can be expressed as a mighty exultation, as it is written, "Yea, my soul is enraptured" (Psalms 84:3). In all these instances, the soul is striving to escape the bounds of this world, and, out of an excess of yearning, it totters at the edge of self-destruction. Not out of any destructive urge, of course, but because all of this material reality is so absurdly meaningless for the person who loves so ardently that he desires only to break through to the other side of existence.

We have only hinted at the root of the difference between the role of the Priest and the role of the Levite in the Holy Temple. The first level of love, that of the Priest, corresponds, as mentioned, to Grace or Chesed; the Levites' level of love corresponds to Severity or Gevurah. When the world will be redeemed, the love of the Levites will be higher than that of the Priests; the Ari said: "The Levites of today will be the Priests of the future." That is to say, the task of the Levite was to raise his voice in song and praise, and to play on instruments with melody and harmony, in a manner of "advance and retreat," which is the expression of intense love, like "the flame that flashes out of the lightning" as mentioned in the Talmud (Chagigah 13b).

This kind of loving is different from the quiet yearning of the steadfast heart; it is a stormy and restless passion, with an aspect of torment as well as ecstasy. In our world it cannot be superior to the first; but in a redeemed world, the Priests and the Levites will change roles and the love of the passionate heart will be able to be expressed without restraint, immune to the perils of frenzy and safe in its boundless delight.

All of the above can hardly be described adequately in words, of course, and especially in writing; the soul's excessive longing cannot be manifested in language. As the Baal Ha-Tanya says, only he who "is warm-hearted and intelligent, gifted with understanding, who deeply binds his mind and contemplation to God, will discover the goodness and light that are treasured up in his intelligent soul, each according to his capacity. . . ." In short, a person who has not had the experience of such intense love will be unable to grasp it, and no words can convey its bliss. On the other hand, someone who can presume to say that he understands what is being described will find much more than he expects in any true witnessing. Every person is different and each, according to his own personality, finds the wonderful and the exhilarating somewhere else.

To be sure, Divine love can be known in any number of ways—even through the simple morality of "depart from evil and do good." The intense passion for God, however, has to be achieved by effort and a more profound fear of sin. Otherwise, it will be a false love or a love that is built on corruption. The heart has to be purified of all its uncleanness, and a place must be prepared for such an overwhelming feeling. Thus, one needs to include Torah and mitzvot in the order of priorities.

The above notwithstanding, what happens when a person runs ahead and attains this ecstatic love of God before his life is fully prepared for it? Sincerity and ardor can often perform strangely unanticipated feats, and the soul may find itself suddenly in advance of the rest of the being, out of tune with the world. As it is related in the esoteric wisdom, the soul tends to "advance and retreat" in a to-and-fro movement that is unique to each individual. Also the order of Divine worship, the connection between man and God, is of the order of "advance and retreat," in two directions, raising oneself up from below and the descent from above. The two movements are the life beat of man; on the other hand, once a man reaches the ecstatic love of God that is like flames of fire, he does not want to retreat, to go back to the ordinary existence. As the Baal HaTanya says: "If thy heart hastens and becomes so exceedingly enraptured that the very soul is consumed with a desire to pour itself out into the embrace of its Father, the blessed Life of Life, and to leave its confinement in the corporeal, physical body in order to attach itself to Him, may He be blessed, then one must take to heart the teaching of the rabbis of blessed memory: 'Despite thyself thou livest . . .' (Pirkei Avot 4:29)."

There is no choice, of course, for "despite thyself thou livest"; the soul dwells in the body and cannot go to God at will. It is self-evident that one lives and dies, without being able to decide very much about the situation. The purpose of the rabbinical wisdom here is to explain why this is so, why one does have to go on living in spite of oneself.

The task of man is not only to live but to animate (give life to) the life of the body. That is, the soul has to give life not only to itself and to the body to which it is attached, but also to all of that portion of the world to which it is connected. This is necessary in order to provide a dwelling place in the lower world for His blessed Oneness. It is expressed in the Zohar: "that there be One in One." This means that the hidden unity should cease to be hidden and should be revealed.

A more poetic rendering of the above is implied by the text: "Come, my beloved, to meet the bride" (Sabbath hymn). This is a request to God to show Himself in the reality of the world, that His oneness be united with the oneness of the world. Nevertheless, why should it be demanded of a person to live and to die, whether he likes it or not. Even the paradox of it is not clear: after all, a person wants either to live or to die, not both. "In spite of yourself, you live" has to be understood as: in spite of yourself you give life to reality, you are only an instrument of God. So that if a person would prefer to vacate this life, the Divine command holds him to the task of giving life; and when his task is done, he is removed, for "despite thyself thou diest"; and "despite thyself thou livest" with the support of the Life of Life, blessed be He.

51

The Soul Likened to the Shechinah

o better grasp the nature of man, it may be in place to start by obtaining some insight into the matter of the Shechinah—the fact that the Shechinah rested in a definite place, the Holy Ark, even though all the earth is filled with His glory. Why was a structured Holy of Holies necessary to house that which is not to be limited or located anywhere?

It is the same in man; the body contains the soul: "From my flesh I see God." And the body, all 248 organs, are animated by the soul. No part of the body can exist without this "breath of life," and every organ receives from the soul whatever it needs to function: the eye to see, the ear to hear, the feet to walk. And this is accomplished by the organ that is in the head—called the brain or the mind—which concentrates the disposition of the forces of the soul.

Obviously, then, there is no separate spiritual force for each organ enabling the eye to see, the heart to beat, and so forth. The soul of man is not divided into functions. The soul is a single spiritual essence, and it is not confined to any place or physical limit. Furthermore, if we say that it is concentrated in the head more than in the feet, it is not meant to suggest that its location is related to any particular function. The ability for all functioning, with its 613 "capacities and vitalities" (which is the sum of the 248 positive ordinances and the 365 negative ordinances), can be considered to have its dwelling place in the brain of the head. Thus, there is an emphasis on the CHaBaD (CHochmah, Binah, Daat) as the spiritual factor decisive for human behavior, while recognizing the "concealment of the soul in the body in the process of animating it."

In such manner too, the higher Divine Soul is revealed in the Vital Soul, which is the intermediate essence between the higher soul and the body. The Vital Soul animates the body, being a spiritual essence, even if of a lower level. Each of the organs of the body draws its sustenance from it, getting its special qualities according to its individual structure. To use a lame metaphor, the electric current in a home provides energy to the light bulbs, the refrigerator, the vacuum cleaner, and it does not become something else for each purpose; there is no special current for lights, for refrigerators, and for vacuum cleaners. All the parts of the body thus receive their life force from the Vital Soul, which functions through the central coordinating agency, the brain. Even the heart, which may be considered a center of life and of the blood, receives its "instructions" from the brain.

The conclusion we draw from the above is that the soul is not to be located anywhere in the body, even though it is vital to the functioning of every part of the body. Just as God fills all the worlds and animates them without ever being at any particular place. And in every world, there are myriad creatures with numberless purposes and levels upon levels of existence, from the angelic hosts to the densest matter. The point is that we cannot say that there is more of God in any one place or at any particular level. He is not more present in a higher world than in a lower world. The soul is equally present in every part of the body; it lights the toes as well as the brain. Even in a place where one cannot perceive any light—as it is written in the *Tikunei Zohar*, "He is the Hidden One of all the hidden"—there too is God to be found. This is true of the highest worlds as well as of the lower ones. He is everywhere hidden as well as revealed. The difference between the higher and the lower worlds in this respect is in the degree of vitality streaming forth to each, the measure of inner life and of independent being allotted to each. Every world and every detail receives its light, its own revelation from out of the hidden, according to its own capacity.

This is one of the reasons why this Divine influence is called light—because all light, whether it be reflected or direct, intense or weak, has to have a source. And this source that illumines exists of itself in terms of light, whereas all that receive the light are dependent on it, and each gets a different amount and degree of illumination. So, too, do all the worlds receive varying measures of Divine revelation; the higher worlds get more and the lower worlds, less. None of them, however, can attain to the Divine essence itself; it is only the "garments" that differ. This helps to explain why our own world is so full of concealments, why God seems to wrap Himself in so much mystery. The "garments" in which the Divine hides His light and vitality are so numerous and powerful that very little is visible, and material substance appears altogether lifeless.

"Yet, they contain light," as the Baal HaTanya says, even though it does not show itself directly, but in a roundabout manner. To make an inadequate comparison, the light of the moon is only a partial and irregular reflection of the light of the sun. Men are given a little light from the great Divine light, an obscure version which has gone through a great number of concealments. And even the light that we do perceive is far too difficult, if not impossible, to understand and to relate back to its source. All that we see are the fragments of seemingly lifeless matter in the world; we do not see or feel the spiritual vitality that gives them their unique existence and capacity to be what they are. The inorganic is dead to us, and our comprehension of life is limited to that which reproduces itself. But the Divine light is there to sustain, as well as to give form and substance to all that exists, to keep each thing from reverting to nothingness. The essence of all existence is therefore Divine force and light; everything has its own version of life.

The Kabbalistic image of the above, which is given by the Ari in *Etz Chaim*, places man in the last of the Sefirot in the lowest of the four worlds, and since each Sefirah contains all the Ten Sefirot, we belong to the Malchut of Malchut in the world of Asiyah. Nevertheless, we do have access to all the higher Sefirot and Worlds. Even if it is only through the light we receive from the Malchut of Yetzirah to which we are connected, it is enough to enable us to get to the root and the principle of things. We can thereby also receive something from the ten Sefirot of the World of Atzilut which emanates the Divine light directly.

What we are attempting to point to in all of this is merely the old concept of a parallel between the way that the soul pervades the body and the way God fills the earth with His glory. What is important is to see this personally. In every particular feature and detail of one's existence, the Divine light is there to give it life and reality. But it is not perceptible to the ordinary gaze; only with the eye of revelation can it be known. And for this revelation to take place, a certain renewal of the heart has to occur, the veil covering it has to be withdrawn. The light from within then reveals the glory without. But usually, because we are not able to see the source of this light and glory, we think that each thing is what it is in itself and no more.

52

Descent of Divine Wisdom

$\mathbf{I}$t may be said that the power behind the manifestation of all the worlds is the Divine Will as expressed by His Wisdom. Both of these are revealed in the Torah, in a manner that enables the human mind to comprehend something about them, at least to the extent that man's "wisdom, understanding, and knowledge" make it possible. This revelation, which is simply an extension of His Wisdom, comes from the same life-giving force that is extended to animate all of existence. Just as the sun is the source of all light, which spreads in all directions and illumines earth and planets indiscriminately; just as the brain gives function and vitality to all the organs of the body, so too is there a central origin of all reality in the universe. This Divine source is an essence that cannot be defined or analyzed or located. Nevertheless, we can speak of inspiration, a spark or revelation of truth, reaching us from this source of all life, which enables us to see it in a number of ways and to give it a variety of names accordingly.

In certain Jewish writings, this origin is known as the World of Manifestation, which is the beginning of the myriad grades of existence, from the highest to the lowest, from the spiritual realms to gross matter. In the Kabbalah, this source is also called the "nether matriarch" or "matron," while a more general designation is the "Shechinah." Most of these names, in the Kabbalah, at least, are somehow linked with the life-giving and mother aspect of that which prevails at the conjunction of all "coming out" and becoming manifest. But their use is always related to a specific context; it is not an indiscriminate matter of one or another name for the same Divine origin.

The name Shechinah, which we have been using in our discussion, is derived from the scriptural phrase, "that I may dwell (*shachanti*) among them" (Exodus 25:8). For in the immensity of Divine light, nothing could exist unless the Shechinah protectively extends over it the particular light and vitality it needs for its being; whatever is, is because the Shechinah "dwells" in it. There has to be an intermediate junction to allow the Divine essence to manifest itself as worlds and in the world. Just as there are very great natural forces that could not possibly belong to, or be contained in, any single being because they would simply consume it. Electric circuits of very high voltage, for example, require transforming stations to make them available for common use. Thus, the power junctions of the universe may be seen as "Shechinah," even though there are very many stages or junctions where the Divine light is contracted and not just one. The Shechinah may also be considered another name for that "lower mother" which gives all creatures their being by allowing the Divine light to animate their particularity. The light of the Shechinah dwells in us and nurtures us, and thus it is called the mother of all children, giving birth and suckling. In another context, the same source of life is known as Knesset Yisrael (Community of Israel), because it is the origin of the souls of all worlds, those that come from the higher Worlds of Emanation, Creation, and Formation, as well as from the lower World of Action. That is, the community of men is identified, at its root, with the general life-giving power behind all the worlds. There is, thus, a profound identity factor between Shechinah and Knesset Yisrael. All these souls, all these revelations, are only extensions of life and light from the one source that sends them out like sparks from an inconsumable sun.

Obviously then, the worlds cannot endure or receive the

light directly from the sun or source, without a "garment" to screen and conceal the light. What is more, we can be sustained by the light of the sun only because we receive a very infinitesimal portion of it. So, too, the Shechinah cannot be revealed, for just as we would not last long if the sun were to get any closer, a certain distance is necessary; indeed, screens and protective devices are required for reality to continue to be what it is.

What is the garment that can contain the Shechinah within itself without being consumed? The answer, as mentioned, is Torah and the mitzvot of the Torah. For God's Will and Wisdom are clothed in the Torah and in the mitzvot that are revealed to us; that is to say, the Torah issues from supernal wisdom, which is immeasurably higher than the World of Manifestation. This means that, since the Divine light is clothed in and united with the Supernal Wisdom, He and His Wisdom are one (higher even than the manifested worlds); but "it can descend by means of obscuring gradations, from grade to grade, through the descent of the worlds, until it has clothed itself in material things, namely the 613 commandments of the Torah."

In this way, the Torah expresses a Divine essence which is beyond all reality, but which has descended in the obscurity of gradations. To be sure, this expression of Divine Will and Wisdom is not revealed in every world on the same level; the Torah also adapts itself, it clothes itself in a different garment in keeping with the succession of worlds from higher to lower, until it clothes itself in the material framework of this world, the positive commandments and the prohibitions. Thus, the Torah belongs, in essence, to a much higher sphere of being, beyond all the manifested worlds. It has no place for an ox that gores a neighbor's cow or phylacteries or prayer shawls or anything else of material substance; it is entirely an expression of Divine Wisdom. Only in our world of Action is this Wisdom translated into its appropriate combination of physical things and actions. The Torah can descend from grade to grade of worlds; it can go through one form of expression to another, lower and lower, until it is able to express the system of Divine Will and the order of Divine Wisdom in combinations that are of a physical nature, even to the point of specific statements about doing this and not doing that. Except that these statements are beyond us, even then; we still fail to really understand. To help us get a notion of what is involved, let us say that an idea that is extremely abstract can be written or formulated in terms of symbols with physical instruments on physical paper. These physical marks or symbols are not the idea; they are only tools to communicate the idea, but at the same time, they express it. Thus, the garments of the Torah are the physically written letters, but its essence is above and beyond all the worlds.

In the process of descending, the Torah has to speak in the language of the world it is passing through. As said, in our world it speaks in physical terms because we are corporal creatures of the earth. In the higher worlds, the Shechinah is more central, more apparent, forming a nerve center, so to speak, which is called the shrine of the Holy of Holies in each and every world. Thus, in each world, at every level of reality, there is its own shrine of the Holy of Holies, which is actually the mind of that world, its brain center. From this center or junction, all life and light emanate.

The Shechinah is, therefore, also identified as the Malchut of Atzilut (Kingdom of the World of Emanation) in Kabbalistic terminology, or the sovereign power of the world. The World of Emanation (Atzilut) is the realm of direct manifestation of infinite light and life. The "Kingdom" (Malchut) of that world is the dominion of Divine power. Therefore, the Malchut of Atzilut is the way God relates to the reality of the world in His capacity as Sovereign or King. Consequently, the Shechinah, as Malchut of Atzilut, and as the light that illumines the worlds from within, is called the Word of God.

It is frequently written that by the word of God was something done, or by the breath of His mouth were the hosts of Heaven activated. It may be asked: How can we attribute to God such physical forms as speaking or breathing? The answer is that just as a man, in speaking, communicates that which he wishes to reveal of himself (that is, some aspect of his hiddenness) to the outer world, so may the Word of God be considered a revelation. When we say that the Shechinah is the Word of God and the breath of His mouth, we are saying that the Shechinah is the means of communication between the Divine essence and the worlds.

According to the Zohar and *Etz Chaim*, the Shechinah also clothes itself in the shrine of the Holy of Holies of the World of Creation. This shrine is the CHochmah, Binah, and Daat (CHaBaD) of the World of Creation and acts as a central junction, from which are created, among other things, after clothing themselves in the Malchut of Briah, the souls and the angels which populate this world of Briah. From this same source, but from another root and another level of being, the wisdom of the Talmud comes down to us. That is to say, the Talmud is not a product of the human intellect, but rather of the CHaBaD of the World of Creation, which is the world of higher spiritual beings and the Divine light of intelligence. In this respect, the Talmud is able to provide intellectual clarification of what is written in the Five Books of Moses and makes it Scripture, or Torah, in the broader sense of the word.

53

The Candle of God

The First Temple was built to house the Holy Ark and the tablets of the Ten Commandments. The structure could thus be considered the dwelling place of the Shechinah, which is the Malchut of Atzilut or the manifestation of Divine light. And indeed, for centuries, the spiritual power emanating from the tablets of the Decalogue in the Holy of Holies on earth was stronger and more effective than the emanations from the shrine centers of Holiness in the upper worlds. Difficult as this may be to comprehend, these Ten Commandments inscribed by God radiated a certain depth and fullness of spiritual power that was more influential than that which came from the spiritual worlds themselves. This was possible precisely because they were engraved on stone, the most material of substances, and because the Ten Commandments are the essence of all of the Torah, which is the direct expression of Divine Wisdom. The Temple simply contained the Revelation, which had not yet descended and changed from world to world, but which had been written on stone and given to the people through Moses.

There are two things here that arouse our incredulity. One is the fact that this world to which the Divine revealed His

Wisdom is a material world and relatively dense to penetration of spirit. The other is the fact that this material world is a natural world, with laws of its own. In a sense, however, the stone tablets of the Decalogue were not a part of the material world, even though they were certainly of substance; they did not abide by the laws of nature. The letters were indeed engraved on stone, but they were forces of an entirely different order; they belonged to the dimension of Divine light and emanated an influence that was higher than anything else in the World of Action where they were kept.

In accordance with the original order of things, the World of Action is influenced by the light of the Shechinah through its own "Holy of Holies" or brain center, which in turn descends from the higher worlds. When the Ten Commandments were given to the Children of Israel and subsequently were housed in the Holy of Holies of the Temple, another source of Revelation intervened. The stone tablets do not diffuse their revelation and scatter it in all directions like the light from the higher worlds, which descends from gradation to gradation until it penetrates the World of Action and all its material parts in accordance with natural law. The Ten Commandments made a great leap; originating in Divine Wisdom, they burst through all the intervening worlds—or rather bypassed them—in order to reveal themselves to the material world without paying any attention to the laws of nature in this world. They avoided the various processes of contraction and change that characterize the evolvement of this world; and altogether, it was something that did not belong to this world. It was a material concretization of a much higher mode of existence; its light was far beyond anything else that the world had ever experienced. That is to say, the tablets of the Ten Commandments belonged to the dimension of miracle, an act of God.

Nevertheless, they were limited in space and substance, so that the Shechinah was present only when they were still kept ritually safeguarded in the First Temple. After they were removed, in the time of the Second Temple, the Shechinah was no longer manifest in the same way. The tablets of the Ten Commandments were the last physical remnant of the Divine descent to the people of Israel; they represented enlightenment at its highest level, when Divine revelation burst through the clouds of the rigid reality of worlds upon worlds of existence, and came to the people without altering itself by contraction, deformation, or concealment.

During the period of the Second Temple, therefore, the Shechinah was not dwelling among the people in the same way as when the tablets were present. Nevertheless, the Shechinah did dwell in the Holy of Holies in the way that Divine influence is ordinarily focused—by gradual descent through the intervening worlds and by assuming the forms, or putting on the garments of the Kingdoms of Emanation, Creation, Formation, and finally, of the World of Action. Consequently the light from the Holy of Holies in the time of the Second Temple belonged to the essence of holiness as transmitted through the brain center (Holy of Holies) of the World of Action. It was a light that originated beyond the reality of this world and radiated to all the world, while the Temple itself was the crossroads of the life of this world. No one could enter therein (the Holy of Holies) unless he was the High Priest, and even he was permitted to enter only on the Day of Atonement. Thus, even if the manifestation was not the same as in the time of the First Temple, the Second Temple could still be considered the dwelling place of the highest sanctity.

But when the Second Temple was destroyed, it could no longer function as a focal point of Divine holiness and, as it is written, God transferred this function to the confines of the Halachah. "Hence, each individual who sits by himself and occupies himself with Torah (in thought, word, and action), the Shechinah is with him" (Brachot 8a). The phrase "the Shechinah is with him" means in the order of the gradual descent and investment of the Malchut of Atzilut in the Malchut of Briah, of Yetzirah, and of Asiyah. In other words, it is not a revelation experience—even if the Shechinah is present. The light and inspiration that follows the presence of the Shechinah simply depends on the amount of holiness the person is able to bring down.

What is more, this occupation with Torah is, for the most part, a very practical matter. Most of the 613 commandments are active precepts, even if only in the sense that one must pray

and study with one's lips and voice, recite certain blessings
aloud, keep the Sabbath by doing or refraining from doing
definite actions, and so on. Torah is related to this world
directly by thoughts, speech, and deeds. One cannot be said to
have fulfilled one's obligations by contemplating noble concepts or aspiring to spiritual heights; it is the doing that counts.

"The Lord by Wisdom founded the earth" (Proverbs 3:19)
indicates that Divine Wisdom has established this world of ours
and that His Shechinah is part of it. For man, this Shechinah is
symbolized by speech, which is the word of the mouth; and
"saying" Torah expresses His Wisdom. As the Zohar puts it:
"The father (Wisdom) begat the daughter (Malchut) which is
Oral Law" (Zohar III, 187a), and the Oral Law is the Halachah,
or the way of life according to the commandments.

This brings us back to the recognition that the basis of all
things is Divine Wisdom that reveals itself in Torah. To say that
God's light is now focused in the narrow confines of Halachah
means that the Divine manifests His Will in the ordinary
realities of the world. Once, in the period of the First Temple,
His Will was manifested through the tablets of the Ten Commandments, bringing His Wisdom to the people directly from
the highest height; and in the time of the Second Temple this
was accomplished by the Divine light descending through all
the higher worlds, with all the distortion and contractions this
involved. Now, the Holy of Holies is to be found in the only
place left to the Divine sanctity, in the study of Torah and the
deeds of Torah.

This is what is meant by the passage "always let your clothes
be white, and let there be no lack of oil on your head"
(Ecclesiastes 9:8), which the Zohar explains. For the supernal
light that is kindled on one's head, namely the Shechinah,
requires oil, and "oil" is the symbol of being clothed in wisdom,
namely, in the 613 commandments of the Torah. Man is here
likened to a candle of God; the fire is the Shechinah, giving
light in all directions, and the part that burns is the wick, or the
animal-soul. What maintains the burning is the oil—the holy
symbol of wisdom—the good deeds or the mitzvot of the
Torah. In other words, the physical life and the body of man
have to be burning in the fire of right action in order to enable

the Shechinah to give light. The burning of the animal-soul is not a total destruction, however, because the soul which gives life to the being cannot be demolished. It is rather a transformation, a transmutation from darkness to light, from bitterness to sweetness, which in turns brings about that which is called "ascent of the feminine waters," the ascent of the lower, passive aspects of the universe toward the higher revealed forces above them. Such is the work of the Tzadik—a conversion of evil to good by transforming the animal-soul. That is, the animal-soul remains; it is not annihilated, but its desires and lusts are converted from one extreme to the other. The animal-soul of the Tzadik no longer knows the desires of the flesh; it wants only the holiness of its own consummation. It seeks the transformation of the garments or shells of the animal being in thought, word, and deed, making them into sparks of Divine light.

In this way, the Tzadik removes himself from the eternal conflict between the animal-soul and the Divine Soul and manages to remain fixed in his own essence on the level of the Divine within him. He achieves it by worshipping God with both his bad impulse and his good impulse. The bad impulse thus ceases to be evil and becomes a part of the totality of the Divine oneness in a man.

The person who is not a Tzadik, he who is a Benoni, has to continue to struggle. His life can, nevertheless, be just as holy, for he also demolishes the garments of the animal-soul in all their manifestations in thought, word, and deed. The steady devotion to God extricates the shells from the realm of the animal and transmutes them into instruments of holiness. Indeed, every Jewish person who is occupied wholly with matters that are connected with such devotion, whose speech and actions are directed from within to God, will undergo such a transformation. The sacrificial fire of Divine worship may not be able to change the essence of the animal-soul in a person, but the expressions of his soul are transmuted into something else.

The difference between the Tzadik and the Benoni would then be in the way the essence of the soul is changed. The Tzadik achieves it inwardly; from his own essential being, he effects a total transformation of his animal-soul. The Benoni is more concentrated on the outward manifestations of his animal-soul, even though, as he progresses, the animal-soul changes and becomes something other than what it was. The soul of the Benoni is extricated from the darkness of the shells; it is not annihilated in the light of Divine Wisdom, only its garments in thought, word, and deed are transformed in the 613 mitzvot of the Torah. Thus, the Benoni keeps changing himself constantly; he has to keep transmuting his inner essence by working on the outer manifestations of his being. His efforts are directed to a vigilant struggle to transform his animal-soul; and this is possible because the animal-soul is of Klipat Nogah, which is basically a spiritual category, even if it is not holy.

The core of the difference would, therefore, appear to be bound up with the animal-soul of man. The point is that this animal-soul is not necessarily of the essence of evil; it is of an undefined essence which, if not treated at all, belongs, like everything else neglected by man, to the realm of formlessness or to the realm of the shells. But when such essences are privileged to be corrected by man, they are raised to a higher level and undergo changes that are of the nature of transformation. This happens whenever the animal-soul, which is of Klipat Nogah, is so refined; there is a transformation from darkness to light, from bitterness to sweetness, whether in the fullness of perfection or only in external expression. In a certain sense, with every mitzvah, be it sanctified thought or action, at least at the moment of performance, man is transformed into a vessel of the Shechinah, an intermediary of the Divine light within him. At the same time, he becomes a means for the ascension of the "feminine waters," and in this ascension, and in response to it, there also occurs an augmentation or an extension of the light of the Shechinah, which is a revelation of Divine light in the brain of the head. It is in such manner that the Divine light is drawn to the soul—at the moment when the lamp seems to be burning out, the flame clutches at the oil rising in the wick and reinforces itself again. It is thus that the soul functions as a candle of God.

Indeed, the soul of man, in its wholeness, is an expression of the truth that "the Lord your God is a consuming fire." For "the Lord your God" is that which works on the reality of the world like a consuming fire; it utterly destroys all that it meets, and there is a constant process of such confrontation and burning. Earthly reality is fuel to the flame of Divine reality; everything is consumed by God. But earthly reality is not only matter and animality; it is also man. We too belong to the world. The difference is that the soul of man is capable of using this fire in order to transform and not to annihilate. Man raises things up to a higher level and thus preserves them. We are letting the previous essence burn up and, as in every burning, which is actually an essential chemical change, we are changing the composition of the reality of the world.

For the Lord your God is a consuming fire to be manifested by you. This demands contact with the world. Revelation is not an abstract Heavenly experience; it is a process of correct self-nullification in the greater dimension of an all-embracing reality. The Benoni is he who makes himself a candle of Divine light. He is not simply the average or middle between the good and the evil. He is intermediate between the one who has succeeded in transforming the entire essence of his soul and the one who is still changing. In terms of his daily existence the advanced Benoni behaves like a Tzadik, in spite of the fact that he is in inner conflict. The justification of his life is that, at every moment, he burns in the consuming fire of the Lord, for his soul is the candle of God.